Samuel Orcutt

**Henry Tomlison and his Descendants in America**

Samuel Orcutt

**Henry Tomlison and his Descendants in America**

ISBN/EAN: 9783742810571

Manufactured in Europe, USA, Canada, Australia, Japa

Cover: Foto ©ninafisch / pixelio.de

Manufactured and distributed by brebook publishing software (www.brebook.com)

Samuel Orcutt

**Henry Tomlison and his Descendants in America**

# Henry Tomlinson.

### AND HIS

# Descendants

### IN AMERICA,

WITH A FEW ADDITIONAL BRANCHES OF TOMLINSONS, LATER FROM ENGLAND.

. By

## REV. SAMUEL ORCUTT,

AUTHOR OF THE HISTORY OF THE TOWN OF WOLCOTT, TORRINGTON, DERBY, NEW MILFORD, STRATFORD AND BRIDGEPORT, AND INDIANS OF THE HOUSATONIC, CONN.

---

PRESS OF PRICE, LEE & ADKINS CO.,
NEW HAVEN, CONN.
1891.

# PREFACE.

This volume is the unexpected result of an effort of three ladies to collect a few families in a connected line, to their first ancestor in America, which was Henry Tomlinson. After their labors had proceeded a few months, the materials were placed in the hands of the author of the History of Stratford, Ct., to be incorporated in that book, but they were found too voluminous for it, and a brief outline was substituted in its place. It was neither easy nor satisfactory to end the undertaking in such a manner, and a separate volume was proposed, and the material largely prepared for it, when illness caused the efforts to be laid aside for more than two years.

In the autumn of 1890, the work was resumed; a few circulars were sent out, for the purpose of completing the Henry Tomlinson line, as far as might be, and after a few weeks the returns became more than was expected, for the search revealed Tomlinsons in every direction, and that literally by the hundred instead of the score; and

it is with great regret that the author, in consequence of arrangements for other work and the expense attending a further enlargement of the book, is compelled to close the printing before all the Tomlinson families in America could be collected and put into historic form.

While, therefore, all that could be obtained of the Henry Tomlinson line is here included, numbering, with the children of Tomlinson women who married out of the family name, about one thousand, with a few other short lines, there is left two or three additional lines, numbering nearly as many persons as are herein given, for the reason that the time has been too short for the parties to complete the gathering of names so far as to make the record satisfactory when put in type. It is expected therefore, that the parties mostly interested in those remaining lines, residing largely in Delaware and Pennsylvania, will in a few months hereafter bring out another—a second volume of "Tomlinsons in America," by which the record of this very honorable family shall be well represented in a book.

Considerable pleasure has been taken in this work, believing that the intellectual and moral influence of such records are elevating to the general character of the nation, or any people, for the reason that whoever respects himself will respect his ancestors before him, and seek to instill the same in the minds of those who shall follow.

The declaration of a popular writer is of force in this connection.

"The more thoughtful a man is, and the more conscious of what is going on within himself, the more interest will he take in what he can know of his progenitors, and a regard to ancestral honors, however contemptible the forms which the appropriation of them often assumes, is a plant rooted in the deepest soil of humanity."

GEORGE MACDONALD.

As with many other works of the kind, this has been produced for the pleasure of it and not for the profit, since all income from the sales will scarcely pay half the expense put upon it; yet such as it is it is cheerfully presented for the convenience and gratification, or otherwise, of the Tomlinson family.

# MEMORIAL.

"O Time and Change!—with hair as gray
As was my sire's that winter day,
How strange it seems with so much gone
Of life and love, to still live on!
Ah, brother! only I and thou
Are left of all that circle now,—
The dear home faces whereupon
That fitful firelight paled and shone;
Henceforward, listen as we will;
Look where we may, the wide earth o'er,
Those lighted faces shine no more.
We tread the paths their feet have worn,
  We sit beneath their orchard trees,
  We hear, like them, the hum of bees
And rustle of the bladed corn;
We turn the pages that they read,
  Their written words we linger o'er,
But in the sun they cast no shade,
No voice is heard, no sign is made,
  No step is on the conscious floor!
Yet Love will dream, and Faith will trust,
(Since He who knows our need is just),
That somehow, somewhere, meet we must.
Alas for him who never sees
The stars shine through his cypress trees!"

— *Whittier.*

# AN ACROSTIC.

Together we are bound at last,

O'er the continent we were cast,

Meeting of a family vast,

Locked in under a cover fast,

Increase, the Lord desired of man,

Now grant His wishes all who can,

So let the name so well begun

On earth be heard till the "race is run,"

Name of our family—TOMLINSON.

E. M. T.

Birmingham, Ct., 1890.

# TOMLINSONS IN ENGLAND.

## ARMS OF TOMLINSON FAMILIES.

*From Burke's Heraldry.*

"TOMLINSON—Sa. a fesse between three falcons or.
  Crest. A griffins head issuant out of a ducal coronet or."

"TOMLINSON, (Gateshead co. Durham.) (See Thomlinson.)
  Visitation at Durham, 1815, Per pale wavy ar. and vert, three greyhounds counterchanged; a chief invecked, &z."

"TOMLINSON, (London and Yorkshire: granted 1590). Sa. a fesse between three falcons volant or.
  Crest. Out of a ducal coronet or, a griffins head ar."[1]

"TOMLINSON, (as borne by Frederick W. Tomlinson of Cliffville, near Newcastle, county of Stafford, esq.) Sa. a fesse between three falcons or.
  Crest. Out of a ducal coronet a griffins head ar."

"TOMLINSON, (Birdford co. York) Per pale vert and or, three grayhounds courant in pale counter changed, collared ar.
  Crest. A savage wreathed about the middle ppr. holding in both hands a spear, headed at each end or."

"TOMLINSON, (as borne by John Tomlinson of Everton near Liverpool, esq. heir-male of the Tomlinson's of Cholmondelay, co. Chester.) Per pale wavy or, and vert, three greyhounds courant, counter changed, a chief indented ar."

*From Book of Family Crests, printed by Washburne, London.*

"TOMLINSON, Yorkshire, a savage wreathed about the loins, ppr. holding in both hands a spear, headed at each end or. Plate 35 no. 21."

"TOMLINSON, a griffins head issuing from a ducal coronet or. Plate 25 no. 40." *Non Sibi sed patriæ.*

*Fairbairn's Crests of Great Britain and Ireland.*

"TOMLINSON, ag., out of a ducal coronet or, a griffin's head. *Non Sibi, patr.*"

---

[1] This is e same as the one in colors in the front part of this book, which ith the lettering, is a facsimile of the one brought to America by Henry Tomlinson.

# RECORDS OF PERSONS AND FAMILIES.

*Register of St. Peter's Cornhill, London, Eng.*

"1572, October 10. Friday Christning of Alice Tomlinson, daughter of Mathew."

*Register of St. Dionis Backchurch, London, Eng.*

"1555, Sept. 20. Buried, William Tomlinson."

"1585-6, Feb. 7. Married Thomas Tomlynson, of St. Margarets in new fysh street and Ame More of this par:"

"1611, May 13. Baptized. Richard Tomlinson, son of John Tomlinson."

*Register of St. Antholin, Budge Row, London, Eng.*

"1572, October 20. William Tomlinson married Mary Shingle."

"1616, June 20. Thomas and Ann Tomlins *alias* Tomlinson, son and daughter of John and Joan Tomlins *alias* Tomlinson."

*Register of St. James, Clarkenwell, London, Eng.*

"1602, March 10. Baptized. Susan daughter of Anthonie Tomlinson."

"1637, Aug. 24, George Tomlinson and Jane Jones were licensed to be married."

*Register of St. Thomas, London, Eng.*

"1795, June 10. Arthur Bell married Tymothie Tomlinson.

*From the Book of Dignities....of the British Empire.*

### COMMISSIONERS.

"1655. Hy. Cromwell, commissioner in chief of the army; Matthew Tomlinson, for Ireland, Miles Corbet, Robert Goodwin to whom afterwards was added William Steel, commissioners of the army.

### ADMIRALS.

"Nicholas Tomlinson died in 1847. He was appointed Rear-Admiral in 1830."

### BISHOPS.

"1842. George Tomlinson was constituted by Letters Patent Bishop of Gibraltar, the Bishopric including Gibraltar and Malta."

MEMBER OF PARLIAMENT.[1]

"Tomlinson, William Edward Murray, Esq. of Heysham House, Lancashire; eldest son of the late Thomas Tomlinson, Esq., Queen's Counsel, of Heysham House, a Bencher of the Inner Temple, by Sarah, only child of the late Rev. Roger Mashiter, of Bolton-le-Sands, county of Lancaster, and incumbent of St. Paul's, Manchester; born 1838. Educated at Westminster Ch. Ch. Oxford (B.A. 1859; M.A. 1862); called to the Bar at the Inner Temple 1865; is Capt. 1st Vol. Batt., Loyal N. Lancashire Regt. Elected M.P. for Preston 1882."

---

[1] County Families, by Walford.

## THOMLINSON, OF WHITBY.

[1] ARMS—*Sable, a fess between three falcons rising or.*

John Thomlinson, of Yorke. =[2] ... Thomas Thomlinson, a Mercer at the Ship in Cheapside, died in aᵒ 1603, or thereabouts.

John Thomlinson, of the City of Yorke, died in aᵒ 1616, or thereabouts. == Eleanor, daughter of Mathew Dadsworth, Chancelour to Tobye Mathew, Archbishop of Yorke.

2. Mathew Thomlinson married Pembroke, eldest daughter and co-heire of Sir William Broke, of . . . . . in Kent.

John Tomlinson, of Whitby, in County Ebor, æt 19 ann., 28 Aug., aᵒ 1665. == Jane, daughter of James Boys of Whitby.

1. Jane wife of Sir Thomas Twysden, Kt., one of the Justices of yᵉ Court of Kings Bench.

2. Eleanor, first married to Ralphe Carnaby, of Halton, in County Northumberland, Esq., afterwards to Sir Thomas Carnaby, of . . . . , in County of Northumberland, Knt.

2. Charles, æt. 16 ann.

1. Mathew, æt. 19 an., 28 Aug., 1665.

1. Margaret.

2. Eleanor.

---

[1] Dugdales Visitations of Yorkshire. The Surtees Society, vol. 36, 66.
[2] The parallel lines show that the parties were married.

# THOMLINSON, OF BIRDFORTH, YORKSHIRE, ENG.

### NON PROBAVIT ARMA.[2]

ARMS—*Per pale, wavy, argent and vert., three greyhounds courant, counterchanged, a chief azure.* M. S. 1487. *No arms in Visitation* 1585 *or* 1612.

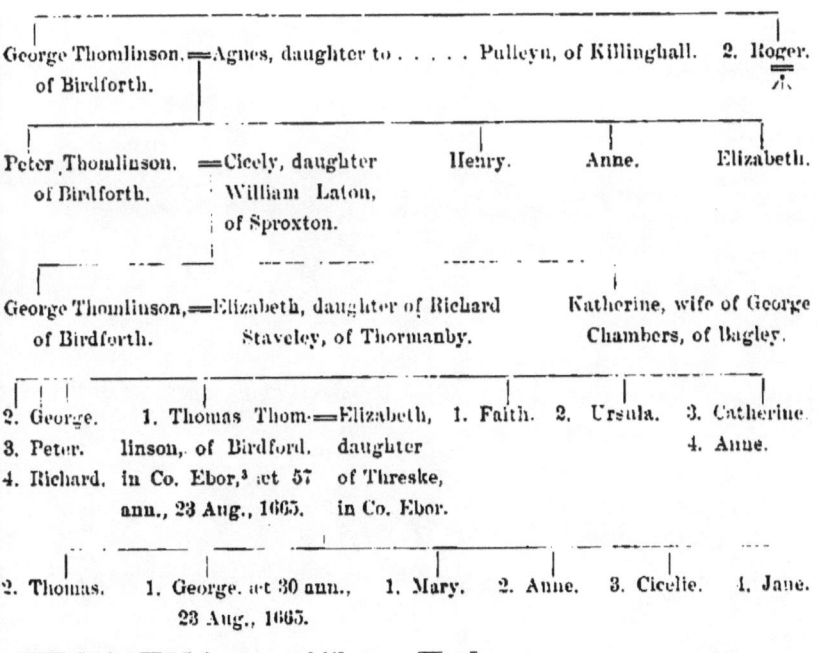

Christopher Thomlynson.══Anne, daughter and co-heir of Thomas Munsell, of Birdforth.

George Thomlinson,══Agnes, daughter to . . . . . Pulleyn, of Killinghall.  2. Roger.
of Birdforth.

Peter Thomlinson.══Cicely, daughter   Henry.   Anne.   Elizabeth.
of Birdforth.    William Laton,
              of Sproxton.

George Thomlinson,══Elizabeth, daughter of Richard   Katherine, wife of George
of Birdforth.    Staveley, of Thormanby.          Chambers, of Bagley.

2. George.   1. Thomas Thom-══Elizabeth,   1. Faith.  2. Ursula.  3. Catherine.
3. Peter.    linson, of Birdford.   daughter                       4. Anne.
4. Richard.  in Co. Ebor,[3] æt 57   of Threske,
             ann., 23 Aug., 1665.   in Co. Ebor.

2. Thomas.   1. George. æt 30 ann.,   1. Mary.   2. Anne.   3. Cicelie.   4. Jane.
             23 Aug., 1665.

[1] As represented in the Visitation of Yorkshire in 1584-5 and 1612, edited by Joseph Foster, p. 217.

[2] Not proved in arms, or not accustomed to war.

[3] Ebor.—*i. e.*, Eboracum, or Yorke.

## THOMLINSON, OF THORGANBY.[1]

ARMS.—*Per pale vert and argent, three greyhounds in pale courant counterchanged, on a chief or, a garb of the first surmounted of a sword gules in saltire.*

It behoveth Captain Thomlinson, being a branch of the Family of Thomlinson, of Byrdforth, to procure a Certificate from Sir Richard Maleverer, that they are descended from his Family, as they pretend (and as Mr. Thomlinson, of Byrdforth, did undertake to prove); which done, he may then beare Arms of Maleverer thus counterchanged, whereunto he pretends, with this Cheife to distinguish himself from Thomlinson, of Byrdforth.

Anthony Thomlinson, of Burne, = . . . . . . . in County Ebor, descended from Thomlinson, of Byrdforth, in County Ebor.[2]

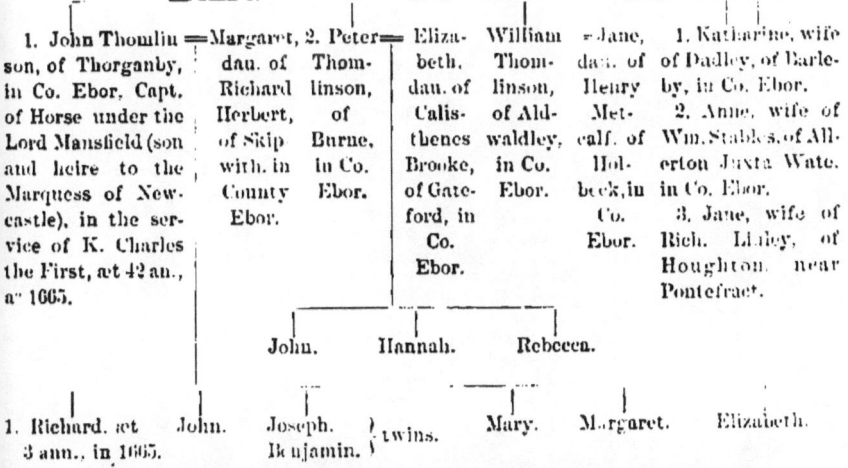

[1] Dugdales Visitation of Yorkshire. The Surtee's Society. 36, 376.
[2] Eboracum, or Yorke.

## Col. Matthew Tomlinson.

St. James Park is replete with historical associations, not the least interesting of which is the fact of Charles First having passed through it on foot on the morning of his execution, from his bedchamber in St. James Palace to the scaffold at White Hall.

The procession was a remarkable one. On each side of the King marched a line of soldiers, while before him and behind him were a guard of halberdiers, their drums beating and colors flying. On his right hand was Bishop Juxon, and on his left hand Colonel Tomlinson, both bareheaded.

Having obtained the watch-word from Colonel Tomlinson, who commanded the guard, Herbert proceeded on a dark night to the house which the king had designated where he readily gained admission to its mistress, who placed in his hands a small cabinet, closed with three seals, which she charged him to deliver to the same person from whom he had received the ring. The next morning in Herbert's presence the king broke the seals, when the cabinet was found to contain a number of diamonds and jewels, most of them set in broken insignia of the Order of the Garter. "This," said the king, "is all the wealth I have in my power to bequeath to my children."[1]

The following refers to the same event: "On Col. Hacker giving the final signal at the door of his apartment his two faithful attendants, Bishop Juxon and Herbert, fell on their knees before him and wept. Charles gave them his hand to kiss, and as Juxon was an old man he kindly assisted him to rise.

To Colonel Tomlinson, a republican officer, who had shown him every attention consistent with his duty to his employers, he presented his gold tooth-pick case, and requested him to attend him to the last. Then desiring that the door might be opened, and telling Hacker he was ready to follow him, he passed with a cheerful countenance through an avenue of guards which lined the galleries to the scaffold."[2]

---

[1] London: Its Celebrated Characters and Remarkable Places. Published in London by Bently. Vol. 1., 133-170.

[2] Ibid. Vol. III., 32.

# THE TOMLINSON NAME.[1]

Thomas of Llwyn Madoc, county of Brecknock, traces his pedigree up to that prolific source of noble and gentle blood, Elyston Glodrydd, Prince of Fferllyn; and Thomas of Welfield, county of Radnor, springs from the same family origin.

Tomlinson and Thomlinson are from the same origin, whatever that may be.

"Son. An exceedingly common termination in English family nomenclature. Observe:

I. That personal or Christian names when introduced into this country, were very likely to become perpetrated by the spirit of imitation among persons who were strangers in blood to the introducers, as well as among their own descendants.

II. When, in process of time, hereditary names began to prevail throughout Christendom, many assumed the patronymic form, and in England Son was the affix employed. So prevalent was this custom in the XIV. century, that there was scarcely a Christian name in use that did not become a surname by this tradition, whether such name was of Saxon, French, Flemish, or Danish birth. No evidence as to race, then, can be adduced from this termination."

"Tom. See Thomas.

Thomas. The Christian name. Though not used here [in England] prior to the Norman Conquest [1066] this has become one of the commonest of baptismal appellations and surnames. It has also been a most abundant source of derivatives and nicknames, represented in our family nomenclature by

| Thomason,  | Thoms,    | Tompsett,   | Thomlin,   |
| Thomerson, | Toms,     | Tomkin,     | Tomlin,    |
| Thomson,   | Thomaset, | Tompkins,   | Tomlins,   |
| Thompson,  | Thomsett, | Tompkinson, | Thomlinson,|
| Tompson,   | Tomsett,  | Thompkisson,| Tomlinson, |
| Thom,      |           |             |            |

In the North, A commonly replaces O, and hence Thampsett, Tampsett, Tamlyn, Tamplin, and probably Taplin.

Some of the Welsh families of Thomas are of antiquity, though the surname is, in all cases, of comparatively recent assumption: e.g.: Thomas of Gellynweruen, county of Carmarthen, descends from Sir Hugh Trehern, one of the Welsh knights who accompanied the Black Prince to the battle of Poictiers: some members of this family have recent exchanged the name for Treherne.

---

[1] *Patrinimic Briton* or a Dictionary of the Family Names of the United Kingdom. Mark Antony Lower, M.A., F.S.A.

## EXPLANATIONS.

A number is given to each Tomlinson, and it is repeated when the same name is taken up again for further record.

The algebraic mark $+$ (plus) indicates that the name is taken up again and further record made.

The small figures at the end of each name show the generation of that name from Henry Tomlinson, the first at Stratford, Conn.

# TOMLINSONS IN AMERICA.

# LINE OF HENRY TOMLINSON.

"*GEORGE TOMLINSON* was married to Maria Hyde, in January, 1600, at St. Peter's Church.

"Henry Tomlinson, son of George and Maria Tomlinson, was baptized at St. Peter's Church, in November, 1606."

The above records were taken from the Parish Register of St. Werburgh, in Derby, Derbyshire, England, by Messrs. William D. Bishop, Jr., and Nathaniel W. Bishop, of Bridgeport, Ct., who, for this specific purpose went to that city, while on a visit in England in 1888. They learned also, what is proved by all the best books on heraldry, that this family belonged to the "Landed Gentry" or class next below the nobility in England. It is also shown by heraldry that this branch was descended from some duke who had received a "coat-of-arms" signifying this honor, which is inherited in a historical sense by all the descendants of the person

receiving it, and that the "coat-of-arms" brought to America by Henry Tomlinson proves, by its ornamentation, the family to have been descended from some line of kings.

Tradition says, "this George Tomlinson was a native of Yorkshire, England," where the family name runs back in history several hundred years, and removed to Derby where his son Henry was bred a weaver, probably to the trade of his father.

It was customary in the fifteenth and sixteenth centuries in England, for this class of families to give their sons trades,[1] which placed them in social life the same as merchants and manufacturers, then and at the present day.

Nearly all the early settlers of New England were of the common or middle class in England, being well informed in the learning, and the religious and political discussions of the times, and came to America for the two specific objects— religious liberty and the possession of lands for an inheritance to their descendants.

---

[1] *From Froude's History of England, Vol. I, 59. A. D., 1536.*

"The children of those who could afford the small entrance fees were apprenticed to trades, the rest were apprenticed to agriculture; and if children were found growing up idle, and their fathers and their friends failed to prove that they were able to secure them an ultimate maintenance, the mayors in towns and the magistrates in the country had authority to take possession of such children, and apprentice them as they saw fit, that when they grew up 'they might not be driven' by want of incapacity 'to dishonest courses.'

Such is an outline of the organization of English society under the Plantagenets and Tudors."

*Line of Henry Tomlinson.*

*1. HENRY TOMLINSON*, with his wife Alice, and probably two or three children, came from Derby, in Derbyshire, England, to America, and, in 1652, settled in Milford, Ct. What year he came or what ship he came in is unknown. Tradition says he came to New Haven and thence to Milford.

There was a Thomas Tomlinson who took the freeman's oath in New Haven in April, 1644, but whether he was a relative or not of Henry has not been ascertained.\*

There was also a Robert Tomlinson in Milford, Ct., whose wife was dismissed from the church in that place in 1648, to unite with the church at Stratford, Ct.

Also, a William Tomlinson settled in Derby, Ct., in 1677, who, it has been said was a nephew, and came with Henry Tomlinson to this country, but of this there is room for doubt, since the will of Jonas Tomlinson shows William to have been born in 1643, and, therefore, was quite young when Henry came to Milford, Ct., in 1652. This William, for aught that appears, may have been the son of Robert, of Milford, but if he was it is a little strange that no records indicate that relation.

---

\* New Haven Colonial Records, I, 140.

This Thomas Tomlinson "was in Hartford, Ct., in 1655, and died there in 1685, leaving seven daughters, and so far as can be ascertained, no son." See "Up Neck in 1825," pages 29-31; a Phamplet of Territory near Hartford, Ct., by G. W. Russell, M. D.

Having settled in Milford, Ct.,[3] the next record shows Henry Tomlinson as "Keeper of the Ordinary" at Milford, to which position he was elected by the town, as one of its most honorable offices.

The articles of agreement could not have been very clear, for at the end of two years, when Henry

---

[3] "A General Court at Milford, this 9th of December, 1652.

"Henry Tomlinson propounded to the Court for the gift of a home lott near the water side to sit down in and improve his trade of weaving, which he is resolved to follow wherever he inhabits, which, according to his proposition to follow his trade of weaving, the towne did grant him an acre lott before or against Ensignes lott, out of the land reserved for elders, with this proviso, to follow his trade, and in case of removall from the plantation, he shall resign it to the town, they promising to give him the value of the same as two indifferent men shall Judge thereof."

It was a custom in all the plantations, if a family would settle to stay, to give them a home lot, and especially a person having a useful trade, and often further inducements were offered, as in this case, for seven days later the following record was made at Milford:

"A General Court, Dec. 16, 1652.

"Henry Tomlinson hath taken the oath of fidelity, and also Renewing his motion to the Court for some small accommodation of meadow, the Court gave him a piece of meadow in the Beaverspond meadow that was made use of by John Smith the last year, judged to be about three acres, more or less, on both sides the Creeke, for his Incouragement to dwell and follow his trade amongst us according to his resolution therein."

Here it is expressly stated that he had taken the "oath of fidelity." That meant fidelity to the plantation under New Haven Colony, which oath secured all the rights of an inhabitant as to property and protection, but not the right to vote: to secure which in that Colony it was necessary to become a member of the Church. This he does not appear to have done, but afterwards united with the Church at Stratford.

Tomlinson claimed the house as his property, both Alexander Bryan, of whom the property was obtained, and the town disputed the claim. The matter was taken to the court, where it was amicably settled.

On June 13th, 1654, Henry Tomlinson, Ensign Alexander Bryan, and Mr. East were summoned before the court of New Haven for non-payment of duties on imported wines. The two latter paid their fines, but Henry Tomlinson made decided opposition, claiming that he had paid all legal duties, and under a legal process, caused the arrest of the Governor of the New Haven Colony, believing that the Governor was acting above all law. For this he was called before the court and fined one hundred pounds, which seems to have been only a show of honor for the Governor, as payment was never demanded.

In the autumn of 1656, or the next spring, Henry Tomlinson removed with his family to Stratford, Ct., and, on April 1, 1657, purchased of Joshua Atwater the estate which Mr. Atwater had bought of William Quenby, one of the original proprietors of the township.

In 1668, he and Joseph Hawley purchased a considerable tract of land in Derby, Ct., of the Indians, and this land in whole or part he gave to his son Jonas, who, with many of his descendants, resided on it for several generations.

In 1671, he and others purchased a large tract of land of the Indians at Weantinock, now New Milford, Ct., sufficient for a township, but his sons to whom he gave it never realized much from it because of trouble with the Indians and the General Court.

The record of the town meeting of Stratford, Ct., for January 2, 1670, says: "Henry Tomlinson is chosen and desired to bee an ordinary keeper, ye which he accepts," and which he accepted several years.

Henry Tomlinson died at Stratford, Conn., March 16, 1681, leaving a widow, two sons, and five daughters, all married except Agur, his younger

---

*"Be it known to all Christian people, Indians and others whom it may concern, that I Pocono, and Ringo, and Quoconoco, and Whimta, who are right owners of one island in the great river Oantenock where Mr. Goodyear had a trading house, and also the lands on both sides of the river, we do by this present writing grant . . . unto Henry Tomlinson of Stratford, the above mentioned island and the land on both sides of the river, three miles down the river south-east, and the land on both sides of the river upward north-west, which amounts to seven miles in length, and accordingly of three miles in breadth, which amounts to six miles in breadth; all which tract of land and island to have and hold. . . . We confess to have received one piece of cloth and other good pay to our satisfaction.

April 25, 1671.

| | |
|---|---|
| Pocono, his mark. | Tomo, his mark, the second son of Mataret. |
| Ocomunhed, his mark. | |
| Wesonco, his mark. | Quocanoco, his mark. |
| Pomentock, his mark. | Weekpenos, his mark. |
| Ringo, his mark. | Toto, his mark. |
| Coshushamock, his mark. | Mohemat, his mark. |
| Mataret, the Sachem's eldest son. | Chetemhehe, his mark. |
| | Othoron, his mark. |
| | Papisconas, his mark." |

son. The remains were probably buried in the first burying ground adjoining the first meeting-house near Sandy-Hollow.

In his will, which is given below, the closing paragraph contains most beautiful and perfect commendation to his children, such as is seldom seen in a will.

*The Will of Henry Tomlinson* copied from *The Fairfield Probate Records.*

"March 15, 1680-81.

"In the name of God Amen. I Henr. Tomlinson of Stratford in the county of Fairfield and in the Colloney of Conecticut being weak in body but I bless God for His mercy and goodness unto me, I am in good understanding. I doe make this my last will and Testament in maner and form as followeth:

"Imp'mes. I give my soul into the hands of my Merciful Father Almighty God; and unto Jesus Christ in whom I doe believe that he hath redeemed my soul from sin death and hell by his own merits and blood shedding: notwithstanding all my unworthyness, and hath prepared a rest for my soul in heaven to live with him and remain with him in joy unto all eternity.

"Item. I give my body after death to a decent burial in the earth from whence it came and thereto remain till the great day of the resurrection.

"Item. As concerning my worldly goods I am possessed of under God at my death after my debts are payd and my funeral accomplished, I doe dispose of them as followeth:

"Item. I give unto my loving wife Allice Tomlinson and to my sonn Agur Tomlinson all my houslug and buildings with all my lands in Stratford during her natural life. And yf my wife incline to live alone by herself then my will is that shee shall make her choyce which end of the house and what of the sellars she will reserve for herself. And yf my wife shall see cause to change her condition after my death then I leave her to the thirds of my estate and the other two parts to remain to my son Agur; and after the death of my wife then the land to return unto my son Agur Tomlinson for him and his heirs to enjoy forever provided as followeth:

"I have given unto all my children that are married my sonn Jonas, my daughter Harger, my daughter Mary Pierson, my daughter Tabatha Worster, my daugater Phebe Worster, and my daughter Bashua Stiles already such portions as God did enable me and as I saw cause yet this is my will that my son Agur after the death of me and my wife shall pay unto my daughter Margaret five pounds the next year after our death, and four pounds to my son Jonas Tomlinson the second year after our death, and five pounds to my daughter Mary Pierson the third year after our death, and five pounds to my daughter Tabetha Worster the fourth year after our death, and five pounds to my daughter Phebe Worster the fifth year after our death, and to my daughter Bathshua the sixth year after our death. Yf any of these my children should be taken away by death before payment be made then it shall be to the children of the deceased. Yf God in his providence should take away my son Agur by death and leave no heirs or heir to inherit this land then it is my will it shall return to Jonas my sonn and his heirs to enjoy forever my sonn Jonas paying unto Margaret Harger my daughter twenty pounds the first year, and to my daughter Tabathy Worster twenty pound the second year after his decease and to my daughter Mary Peirson twenty pound the third year; to my daughter Phebe Worster twenty pound the fourth year and to my daughter Basshua Stiles the fifth year after our decease.

"I give to my two sons and the Longer Liver of them my Indian purchases of Wyantenuck. I give to Jonas and Agur my two sons all my guns to be divided between them as they best can agree. Moreover I give to my sonn Agur a horse fit for draught, two young oxen, one bed and furniture, all husbandry Tackling, that my wife hath not occasion to use and what else my wife sees cause to give him.

"Moreover I give to my grand child Timothy Worster if he continue with my wife or Agur four years one mare, and likewise to Abigail Harger I give one mare yf she continue with my wife four years; And my wife to add what she please; and I make my wife executrix of this my last will and Testament. And I do request my loving friends Richard Blaklidg and Joseph Hawley to joyn with my son Ephraim Stiles to be my overseers of this my last will: and I declare this to be my act by subscribing my name.
" Witness                              " HENRY TOMLINSON.
    " JOSEPH HAWLEY,
    " RICHARD BLACKLIDG.

"And this last of all I commend to you all my children as my last blessing: Live in love and peace and the God of love and peace shall be with you."

*The Will proved in Fairfield Court.*

"28 April 1681. Mr. Joseph Hawley and Mr. Richard Blacklidg make oath before the Court that the above said will to which they are witnesses was signed by Henr Tomlinson in his life time in their presence and witness of his last will; and that the said Tomlinson when he signed as above was of good understanding.
"WILLM HILL, Clerk."

"An Inventory of the estate of Henry Tomlinson deceased March 16: 1680 or 1681. Taken by the Townsmen of Stratford this 26th of March 1681.

| | | |
|---|---|---|
| Impr. By his wearing apparel | £13 13 | 0 |
| In money and plate | 7 00 | 8 |
| Books | 4 00 | 0 |
| 2 oxen 20lb 3 cows 11th 3 calves 9/6 | 40 00 | 0 |
| 2 yearlings     horses 8 | 10 10 | 0 |
| 14 sheep | 6 00 | 0 |
| 3 yds. of cotton 9/6, bed, bedstead blanket sheets upon it and off | 16 00 | 0 |
| Trunckle bed and bedding upon it all | 3 10 | 0 |
| In the chamber a bed and furnishings | 11 00 | 0 |
| Another bed in the chamber | 5 00 | 0 |
| Another bed | 1 10 | 0 |
| A loome and the rest of weavers tackling | 5 10 | 0 |
| A loome and the rest of weavers tackling | 5 10 | 0 |
| Chest and linin in the chamber | 18 10 | 0 |
| Old chest in the parlor and linin in it | 1 5 | 0 |
| Pins great and small | 1 15 | 0 |
| Pepper — and other spices | 0 10 | 0 |
| Buttons fidsting and othe small things | 0 8 | 0 |
| Hony, Sugar and the things they want in coffee and sweetings | 1 00 | 0 |
| Cu—— and other small things | 2 00 | 0 |
| Amunition | 0 16 | 0 |
| In Pewter, scales and other things | 1 06 | 0 |
| Chest and box | 1 05 | 0 |
| Hetchels | 1 00 | 0 |
| Sope | 1 10 | 0 |
| Pilleon and cloth | 0 15 | 0 |

| | | |
|---|---:|---|
| Chains and cushings joint stools | 2 10 | 0 |
| Augurs Chissels and other tools and old Iron | 5 10 | 0 |
| Shovels and other small things 10lb 13s fiels 6lb | 0 17 | 0 |
| Guns and sword | 5 00 | 0 |
| Iron pots and kettels and old iron | 7 10 | 0 |
| Brass kettles great and small | 5 5 | 0 |
| Wooden and tin ware | 1 10 | 0 |
| Cart, plowe and other husbandry tackling | 4 15 | 0 |
| Earthen and wooden vessels | 1 14 | 0 |
| Cider | 1 00 | 0 |
| Butter and hogs fat 1lb 13s, barrels and other things | 7 05 | 0 |
| Tobacoe, flax crackled and uncrackled | 5 03 | 0 |
| 2 frying pans, clock and other things | 1 00 | 0 |
| Wool, corn and meal—hay and cart rope | 6 00 | 0 |
| Hogshead and barrels, sope, ziddler and sives | 3 10 | 0 |
| Oats £1 10s. Rye and barley £2 10-6, Wheat 3lb 10s. | 7 10 | 0 |
| Hops and ——, bees and hives—beef and porke | 8 08 | 0 |
| —— looking glass and paper | 2 01 | 0 |
| Ink—Penknife and spectacles and other —— | 0 06 | 0 |
| Wheels and baggs | 1 15 | 0 |
| Ciderpress and tackling | 4 00 | 0 |
| House lot and buildings, rear lot trees upon it | 140 00 | 0 |
| 5 Acres of meadow 50lb 11 acres upland New pasture | 61 00 | 0 |
| 2½ acres upland in the great neck | 1 00 | 0 |
| 2½ acres in the old feild | 12 00 | 0 |
| 2½ acres in the new feild | 28 00 | 0 |
| 64 acres of division in the woods | 16 00 | 0 |
| Division, the town 1½ acres and 16 rods | 4 00 | 0 |
| | **£509 15** | **8** |

| | | |
|---|---:|---|
| An Indian Coat | £0 12 | 0 |
| 9 —— of land | 0 4 | 6 |
| Hogs land | 0 4 | 0 |
| Pasture | 2 00 | 0 |
| 6 acres and ½—new: | 6 00 | 0 |
| | **9 00** | **6** |

"A tract of land at Weantenuck we know not what value to put upon it.

    By us Townsmen of Stratford
                JOSEPH HAWLEY,
                SAMUEL SHERMAN,
                JAMES CLARKE,
                TIMOTHY WILCOCKSON,
                JOHN BURRIT."

After the decease of Henry Tomlinson, his widow Alice married John Birdsey, Sen., in 1688.[5] He died April 4, 1690, aged 74 years. She died January 25, 1698, probably about 90 years of age.

Henry Tomlinson brought with him "a coat-of-arms," painted in colors according to the rules of heraldry, which is still preserved, and is in possession of Mrs. Catherine (Plant) Sterling, of Stratford, Ct. This lady, whose mother was Catharine Tomlinson, had a copy of the original, some years ago, which she supposed was the original, and gave it to Mr. William Agur Tomlinson, of Kalamazoo, Michigan. Afterwards the present one

---

[5] "This indenture witnesseth that John Birdsey and Alice Tomlinson, upon consideration of marriage intended, have come to this agreement for prevention of any after trouble between relatious, on one or the other side, as follows: That John Birdsey shall have, enjoy, possess and dispose of any or all of his own estate, in life or death, and Alice Tomlinson shall have full power to dispose of all or any part of her estate of which she is now possessed, in life or death, without any interposition of John Birdsey, or any under heir, or if either of them should be disabled by sickness, then they would mutually contribute out of both of their estates for maintainance of each other during life time, or while they live together. It is furthermore agreed that should Alice Tomlinson outlive John Birdsey, she shall have and enjoy the dwelling-house, garden and yard of John Birdsey, Sen., during the time of her natural life, and it is agreed that John Birdsey, Sen., during the time of her natural ———— shall winter and summer and have six cows for her use. This is the agreement of all hands before marriage, 8th October, 1688.

    Signed and sealed.

Israel Chauncey,    John Birdsey (T) mark.
Richard Blackleach,   Alice Tomlinson (A) mark."
  *Witnesses.*

came into her possession, which in itself, and by the family who preserved it, is known to be the original one brought by Henry Tomlinson to America. Of this "coat-of-arms" a print of a carefully executed engraving is presented as "Frontispiece" in this book. For further account of the Tomlinson coat-of-arms, see introductory pages of this book. Governor Gideon Tomlinson had also a copy of the original.

*The children of Henry and Alice Tomlinson were:*

2   I. ABRAHAM,[2] born in England and died on his way to America.
3  II. JONAS,[2] settled in Derby, Ct.—
4 III. MARGARET,[2] born about 1642; married, November 5, 1662, Jabez Harger, a Huguenot from New Rochelle, N. Y. They settled in Stratford, Ct., where they resided eight or nine years, then removed to Derby, Ct., on Sentinel Hill, where he died in 1678. His widow, Margaret, died Mar. 17, 1698, aged about 56 years. *Their children were:*

    I. Samuel[3] Harger, born Sept. 29, 1663; married, and had three daughters, who were married.
    II. Sarah[3] Harger, born Feb. 5, 1666.
    III. Anna[3] Harger, born Feb. 23, 1668; married John Chatfield Feb. 15, 1684, when she was fourteen years of age, and from them were descended A. Bronson Alcott and his daughter Louisa M. Alcott, the well-known authoress.
    IV. Mary[3] Harger, born Feb. 17, 1669; died Sept. 17, 1673.
    V. Abigail Harger, born March 2, 1671-2.
    VI. Mary Harger, born Mar. —, 1673. No account of her.
    VII. Ebenezer Harger, born Dec. 25, 1674; married and had four sons.

VIII. Abraham³ Harger, born April 1, 1677; married and had sons and daughters.

IX. Jabez³ Harger, born after his father's decease; married and had eight children.

5 IV. MARY,² born ——; married Stephen Pierson, of Derby, Ct., about the year 1675. She died Sept. 25, 1715. He married 2d Esther ——, and he died in Oxford, Ct., May 14, 1739, aged 94 years. They had:

    I. Stephen³ Pierson, married, and had a family.

    II. Sarah³ Pierson, married John Twitchell, ancestor of the Rev. Joseph Twitchell, of Hartford, Ct.

    III. Abraham³ Pierson, whose daughter Hannah married Solomon Chatfield, ancestor in the line of his mother, of A. Bronson Alcott, of Massachusetts, and his daughter, the authoress, Louise M. Alcott.

    IV. John³ Pierson, died before 1704.

    V. Mary³ Pierson, married Josiah Baldwin.

    VI. Bathsheba³ Pierson, married Adam Blakeman, of Stratford, Ct., April 6, 1708.

6 V. TABITHA,² —— ——; married Edward Wooster, of Derby, as second wife in 1669. She had several children probably. Timothy, her son, is mentioned in his grandfather Tomlinson's will.

7 VI. PHEBE,² born Aug. 14, 1656 in Milford; married Lieut. Thomas Wooster, of Derby, about 1672. Her husband was son of Edward Wooster, and hence step-son of her sister Tabitha. Their children were:

    I. Phebe Leavenworth³ Wooster, died Mar. 26, 1696.

    II. Zervia³ Wooster, died Aug. 19, 1682.

    III. Alice³ Wooster, born Sept. 6, 1680; died in 1682.

    IV. Elizabeth³ Wooster, born Sept. 1, 1685; married her first cousin, John Tomlinson, son of Jonas, (No. 12.)

    V. Thomas³ Wooster, born Feb. 18, 1692.

VI. Thankful Webster, born Nov. 7, 1695; died Nov. 18, 1706.

8 VII. Agur,² born Nov. 1, 1658, in Stratford, Ct.—

9 VIII. Bathsheba,² born Jan. 3, 1661, in Stratford; married Ephraim **Stiles**, of Stratford, Ct., as second wife, about 1685. He was a prominent citizen of Stratford, a representative to the General Assembly several years. His first wife was Ruth, widow of Obadiah Wheeler. He died June 21, 1714, and she married (2d) Benjamin **Curtis**, and died in 1735, aged 74 years.

    *His children by the second wife:*
    I. Elizabeth **Stiles**, born Feb. 18, 1687; married June 26, 1707, Ephraim **Curtiss**, of Stratford, and had ten children.
    II. Sarah³ **Stiles**, born Nov. 4, 1693; married Aug. 31, 1710, Thomas **Welles**, of Stratford; had nine children.
    III. Phebe³ **Stiles**, born Mar. 25, 1696; married Oct. 29, 1713, David **Judson**, of Stratford; had ten children, and died May 20, 1765.

10 IX. Abraham,² born May 30, 1662; died same day.

**3. JONAS² TOMLINSON**, son of *Henry¹* and Alice Tomlinson, married Hannah ——. He settled on Great Hill, in Derby, Ct., about 1675, on a tract of land given him by his father, where he resided until his death, in the latter part of the year 1692, or the first part of 1693.

The New Haven Probate Records have the following, concerning Jonas Tomlinson's will:

"June Court, 1693. The deposition of William Tomlinson, aged about 50 years, and Mary Washburn, aged about 22 years.

"These deponents testify and say that upon the 27th of November, 1692, we heard Jonas Tomlinson, of Derby, County of

New Haven in New England, say and declare as his last will, that his will and desire [was] that his wife Hannah, after his decease should have full power to dispose of any part of his estate to pay his debts, and named two parcels of land at a place called White Hills in Stratford bounds, and a parcel of land in the bounds of Derby, called the Great Hill, or any other of his land to pay his debts. He has expressed as his last will that the said Hannah, his wife, should after his decease have full power as he himself, to proportion what estate remained when his debts were paid and the children came of age, only she should give to the eldest a double portion; that the whole estate should be lawfully at her disposal. He said it over and over, for said he, she hath been a loving wife and mother.

    her
MARY W WASHBURN,    WILLIAM TOMLINSON.
   mark.

Jonas Tomlinson's tax list in Derby in 1681, on improved land, was the fifth from the highest, but he held considerable unimproved land, both in Derby and Stratford, now Huntington, which was not taxed in those days.

Administration was granted on the estate of Hannah Tomlinson of Derby, a widow [of Jonas], to Abraham Tomlinson, her eldest son, Feb. 4, 1722-3, there being only four children. On May 6, 1723, Abraham and Samuel agree to support their mother. What her maiden name was is not known.

*Their children were:*

11 I. ABRAHAM.[3]+
12 II. JOHN,[3] born in 1686.+
13 III. ISAAC,[3] born in 1687.+
14 IV. SAMUEL,[3] baptized Dec. —, 1687.+

*8. LIEUT. AGUR² TOMLINSON*, son of
*Henry¹* and Alice Tomlinson, married (1st) Elizabeth, daughter of Jeremiah *Judson*, Dec. 13, 1681.
He married (2d) Sarah, widow of Ephraim *Hawley*,
Oct. 19, 1692. She was the daughter of Samuel
*Welles*, of Wethersfield, Ct., and granddaughter of
Governor Thomas Welles, and died June 29, 1694.
He married (3d) widow Abigail *Brown*, April 14,
1702. He died Mar. 5, 1727-8, in the 70th year of
his age.

His residence was in Derby several years, where
the births of two or three of his children were
recorded, but he returned and remained on the old
homestead in Stratford until his decease.

*Their children were:*

15  I. ALICE,³ died Oct. 11, 1684.
16  II. ELIZABETH,³ born Aug. 11, 1684; married John **Willcoxson**,
    Jun., in June, 1707. They had:
        I. John⁴ **Willcoxson**.
        II. Timothy⁴ **Willcoxson**.

*By second wife:*

17  III. ZECHARIAH,³ born Oct. 31, 1693.+
18  IV. SARAH,³ died June 29, 1694.

*11. ABRAHAM³ TOMLINSON*, son of
*Jonas*,² (*Henry*.¹) and Hannah Tomlinson; married
(1st) Mary *Lockin*. He married (2d) Lois, widow of
Samuel *Wheeler*, of Oronoke in Stratford, July 4,
1728. She was the widow of Ebenezer Riggs, of
Derby, when she married Samuel Wheeler, but her
maiden name is not known. She was the mother of

## Line of Henry Tomlinson.

Capt. James Wheeler, of Derby, where she died Sept. 11, 1767, in her 87th year. Abraham Tomlinson was a prominent citizen of Derby, Ct., and served the town frequently in public office. He was a farmer on Great Hill. His will was dated March 27, 1739, and proved April 27, 1739, and in it he mentions his wife Lois, and all of his children given below, except Mary. The dates of the births of his children are from the Derby town records. The following is on the New Haven Probate Court records: "Division of the estate of Abraham Tomlinson, October, 1761. Jonah, £616 13s. 4d.; Agur Tomlinson, £616 13s. 4d.; Ichabod, £606 13s. 4d."

*Their children were:*

19    I. JONAH,[4] born April 6, 1712, in Derby.+
20    II. AGUR,[4] born Nov. 10, 1713, in Derby.+
21    III. ABRAHAM,[4] born Sept. 2, 1715, in Derby; married Mary, daughter of David Gibson, of Woodbury, Nov. 11, 1760.
22    IV. ICHABOD,[4] born in Derby; died unmarried in 1792.
23    V. MARTHA,[4] born Sept. 22, 1719; is said to have married John Canfield, of Derby.
24    VI. MARY,[4] born December 18, 1721, in Derby.

**12. JOHN[3] TOMLINSON,** son of *Jonas,[2] (Henry,[1])* and Hannah Tomlinson, married March 27, 1712, his cousin, Elizabeth, daughter of Lieut. Thomas *Wooster* and his wife, Phebe (Tomlinson) Wooster. He was a farmer in Derby, Ct., and died in November, 1756, aged 70 years. The birth of six of his children is found on the Derby town records;

the other names, Benjamin and Isaac, are found in his will. In the distribution of his estate in 1756 his children, Phebe, Bathsheba and Hezekiah, are not mentioned.

*Their children were:*

25  I. PHEBE,[4] born Jan. 27, 1713.
26  II. BATHSHEBA,[4] born Dec. 24, 1714.
27  III. JOSEPH,[4] born Dec. 27, 1716.+
28  IV. ELIZABETH,[4] born Dec. 9, 1720, and she married Joseph Twitchell, of Derby, Dec. 6, 1738. She died Feb. 7, 1787, aged 67 years.
29  V. HEZEKIAH,[4] baptized Oct , 1722.
30  VI. ABIGAIL,[4] born July 18, 1723; married Elias Davis, of Derby.
31  VII. JOHN,[4] born Sept. 23, 1725.+
32  VIII. BENJAMIN.[4] His brother John became his guardian in 1756.
33  IX. ISAAC.[4] His brother Joseph became his guardian in 1756.

**13. SERGT. ISAAC[3] TOMLINSON,** son of *Jonas*,[2] (*Henry*[1]) and Hannah Tomlinson, married Patience *Taylor*, March 25, 1712. He died Jan. 27, 1754. His will was dated Jan. 9, 1754, and proved February, 1754, and in it he mentions all of his children given below. He was a representative to the legislature from Derby, and a prominent man in other offices in that town. His widow, Patience, died Sept. 16, 1763.

*Will of Isaac Tomlinson,* Proved in the New Haven Probate Court, First Monday of February, 1754.

In the name of God, Amen. I, Isaac Tomlinson, of Derby, in the County of New Haven, in the Colony of Connecticut in New England, being weak and low in bodily estate, but of sound mind and memory (thanks be given to God for it) see cause to make this my last will and testament in manner and form as followeth:

First of all, I resign and give my soul to God, who gave it hoping and trusting in ye merits of Jesus Christ, my Redeemer, for an Inheritance incorruptable among the blessed; and as for my Body, I desire may be committed to the Earth by Christian Burial; and as for that outward estate of worldly goods which God hath blessed me with, I order and dispose of as followeth:

First of all, I order my funeral expenses and just debts to be paid out of my estate by my executors hereinafter named.

Item. I give and bequeath unto my beloved wife, Patience Tomlinson, my dwelling house with my orchard or four acres of land adjoining to my House with all my Household movables during her natural life; and also two cows with the improvement of my Hill Side Lot during her natural life.

I give and bequeath unto my Daughter, Ann Durand, fifty pounds old Tenor to her and her Heirs forever.

I give and bequeath unto my Daughter, Patience Tomlinson, and to her Heirs forever fifty pounds old Tenor.

I give and bequeath unto my Daughter, Rachel Smith, and to her Heirs forever the sum of fifty pounds old Tenor.

I give and bequeath unto my Daughter, Mary Hawkins, and to her Heirs forever the sum of fifty pounds old Tenor.

I give and bequeath unto my Daughter, Zervia Chatfield, and to her Heirs forever fifty pounds old Tenor.

I devise, give and bequeath unto my Son, Noah Tomlinson, and his Heirs forever my Barn and Half an acre of land adjoining thereto.

I devise, give and bequeath unto my two sons, namely Isaac Tomlinson and Noah Tomlinson, them and their Heirs and Assigns forever all my estate, both real and personal, whatsoever yt might acrue to me, to be equally divided between them.

Lastly my will is, and I do hereby appoint my two sons, namely, Isaac Tomlinson and Noah Tomlinson to be Executors of this my last Will and Testament, and I do hereby utterly disallow, revoke and disannul all and every other Testaments, Wills, Legacies and

Bequests and Executors, by me in any wise before named, willed and bequeathed, ratifying and confirming this and no other to be my last Will and Testament. In confirmation of all that is above written, I, the sd. Isaac Tomlinson, have hereunto set my hand and seal this 9th day of January in the year 1754, &c.

*Witness:*                   his
                                     ISAAC   X   TOMLINSON.
  DANIEL HUMPHREY,                     mark
  SAMUEL BASSET,
  ABIRAM CANFIELD.

*Their children were:*

34  I. ANN,[4] born March 8, 1713; married Joseph **Durand**, of Derby, a son of Doct. John Durand, a Huguenot, who married Elizabeth, daughter of Richard Bryan, of Milford, Ct. Ann (Tomlinson) Durand died Feb. 14, 1778, aged 64 years. Joseph Durand died Aug. 6, 1792, aged 81 years.

*They had six children:*

    I. Samuel[5] **Durand**, born Feb. 28, 1735.
    II. Joseph[5] **Durand**, born March 28, 1737.
    III. Noah[5] **Durand**, born May 12, 1740.
    IV. Ann[5] **Durand**, born Dec. 3, 1742.
    V. Isaac[5] **Durand**, born Aug. 14, 1745.
    VI. Eleazer[5] **Durand**, born Oct. 5, 1754.

35  II. PATIENCE,[4] born Sept. 6, 1715; married Henry Tomlinson (No. 41).
36  III. RACHEL,[4] born Feb. 2, 1718; married Jonathan **Smith**.
37  IV. MARY,[4] born Feb. 18, 1721; married Zechariah **Hawkins**.
38  V. ISAAC,[4] born Oct. 16, 1723.+
39  VI. NOAH,[4] born Mar. 6, 1727.+
40  VII. ZERVIAH,[4] born ——; married Oliver **Chatfield**, of Derby, as second wife.

*Line of Henry Tomlinson.* 23

**14. SAMUEL[3] TOMLINSON**, son of *Jonas*,[2] (*Henry*,[1]) and Hannah Tomlinson, married Hannah ———. He was a selectman several years in Derby, a representative to the legislature from 1730 to 1740. The inventory of his estate, August, 1773, amounted to £366 9s. 11d.

*Their children were:*

41   I. HENRY,[4] born April 18, 1712.+

42  II. ELIZABETH,[4] born October 10, 1713; married Jonathan **Lum**, Jr., of Derby, March 13, 1734. They had eight children:
    I. Anne[5] **Lum**, born March 7, 1735.
    II. Ann[5] **Lum**, born March 22, 1737.
    III. Lemuel[5] **Lum**, born March 2, 1742.
    IV. John[5] **Lum**, born September 5, 1743.
    V. Sarah[5] **Lum**, born November 21, 1745.
    VI. Henry[5] **Lum**, born June 1, 1748.
    VII. Adam[5] **Lum**, born November 11, 1753.
    VIII. Olive[5] **Lum**, born December 9, 1758.

43 III. EUNICE,[4] born December 7, 1715.

44 IV. HANNAH,[4] born September 2, 1718; married Benjamin **Ingraham**, of Derby, February 18, 1742. They had:
    I. Benjamin[5] **Ingraham**, born April 9, 1747.
    II. Samuel[5] **Ingraham**, died September 14, 1751.
    III. Hannah[5] **Ingraham**, born March 12, 1753; died September 20, 1753.
    IV. Abijah[5] **Ingraham**, born May 12, 1755; died September 20, 1761.

45  V. SAMUEL,[4] born December 13, 1720.

46 VI. CALEB,[4] born March 30, 1723.+

47 VII. SARAH,[4] born February 11, 1726; married Isaac **Nichols**, Jr., of Derby, July 22, 1747. She died November 23, 1754.

*They had two children:*
    I. ISAAC[5] **Nichols**, born May 8, 1748.
    II. SARAH[5] **Nichols**, born February 12, 1751.

17. **ZACHARIAH³ TOMLINSON**, son of Lieut. Agur² (Henry¹) and Sarah (Welles) (Hawley) Tomlinson, married (1st) Hannah, daughter of Joseph Beach, March 23, 1718-19. She died Oct. 3, 1740, aged 37 years. He married (2d) widow Mary *Holmes*. She was the daughter of John *Morse*, of Stratford. By tradition and records in the family she was the widow of Daniel Holmes, who died in 1738. Zachariah Tomlinson died Mar. 15, 1768, aged 75 years. He was a prominent citizen of Stratford, and was the only grandson of Henry Tomlinson, resident in the town of Stratford. He was born a little over twelve years after his grandfather died, and thirty-five years before the death of his father, Agur, and the coat-of-arms, painted in large size, is traced to his possession, as having descended to him from his grandfather, Henry Tomlinson, and hence the historical certainty that it was brought hither by the said Henry Tomlinson.

The inscriptions on the gravestones of these persons in the Stratford old cemetery are:

"In memory of Mr. Zachariah Tomlinson, who Departed this Life on y$^e$ 15$^{th}$ day of April, Anno Domni, 1768, in y$^e$ 75$^{th}$ Year of His Age."

"Here lyes y$^e$ Body of Mrs. Hannah Tomlinson, Wife of Mr. Zachariah Tomlinson, who departed this life Octo$^{br}$ 5$^{th}$, 1740, in y$^e$ 37 year of her age."

*The Will of Zachariah Tomlinson, of Stratford village, 1768.*

"IN THE NAME OF GOD, AMEN."

I, Zachariah Tomlinson, of Stratford, in the County of Fairfield and Colony of Connecticut in New England, being sick and weak of body, but of sound mind and memory, and being mindful of mortality, do make and ordain this my last Will and Testament.

FIRST of all, I freely resign my soul into the hands of God who gave it, and my body to be decently buried in a Christian manner at the discretion of my executors hereafter named, hoping in the merits of Christ Jesus my Savior to receive the same at the resurrection.

AND as to the worldly goods and estate which it hath pleased God to bestow upon me in this life, I give and bestow in manner following:

*Imprimis.* I will that my debts and funeral charges be first paid and answered, and having heretofore in marriage articles with my beloved wife Jemima, dated the 30th of November, 1758, settled upon and given her fifty pounds lawful money and the use of two rooms in the house where I now dwell, with household furniture, the use of which she is to accept in lieu of dowry, I do hereby ratify and confirm said articles, and order that the same be punctually performed; which rooms shall be in such part of my said house as she shall choose. And I do hereby give unto my said wife over and above what I have given her in said agreement, the use and improvement of convenient room in my cellar under said house for her use, with liberty of passage for said use, and the use of two good milk cows and a horse proper for her use, and the use of the garden adjoining south of my said house, and the use of my Negro woman called Hannah, if she see cause to have her, during the time she remains my widow and lives in my said house and no longer; said two cows and horse to be provided for with hay, sheltering and pasturing, and said Negro with boarding and clothing during the time aforesaid by my executors and my grandson Jabez Huntington Tomlinson. And also, I give unto my said wife during said time necessary food and support, and firewood convenient and sufficient for her spending brought to her door, cut fit for her use during the time she remains my widow.

*Item.* I give and bequeath unto my loving son Agur Tomlinson twenty pounds out of my moveable estate over and above what I have given him in education in consideration of his being my

eldest son. And also, I give and bequeath unto my said son, over and above what I have given him by deed, all my lands and meadows southerly of the line lately called the general line inclosing what was lately called the general field south of the country road, saving two pieces of lot meadow in the Great Neck and one piece of upland of about two acres; and all my land on Clabboard hill north of said country road lately inclosed with fence; to him and his heirs forever. Also about an acre and quarter of meadow on Carting Island adjoining to what I have already given him there.

*Item.* I give and bequeath to my loving son, Joseph Tomlinson, over and above what I have already given him by deed, all my part of that farm and tract of land and buildings where he now lives. I having heretofore given him one-half thereof; also one acre of meadow on the upper island, it being the remains of that meadow which I have already given him by deed; also my lot of land on Long hill which I purchased of Wakelee; also all my land in Wells Hollow and Wells Hill, be it more or less; to him and his heirs forever.

*Item.* I give and bequeath unto my loving son Beach Tomlinson over and above what I have already given him by deed, all my lands and buildings lying on the lower White hills, excepting Summer's lot, to him and his heirs forever.

*Item.* I give and bequeath unto my loving son Zachariah Tomlinson, over and above what I have already given him by deed, one hundred acres of land lying at Bank's Wigwam or Webb's Rocks, adjoining what I have given him by deed, to lie in proper form to him and his heirs forever.

*Item.* I give and bequeath to my loving son Abraham Tomlinson, over and above what I have given him by deed, and over and above the three hundred pounds which I paid to the Reverend Mr. Hezekiah Gold for the house and homestead where my said son now dwells, the said three hundred pounds to be recoued and deemed as so much in partition of my estate; also my meadow in the common meadow in the Great Neck in the salt ponds; and also about two acres of upland which I bought of Josiah Beardslee.

*Item.* I give and bequeath unto my grand-son Jabez Huntington Tomlinson, son of my late beloved deceased son, Gideon Tomlinson, over and above what I have given by deed to my said son Gideon, in his life time, the one-half of my homestead with the one equal half of all the buildings and appurtenances thereon standing and thereto belonging, the other equal half I have given to his said father, the said Gideon, deceased; also two acres of meadow lying

in Oronoque meadow, called Griffin's meadow, the which he is to possess when he arrives to the age of twenty-one years as is here after expressed.

My will further is that in consideration of that money I owed his father the said deceased Gideon, he have divided, and set off to him so much of my lands as shall be deemed equivalent to said sums of money, and that my said grand-son do possess the same as his own proper estate, his heirs and assigns forever, which is so to be set off out of my lands lying on Oronoque hills.

*Item.* I give and bequeath to my daughter, Sarah Olcott, the wife of Thomas Olcott, besides what I have given her already in household stuff and portion, three lots and pieces of land lying in the Society of Westbury, in the township of Waterbury and County of Newhaven, containing about one hundred acres in the whole; also ten pounds in money and ten sheep out of my movable estate, besides what household furniture may be now in my dwelling house belonging formerly to her mother, which last article shall not be reconed a part of her portion.

*Item.* I give and bequeath unto my daughter Mary Kellogg, wife of Judah Kellogg, all my land, lying in the place called Scatacook in the town of Kent, which I bought of the Government, to her and her heirs forever. Also I give to my said daughter Mary, two cows with calves by their sides; also two neat kine of one year old each; also my sorrel mare now called Molly's mare; also I give to my said daughter ten sheep; and also I give her the use of that part of my dwelling house and buildings not before herein given to my said wife with the use of a garden near or adjoining thereto, for her and hers to live in until my abovesaid grandson shall arrive to the age of twenty one years, but not to lease it or let the same upon hire when she and hers shall depart from said house and not dwell there; and also the use of all my land in my said homestead in that part which I have herein given to my said grandson and the use of that meadow called Griffin's, lying in said Oronoque meadow. Also I order her to find my said wife with hay, viz: her equal proportion with my said executor grandson, for her proper use off said meadow, and also liberty to cut wood off any of my woodland which I have not heretofore disposed of and that I shall die seized of; that is, so much wood as shall be needful for fire wood to burn in the fire that my said daughter shall prudently keep in her part of said house; the said Mary doing her proportionable part in keeping said house and barn and fences in good repair.

Also I give and bequeath unto my said daughter Mary, one hundred and fifty pounds lawful money, to be paid her out of my movable estate by my executors within one year after my decease.

Also my will further is that my said daughter shall have all the things that were her own mother's, in my said house; and all the linen that she hath spun over and above not to be reconed as part of her proportion.

Also, my will is that my said daughter and wife shall have family provisions found them out of my stores one year.

*Item.* My will is that my executors deliver unto the Rev. Mr. Izrahiah Wetmore, our minister, two loads of walnut wood yearly, and every year for six years after my decease.

And I give and dispose of all the residue of my estate, both real and personal, to my said five sons and my said grandson, to be divided amongst them in manner following, viz.: that all the estate I have heretofore by deeds of gift and now by this my will, given them as above, be properly appraised, and that son or grandson that shall appear to have had by deed of gift, or by this my will, the greatest share and portion, his estate shall be the standard, and the rest of my sons or grandson shall have portions of their said residue so as to make them equal to him that so appears to have had the greatest share and portion, and then the rest or residue to be equally divided amongst them, so as that in the whole and final settlement all my said sons, with said grandson, shall be equal in their shares of my estate.

My will further is that my said grandson do not take possession of such estate, as I have herein bequeathed him until he shall arrive to the age of twenty-one years (he being at this time a minor) but that the same shall be improved by my executors hereafter named for the benefit of the estate in general for the payment of the debts of the estate and settlement of the same, and if it should be so ordered that my said grandson, Jabez Huntington, should decease and not arrive to the age of twenty-one years to take possession of the same that then my will is that said estate be so divided between my said five sons, Agur Tomlinson, Joseph Tomlinson, Beach Tomlinson, Zachariah Tomlinson and Abraham Tomlinson, their heirs and assigns forever.

My will further is that my said five sons and my said grandson, in equal proportions do at all times support and supply what I have herein made necessary for my said wife, except the hay for my wife which Mary is to bear her equal portion of; also, in providing the wood that I have herein ordered for the Rev. Mr. Wetmore.

Also, if it should so happen that if any of my lands herein devised, or otherwise, such lands as are not divided herein may be contested in law, my will is that my said five sons and my grandson shall in equal proportion bear the cost and expense of said determination in law, if may be.

Also, my will is, that all such estate as is herein given to my said grandson, both real and personal, shall be and remain in the hands of my said executors, to be improved by them for the use of settling my estate until he arrive at the age of twenty-one years, and that he is to receive it without the benefit of any previous improvement to that time.

And I do hereby constitute, ordain and appoint my said sons, Agur Tomlinson, Joseph Tomlinson, Beach Tomlinson, Zechariah Tomlinson and Abraham Tomlinson, executors of this my last will and Testament, revoking all other wills by me made, and confirming this to be my last will and testament.

In witness whereof I have hereunto set my hand and seal this 8th day of April, A.D. 1768.
ZACH[H] TOMLINSON.

Signed, sealed, published, pronounced and declared by the said Tomlinson to be his last will and testament in presence of

STILES CURTISS,
GEORGE THOMPSON,
JOSEPH BIRDSEY.

*Children of Zachariah and Sarah (Welles) Tomlinson:*

48 I. AGUR,[4] born September 13, 1720.+
49 II. SARAH,[4] born Sept. 23, 1722; married (1st) Hezekiah **Thompson**, of Stratford, in 1748. He died in September, 1750, aged 28 years. She married (2d) Thomas Olcott, in 1757.

*The children of Zachariah and Sarah (Tomlinson) Thompson were:*

  I. Zechariah[5] **Thompson**, born October 22, 1749.
  II. Sarah[5] **Thompson**, born February 15, 1750-51; married Hezekiah **Curtiss** in 1771, and had one son and four daughters.

*The children of Thomas and Sarah (Tomlinson) (Thompson) Olcott were:*

    III. Thomas **Olcott**,⁵ born October 5, 1758, married Mary, daughter of Andrew **Thompson**, of New Haven, and had William, Thomas and George.

    IV. Josiah **Olcott**,⁵ born July 19, 1760; married and had 13 children, and died at Hudson, N. Y.

    V. Anna **Olcott**,⁵ born April 28, 1761; married Doctor Isaac **Bronson**, of Greenfield Hill, Fairfield County, Ct. He was the first president of the first bank in Bridgeport, and held the office for many years. His descendants still reside at Greenfield Hill.

    VI. Hannah **Olcott**,⁵ born January 25, 1762; married Beach **Judson**, of Stratford, March 31, 1780.

    VII. Mary **Olcott**,⁵ born August 3, 1763; married Nehemiah **Gorham**, March, 1784.

50    III. JOSEPH,⁴ born November 13, 1724.+

51    IV. BEACH,⁴ born December 3 or 7, 1726.+

52    V. ZECHARIAH,⁴ born March 23, 1729-30.+

53    VI. GIDEON,⁴ born March 16, 1730-1.+

54    VII. ABRAHAM,⁴ born April 28, 1733.+

55    VIII. HENRY,⁴ born July 21, 1735; died November 19, 1738.

56    IX. DAUGHTER,⁴ born August 15, 1737; died the same day.

57    X. HENRY,⁴ born April 6, 1739; died February, 1739-40.

58    XI. MARY,⁴ baptized in November 1744; married Judah **Kellogg**, who was graduated at Yale College in 1763, and soon after came to Stratford, where he taught school several years. In 1774 he purchased a home in Cornwall, Conn., where he resided until his decease in 1820, aged 80 years. He was a representative from that town, a justice of the peace many years, and town clerk 36 years. He with his sons, William and Frederick, held the office of town clerk 69

*Line of Henry Tomlinson.* 31

years. His widow Mary died August 24, 1836, aged 91 years. *Their children were:*

I. Mary⁵ Kellogg, married Eliphalet Shepard and died July 19, 1862, aged 79 years.

II. William⁵ Kellogg, was a prominent man in Connecticut, had four sons, and died May 28, 1829, aged 60 years.

III. John⁵ Kellogg, married, had a family of ten children, all of whom emigrated to the Western States,— Wisconsin, Minnesota, and Kansas.

IV. Frederick⁵ Kellogg, was a merchant and succeeded his father as town clerk, was Judge of Probate and held other prominent offices.

V. Lucius Kellogg settled at Oyster Bay, L. I., where he became eminent as a physician.

**19. JONAH⁴ TOMLINSON**, son of *Abraham,³ (Jonas,² Henry,¹)* and Mary (—) Tomlinson, married Mary, daughter of the Rev. Joseph *Moss*, of Derby, Ct., Nov. 26, 1734. He resided in Derby, and died Oct. 2, 1796. The amount of the inventory of his estate, Oct. 11, 1796, was £2,488 10s. 2d.

*Their children were:*

60  I. ABRAHAM,⁵ born July 20, 1738.+
61  II. MARY,⁵ born Sept. 26, 1740; married —— Poole.
62  III. MARTHA,⁵ born May 13, 1743; married —— Woodruff.
63  IV. SAMUEL,⁵ born April 26, 1745.
64  V. NABBY,⁵ born April 21, 1747.
65  VI. CALEB,⁵ born Sept. 11, 1749.+
66  VII. ANNE,⁵ born Sept. 1, 1753.
67  VIII. SAMMY, LORD MOSS,⁵ born Dec. 15, 1757.+
68  IX. ABIGAIL,⁵ married David Bassett, Oct. 2, 1773.

**20. AGUR TOMLINSON,** son of Abraham,³(Jonas,² Henry,¹) and Mary(—) Tomlinson, married Dec. 4, 1734, Sarah, daughter of Rev. Nathaniel *Bowers*, of Rye and Greenwich, N. Y. and of Newark, N. J. He died Feb. 7 (?) 1800, aged 87 years. He was the Agur Tomlinson referred to by J. W. Barber in his Historical Collections, as having brought up and educated Chuse, who in later years was the Indian Chief at Chusetown, afterwards Humphreysville, now Seymour, Ct. Mr. Barber says:[6] "His father, Gideon Manwehu, wishing to have his son brought up among the white people, sent Joe to Agur Tomlinson, of Derby, with whom he lived during his minority."

*Agur Tomlinson's Will.*

"IN THE NAME OF GOD, AMEN.

I, Agur Tomlinson, of Derby, in the County of New Haven and State of Connecticut, being advanced in age and, in my own view, drawing towards the close of life, though at present in full exercise of Reason and sound memory, would first of all commit my immortal soul to God, who gave it, hoping through divine grace to be finally accepted of him thro' Jesus Christ the great Redeemer, and would with the worldly estate God in his providence has been pleased to Bless me with make the following disposition of which is my last Will and Testament:

1. I would recommend that my Executors, hereafter Named, shall pay out of my estate my funeral charges and all my just debts, giving me a decent and Honorable Burial.

2. My Will and Testament is, and I give it in Charge, that my Executors see that my Negro man named Quosh and his wife named Rose be made free, and I hereby order my Executors to give my said

---

[6] Hist. Coll., 199-200. Also Derby History, xliv.

Negro man the use and improvement of one Hundred pounds worth of land to be set out to the said Quosh for him to use and improve as long as he, the said Quosh and his wife Rose may live together, with one Yoke of Oxen and one good cow, with needful farming Utensils, such as Plough, Chain, Ax, hoe, and Sythe, &c.

I give and bequeath to my three sons, Joseph Tomlinson, Web Tomlinson, and to the heirs of David Tomlinson deceased, my estate both real and personal, a double share to what either of my Daughters, viz.: Sarah Tomlinson and Hannah Hawkins, widow and relict of Freegift Hawkins deceased, shall have, that is to say, I give unto my eldest son Joseph just as much again as I give to either of my daughters of my real estate and personal estate, taking into consideration what he the said Joseph has already received of me as part of Portion, to be estimated according to its value when he received it, near as possible.

I also give unto my son Web Tomlinson, my second son, an equal share with my eldest son Joseph of my real and personal estate, taking into consideration whatever I have already given unto him, the said Web, viz.: to the avails of a piece of land lying at Squontuck so called, sold to Jonathan Lum. Jr., and to the avails of one piece of land at said Squontuck sold to Nathan Mansfield, and to the avails of one piece of land at the falls so called, to one right in Mumphrymagog, and to the avails of other lands given by me to the said Web, and also to the avails of one Negro Boy named James.

I also give and bequeath unto the heirs of my Third son David an equal share of what I give unto my other sons, viz.: Joseph and Web, that is to say, to the whole of the heirs of my son David, considered compoundedly as unto either Joseph or Web, to be distributed in manner following, viz.: David and Agur, my two grandsons, to have a double share to either of their sisters, of my estate, both real and personal, and my two grand-daughters, viz.: Nancy and Betsy Tomlinson, heirs of my son David deceased, one Half as much of my estate as either of my grandsons, viz.: David and Agur, shall have.

Also, I give of my estate unto my eldest daughter Sarah Farmer, one half as much of all my estate, real and personal, as I give unto either of my sons, taking into consideration what I have already given to my daughter Sarah, viz.: one Negro girl named Jude, and notes of hand to the amount of fifty-three pounds and other things.

And lastly, I give unto my youngest daughter, Hannah Hawkins, an equal share or right in all my estate, both real and personal, which I give unto my eldest daughter, Sarah, that is half as much as I give to either of my above-named sons, taking into consideration what she, the said Hannah, hath already received as portion.

And moreover, I do by this presents in this my last will and testament constitute and appoint my son Joseph Tomlinson to be, and he is hereby appointed and authorized to be my Executor to put this my last Will and Testament of mine in execution, as soon as may be convenient after my decease.

In witness whereof I have hereunto set my hand and seal this 6th day of April, A.D. 1795.

AGUR TOMLINSON.<br>Proved Feb. 5, 1800."

In presence of
    THOMAS YALE,
    NOAH DURAND,
    BENJAMIN BASSETT,
    JOSIAH SMITH.

Before RUSSELL TOMLINSON, Justice of the Peace.

The "Negro Man named Quosh" became quite a noted character in Derby, Ct., as set forth in the *History* of that town, on page 548.

"Near the old road that winds its way through the woods above Derby Neck, there stands a rude domicile, built nearly one hundred years ago. So secluded is the spot that its dwellers within could never see the rising sun, though surrounded by romantic, beautiful and poetic scenery. Here was born, reared and educated, the last sable governor of Connecticut, Roswell Freeman, who died October 6, 1877, aged 74 years.

His father was the slave of Agur Tomlinson, although he "bossed" the master, and when young was known only by the name of Quash. His mother, whose name was Rose, was a slave to the Rev. Thomas Yale, a minister of the Congregational Church. When the State threw off the yoke of human bondage Quash took the name of Quash Freeman, which he always retained. Tomlinson gave him with his freedom the above-named hut, a cow and the use of some thirty acres of land."

"According to the custom of the colored freemen of that time, Quash was elected their governor of the State. He held the office many years. He possessed herculian strength, a giant six-footer, and it is said of him that he could take a bull by the horns and the nose and at once prostrate him to the ground. No one ever dared to molest, or tried to make him afraid, and when he was approaching in the distance he awakened the sense of a coming thunder cloud.

"Tradition says that one dark night when he was out with his son Roswell, on the Housatonic fishing, and a party from the other side came in collision with his skiff and were much damaged, they sang out: 'There is a lot of niggers over this side, and if you don't keep your net out of our way we will come over and flax you out.' Quash coolly replied, 'Nigger this side too.' Enough was said, for

they knew his voice and dared not trouble him.
Physically speaking, Quash was probably the strong-
est and largest man that ever shared the guber-
natorial honors of this commonwealth."

"After Connecticut in 1789 or 90 made a law to
free all persons born in slavery, it was required that
such persons, with their ages, should be entered
upon the town records, and therefore the following
is on the Derby records:

"New Haven County, February 7, 1791.

Personally appeared Mr. Agur Tomlinson and made oath that
he has in his possession a negro boy named Peter, belonging to
David Tomlinson [Agur's son] deceased, aged five years and three
months wanting one day.

Entered per John Humphreys, town clerk."

"In December, 1792, Mr. Agur Tomlinson made oath to the
possession of a negro boy named Timothy, aged one year and
twenty-five days."

"On April 20, 1795, Mr. Agur Tomlinson made oath that he
was possessed of a negro girl named Olive, aged eight months the
first day of May, 1795."

The inventory of Agur Tomlinson's estate,
amounted to £1,840 12s. 4d., including "one Negro
man, named Shubel Et., 22 years, at £30," and the
"avails of one Negro boy named James," by which
he meant the value of his time until he should be
twenty-five years old, when he became free by limi-
tation of the law at that time, concerning young
persons who were slaves.

## Line of Henry Tomlinson. 37

The inventory of his Books is as follows:

| | |
|---|---|
| Mr. Samuel Hopkins, Body of Divinity, 2 volumes folio, | £0 12 0 |
| 1 vol. by Doct' Edwards on religious affections, 1'6, A-adominum, 19, . . . . . . . | 0 2 3 |
| 1 vol. by Doc'r Watts on the improvement of the mind. | 0 2 6 |
| 4 small vols. on various subjects in Divini'y, | 0 4 6 |

*The children of Agur and Sarah Tomlinson were:*

69   I. NATHANIEL,[5] born April 9, 1736; not mentioned in his father's will, yet he is said to have married and had a son Truman.

70  II. JOSEPH.[5] +

71  III. WEBB.[5] +

72  IV. DAVID.[5] +

73  V. ABRAHAM.[5]

74  VI. SARAH,[5] married ——— Farmer.

75  VII. HANNAH.[5] married Freegift Hawkins, of Derby, and had Mercy, who married ——— Fowler.

**27. JOSEPH[4] TOMLINSON.** son of *John*[3] (*Jonas*,[2] *Henry*[1]) and Elizabeth (Wooster) Tomlinson, married Sarah *Beers*, May 24, 1743, who died Feb. 22, 1776.

*Their children were:*

76  I. BETTY,[5] born Mar. 23, 1744; married Benjamin Davis.

77  II. JOSEPH.[5]  (A Joseph Tomlinson, of Oxford, Ct., married Elizabeth Hull, of Derby, Ct., Oct. 14, 1776.)

78  III. WEBB.[5]  Derby Church Record of Baptisms says: "Joseph Webb, baptized Aug. 4, 1765," but probably it was not this person.

79  IV. DAVID.[5]

80  V. POLLY,[5] baptized Mar. 29, 1767, in Derby.

**31. CAPT. JOHN TOMLINSON**, son of John,³ (Jonas,² Henry,¹) and Elizabeth (Wooster) Tomlinson, married Deborah, daughter of Capt. Samuel *Bassell*, of Derby, Ct., April 28, 1748. Their home was on "Great Neck" (now Birmingham) in Derby, Ct.

"May, 1770. This Assembly do establish John Tomlinson to be Captain of the 18th company or trainband in the second regiment in this Colony." (Col. Rec. XIII., 297.)

The Derby History has the following concerning Captain Tomlinson in 1779, when General Tryon invaded New Haven:

"When Tryon's forces arrived at New Haven, Capt. John Tomlinson, who then lived at Derby Neck, in the old mansion now owned by Truman Piper, happened to be in that city, and, mistrusting the object of their mission, quickly mounted his horse and spurred him on in hot haste over the hills until he reached the peaceful hamlet of Derby Narrows, when he shouted at the top of his voice, 'The British are in New Haven, look out for your pork, look out for your pork'!"

Now this Captain Tomlinson was a reliable man, a convert to the Whitefield doctrine, and it is said he did more praying and exhorting than half the town. He labored for the good of his fellow-men and lived to be over ninety years old. In his last sickness a neighbor was called in to watch with him, who was not particularly a religious man, and who had on a short coat, but he was soon relieved of his expected night's work. When he entered the sick chamber the Captain greeted him with the salutation, 'Be gone, thou enemy of all righteousness, the Devil never looked worse than when in a short coat.'

---

† War provisions stored there.

When the Captain brought the news to Derby Narrows concerning the British, the day was far spent, but in those times Yankee Doodle, ever on the alert, ready to fight for country and fireside, was equal to the emergency. Alarmed at the near approach of the enemy, men, women, and even boys sallied out, and soon the work of removal to a place of safety commenced. Among others, a tall, slender lad aged sixteen years, named Isaac Smith, was signaled out to assist in taking care of the military stores. His father was then an officer in the military company from Derby stationed at Danbury, and we may here mention that the old slave Quash, (of Agur Tomlinson) father of Governor Roswell Quash (colored), who died about two years ago [1880] was his body guard. Young Smith full of patriotic fire, yoked his father's oxen, hitched them to his cart, and soon the work of hauling the pork from the old building was in lively operation. Load after load was conveyed up the lonely cart and cow paths, zigzag here and there among the shrub oaks, guided only by the glittering stars, and dumped into the famous hollow about a quarter of a mile below the present almshouse on the right of the main road as you now go to Seymour in West Ansonia. This hollow was dense with low shrub oaks, and furnished a capital hiding place, and ever afterwards was known as Pork Hollow."

The grave-stone inscriptions in the old cemetery at Derby, Ct., read:

"In memory of Capt. John Tomlinson, who died Nov. 18, 1817, aged 92 years."

"In memory of Mrs. Deborah Tomlinson, Consort of Capt. John Tomlinson, and daughter of Samuel Bassett, Esqr., who departed this life Sept. 29, 1796, in the 71st year of her age."

"She lived beloved and died lamented by all her acquaintance."

*Children of Capt. John and Deborah Tomlinson:*

81   I. DAMARIS,⁵ born in 1748; died Dec. 28, 1825, aged 77 years.
82   II. PHEBE,⁵ born Sept. 23, 1750.
83   III. LEVI,⁵ born Feb. 15, 1752.+
84   IV. LUTHENE,⁵ born Jan. 27, 1755.
85   V. JOHN LEWIS,⁵ born Jan. 24, 1757.+
86   VI. DANIEL,⁵ born May 20, 1759.+

*38. CAPT. ISAAC⁴ TOMLINSON,* son of *Sergt. Isaac³ (Jonas,² Henry¹)* and Patience (Taylor) Tomlinson, married Sibyl ("Sibillia") *Russell,* Jan. 17, 1749-50. She died May 29, 1775, and he married (2d) Mary ——. He removed from Derby to Woodbury. Ct., in 1758 or 9, where he died Dec. 20, 1806, aged 84 years. His second wife, Mary, died Sept. 15, 1843, aged 83 years.

"This Assembly do establish Mr. Isaac Tomlinson to be Captain of the first company or trainband in the town of Woodbury. Ct., October, 1767." ⁸

Isaac Tomlinson, of Derby, marched "for the Relief of Boston in the Lexington Alarm, April, 1775." He was two days in the service, at that time, the same as all his company that went.

He was in the 3d Company under General David Wooster in 1775; enlisted May 15, discharged Dec. 1, 1775. This company served at the siege of Boston.⁹

---

⁸ Col. Records, vol. XII., 613.

⁹ See Adjutant General's Report of Soldiers in the Revolutionary War.

## Line of Henry Tomlinson.

*Children of Capt. Isaac and Sibyl Tomlinson:*

92    I. SIBYL,⁵ born September 10, 1750, in Derby.

93    II. ISAAC,⁵ born August 31, 1752, in Derby.+

94    III. RUSSELL,⁵ born December 23, 1754, in Derby.+

95    IV. TIMOTHY,⁵ born June 18, 1757, in Derby.+

96    V. SAMUEL,⁵ born July 9, 1759, in Woodbury; died May 25, 1809. His widow Jerusha, died April 1, 1804, aged 49.

97    VI. DAVID,⁵ (Hon.), born March 29, 1761.

98    VII. MARY ANN,⁵ born February 11, 1763; died March 29, 1777, of small pox.

99    VIII. SARAH,⁵ born May 12, 1765; married Dr. Phineas *Meigs*. One of her children was the Rev. Benjamin C. Meigs, missionary to Ceylon. Other descendants lived at Waterbury, Conn.

**39. *NOAH TOMLINSON*,** son of *Isaac*,³ (*Jonas*,² *Henry*,¹) and Patience (Taylor) Tomlinson, married Abigail *Beers* July 2, 1747. They resided in Derby, Ct.

*Their children were:*

100    I. AMARILLA⁵, born June 28, 1748; died July 12, 1748.

101    II. DAN,⁵ born July 30, 1749.+

102    III. NABBY,⁵ born October 22, 1751; died April 22, 1753.

103    IV. NOAH,⁵ born June 8, 1753; died June 16, 1753.

104    V. BEERS,⁵ born March 13, 1755.+

105    VI. NOAH,⁵ born August 3, 1757.

106    VII. NATHAN,⁵ born August 4, 1760.+

107    VIII. LUCY,⁵ born July 19, 1767; died September 16, 1767.

108    IX. LUCY,⁵ born July 18, 1769; died March 30, 1791.

**41. HENRY[4] TOMLINSON,** son of *Samuel,* (*Jonas,*[2] *Henry.*[1]) and Hannah (—) Tomlinson, married Patience, daughter of Sergt. Isaac Tomlinson. They were first cousins. (No. 35.)

*Their children were:*

- 109    I. SIBYL,[5] born April 11, 1738.
- 110    II. SAMUEL,[5] born Jan. 4, 1739; died Sept. 13, 1742.
- 111    III. HANNAH,[5] born Dec. 16, 1743; married —— Waters.
- 112    IV. EUNICE,[5] born Feb. 27, 1746.
- 113    V. SARAH,[5] born June 4, 1747.
- 114    VI. PATIENCE,[5] born in 1748, married Yelverton Perry, of Derby, Ct. He died June 30, 1821, aged 83 years. She died Sept. ——, 1823, aged 75 years. Both were buried in the Lower White Hills cemetery, in Huntington, Ct.

*Their children were:*

I. John[6] Perry, married Anna Beardsley, of Monroe, and settled in Amenia, Dutchess county, N. Y., and had Charles, John and Nancy.

II. Herman[6] Perry, a sea captain, who sailed from Baltimore. He married Susannah Henrys, of Baltimore. He contracted yellow fever in Havana and died soon after reaching home. They had children: Herman, Albert, William, Susannah.

III. Frederick[6] Perry, married Mary Strong of Southbury, Ct., where they resided.

IV. Hawley[6] Perry, married Polly Leavenworth, of Huntington, Ct. They had only Jane, who married David Shelton, of Huntington, Ct.

V. Nancy[6] Perry, married Truman Tomlinson.

## Line of Henry Tomlinson. 43

VI. Laura⁴ **Perry**, married David **Smith**, of Kent, Ct., a Baptist minister, removed somewhere near Lake Ontario, New York.

115   VII. HENRY,⁵ born Oct. 20, 1752.+

116   VIII. ANNE,⁵ married Nathaniel **Mansfield**, who kept a tavern at Squantuck, in Derby.

117   IX. BETTY.⁵

**46. CALEB⁴ TOMLINSON**, son of *Samuel³* (*Jonas,² Henry¹*), married Mary ——. He died June 28, 1764.

*Their children were:*

118   I. SAMUEL,⁵ born Oct. 18, 1747.

119   II. ABIGAIL,⁵ born Mar. 30, 1750; married Noah **Durand**, grandson of Doct. John Durand and his wife Elizabeth **Bryan**, of Derby. They lived on Great Neck in Derby. Noah Durand died April 12, 1818. Abigail, his widow, died Nov. 2, 1831.

*Their children were:*

I. Anna **Durand**,⁶ born Jan. 4, 1772; married Lewis **Hawkins**, and died Nov. 18, 1840.

II. Polly **Durand**,⁶ born July 11, 1775; married Samuel **Yale**, a merchant, son of Rev. M. Yale. She died Jan. 6, 1841.

III. Joseph **Durand**,⁶ a tailor, born July 17, 1778; married Margaret **Chamberlin**, of New York City. He returned to his father's house, and died Oct. 12, 1821.

IV. William **Durand**,⁶ born May 29, 1780; married Sarah **Ambler**, of Bethlehem, Conn., where they lived. He was a tailor.

V. Samuel **Durand**,⁵ born July 13, 1788; married four times; was a farmer in Derby.

VI. David **Durand**,⁶ born May 1, 1790; married Maria, daughter of Edmund **Leavenworth**, of Huntington. He lived on his father's homestead on Derby Neck.

120 III. ANNE,⁵ born Sept. 7, 1752.
121 IV. REBECCA,⁵ born Nov. 14, 1760.

*48. DOCT. AGUR⁴ TOMLINSON*, son of *Zachariah³ (Agur,² Henry¹)* and Hannah (Beach) Tomlinson, married Mary, daughter of the Rev. Hezekiah *Gold*. She was born Feb. 29, 1723-4, and died June 23, 1802, in her 79th year. He died Feb. 15, 1774, aged 53 years. He was graduated at Yale College in 1744, in the class with Timothy Dwight, Leverett Hubbard and Samuel Tracey. He studied medicine and practiced his profession in Stratford, where he was noted for his eccentricities and keenness of observation. His home was on Main street, on the corner occupied by the late George A. Talbot.

Agur Tomlinson was Representative from Stratford, Oct. 1752, Oct. 1755, Jan. 1756, Feb. 1756, March 1756, May 1757, October 1757, March 1758, May 1758, October 1767, October 1768, January 1769, October 1769.

He was appointed Justice of the Peace, and reappointed as follows:

May 1758, May 1759, May 1760, May 1761, May 1762, May 1763, May 1764, May 1765, May 1766, May 1767, May 1768, May 1769, May 1770, May 1771, May 1772 (Colonial Records.)

"This Assembly do establish and confirm Mr. Agur Tomlinson to be of the 1st company or trainband in the town of Stratford, and order that he be commissioned accordingly." May, 1754. (Col. Rec., vol. X., 264.)

"Here lies interred the Remains of Agur Tomlinson, Esq., who departed this Life, February the 15th, A. D. 1774, in the 53d year of his age.

> You pass with melancholy state
> By all these solemn heaps of fate,
> And think as soft as sad you tread above the Venerable Dead,
> Time was like you Life possessed
> And time will be when you shall rest.

"In Memory of Mrs. Mary Tomlinson, Relict of Agur Tomlinson, Esq., who died June 23d, 1802, in the 79 year of her age.

"In Memory of Mary Alace, the Daughter of Agur Tomlinson, Esq. and Mrs. Mary his Wife, who died Oct. 8th, A. D. 1771, Aged 5 years and 1 month; and 5 other infant children of the above Parents, who lie here interred.

> Sleep lovely Babes and take your perfect rest,
> God called you home because he thought it right."

*Children of Doct. Agur and Mary Tomlinson:*

122 I. KATEE,⁵ baptized in June, 1746; married Abijah **McEwen**, of Stratford, Mar., 1771. She died Dec. 28, 1774. He married (2d) Jerusha, daughter of Abraham **Tomlinson**, and cousin to his first wife, Nov. 28, 1778.

*The children by the first wife were:*

I. Mary Alice McEwen,⁶ born Dec. 1, 1772; died young.

II. Katharine Maria McEwen,⁶ born Mar. 27, 1773; married Victory Wetmore, April 3, 1791. He was a merchant in Stratford, where she died a widow, Oct. 14, 1859, aged 86 years.

*The children by the second wife were:*

III. Charles McEwen, born Sept. 22, 1779.

IV. Maria Katharine McEwen, born Dec. 10, 1781; died Dec. 22, 1843, unmarried.

123 II. HEZEKIAH,⁵ Doct., born Dec., 1747.+

124 III. HANNAH,⁵ born Feb. 1749–50; married Stiles **Lewis**, of Stratford.

*Their children were:*

I. David **Lewis**,⁶ baptized Feb. 11, 1774.

II. Hannah Maria **Lewis**,⁶ baptized Aug. 6, 1787.

III. Stiles **Lewis**,⁶ born Dec. —— 1791.

125 IV. AGUR,⁵ baptized April, 1752; died an infant.

126 V. MARY,⁵ baptized July, 1753; died an infant.

127 VI. AGUR,⁵ baptized Sept., 1754; died young.

128 VII. HENRY AGUR,⁵ born Dec., 1755; died young.

129 VIII. MARY,⁵ baptized Sept., 1758; died young.

130 IX. ANN,⁵ baptized June, 1760; married Judson **Lewis**.

131 X. WILLIAM AGUR,⁵ baptized June, 1763.+

132 XI. MARY ALICE,⁵ baptized July, 1766; died Oct. 8, 1771.

## Line of Henry Tomlinson. 47

**50. CAPT. JOSEPH TOMLINSON**, son of *Zachariah*,³ (*Agur*,² *Henry*,¹) and Hannah (Beach) Tomlinson, married Elizabeth *Curtiss* about 1747. He settled in Oronoke, a little north from Farmill River, in Stratford, Ct., where his descendants still reside. His military standing is indicated in the following records:

"October, 1759. This Assembly do establish Joseph Tomlinson to be Quarter-master of the troop of horse in the 4th regiment in this Colony." (Col. Rec., XI., 336.)

"October, 1762. This Assembly do establish Mr. Joseph Tomlinson to be Cornet of the troop of horse in the 4th regiment in this Colony." (Col. Rec., XII., 85.)

"October, 1768. This Assembly do establish Mr. Joseph Tomlinson to be Captain of the troop of horse in the fourth regiment in this Colony." (Col. Rec., XIII., 100.)

Capt. Joseph Tomlinson died October 5, 1774, aged 50 years. His widow, Elizabeth, died July 28, 1809, aged 80 years. Both were buried in the old Congregational burying-place at Stratford village, Ct.

*Their children were:*

133    I. STEPHEN,⁵ born Oct. 6, 1749; died young.

134    II. PHEBE,⁵ born ——; married Capt. Robert Moore, of Huntington, Ct.

**50. CAPT. JOSEPH TOMLINSON,** son of *Zachariah,*³ (*Agur,*² *Henry,*¹) and Hannah (Beach) Tomlinson, married Elizabeth *Curtiss* about 1747. He settled in Oronoke, a little north from Farmill River, in Stratford, Ct., where his descendants still reside. His military standing is indicated in the following records:

"October, 1759. This Assembly do establish Joseph Tomlinson to be Quarter-master of the troop of horse in the 4th regiment in this Colony." (Col. Rec., XI., 336.)

"October, 1762. This Assembly do establish Mr. Joseph Tomlinson to be Cornet of the troop of horse in the 4th regiment in this Colony." (Col. Rec., XII., 85.)

"October, 1768. This Assembly do establish Mr. Joseph Tomlinson to be Captain of the troop of horse in the fourth regiment in this Colony." (Col. Rec., XIII., 100.)

Capt. Joseph Tomlinson died October 5, 1774. aged 50 years. His widow, Elizabeth, died July 28, 1809, aged 80 years. Both were buried in the old Congregational burying-place at Stratford village, Ct.

*Their children were:*

133    I. STEPHEN,⁵ born Oct. 6, 1749; died young.
134    II. PHEBE,⁵ born ——; married Capt. Robert Moore, of Huntington, Ct.

135   III. CURTISS,[5] +

136   IV. JOSEPH,[5] +

137   V. SALLY,[5] married Samuel Pee' Mills, of Huntington, and had:

>   I. Elisha Mills,[6] who died unmarried in 1886, in New York City.
>
>   II. Samuel Mills,[6] married and had James W. Mills, who resides in Brooklyn, N. Y., and Sarah E. Mills, who married Rev. C. Brewster, resides in Shelton, Conn.
>
>   III. Elvia Mills,[6] married and had Gideon T. and Chester.
>
>   IV. William Mills.

138   VI. ELIZABETH,[5] born Oct. —, 1758; married Philip Welles, of Stratford, in 1776; removed to New Milford in 1792, at what was afterwards called Wellesville, where he owned a gristmill and considerable property. He afterwards removed to Litchfield, where he died Dec. 23, 1818, aged 65. Elizabeth, his widow, died Nov. 27, 1848, aged 92 years. They had:

>   I. Betsey Welles,[6] born Feb. 25, 1777; married Cyrus Northrop, of New Milford, which constituted one of the prominent families of that town. Their daughter, Caroline Northrop, married William Mygatt; Emily Eunice Northrop married Benjamin E. Bostwick; Sarah Northrop married Col. William J. Starr; Sophia Northrop married Eli Mygatt, Jr., and Catherine Northrop married James Hine, M. D.
>
>   II. Hezekiah Welles,[6] born May 10, 1779; married Eunice Blackney.
>
>   III. Joseph Welles,[6] born August 21, 1781; married Anna Marsh.

*Line of Henry Tomlinson.* 49

 IV. Sarah **Welles**,⁶ born Jan. 16, 1784; married Bradley **Marsh**.

 V. Philip **Welles**,⁶ born April 21, 1787; married Nancy **Watson**.

 VI. Stephen **Welles**,⁶ born Sept. 24, 1789; died unmarried Feb. 22, 1815.

 VII. Tomlinson **Welles**,⁶ born Mar. 23, 1793; married Electa **Smith**; resided in Litchfield.

 VIII. Sophia **Welles**,⁶ born June 21, 1796; married John **McMahon**.

 IX. John **Welles**,⁶ born June 19, 1799.

139 VII. HANNAH,⁵ baptized December —, 1763; married Capt. James **Hovey**, of Huntington, Ct.

140 VIII. KATY,⁵ baptized Aug. —, 1771; married William **Shelton**, Jr., M. D., a graduate of Yale College in 1788, and a successful physician in Huntington, Ct., and died of typhus fever Aug. 20, 1819, aged 52 years. His widow Katy died July 14, 1858, aged 88 years.

 *Their children were:*

 I. William **Shelton**,⁶ married —— Thompson, and was a physician in Stratford and died in 1869.

 II. Caroline **Shelton**,⁶ died in Nov. 1864, unmarried.

 III. Cornelia **Shelton**,⁶ married Jan. 4, 1819, Rev. Edmund D. **Barry**, D. D.

 IV. Edwin **Shelton**,⁶ born April 20, 1801; married Susan **Curtiss**, of Stratford.

 V. Catherine **Shelton**,⁶ married Christopher N. **Shelton**, of Huntington.

 VI. James Hovey **Shelton**,⁶ born Mar. 12, 1806; married Hannah **Shelton**.

*51. CAPT. BEACH[4] TOMLINSON*, son of *Zachariah*,[3] (*Agur*,[2] *Henry*,[1]) and Hannah (Beach) Tomlinson, married Charity, daughter of Joseph *Shelton*, Oct. 25, 1752. The inscriptions on their grave-stones in the Huntington cemetery read:

"In Memory of Capt. Beach Tomlinson, who died Nov. 28, 1817, aged 91 years.

> Unvail thy bosom faithful tomb,
>   Take these new treasures to thy trust;
> And give these sacred relics room
>   To seek a slumber in the dust.

"In Memory of Mrs. Charity Tomlinson, wife of Capt. Beach Tomlinson, who died Nov. 19th, 1809; In the 73d year of her age."

They settled in Huntington, Ct., on land given him by his father, where they resided during their lives. He possessed remarkable physical strength, memory and enterprise, which continued to the end of his life. He was a large stockholder in the Derby Turnpike, and owned considerable land in Vermont to which he went yearly on horseback, until after he was ninety years of age, to collect rents. On one of his return trips, being alone and carrying considerable money, he was pursued by robbers, from whom he escaped by jumping his horse down a steep bank into the Onion river, across which his horse swam, bringing him safely home.

Beach Tomlinson was appointed Ensign in the trainband, May, 1771, in Ripton (now Huntington,

CAPTAIN BEACH TOMLINSON

MRS. CHARITY (SHELTON) TOMLINSON.

Ct.), 4th regiment, and Lieutenant in October, 1774, and Captain according to the following record:

"This Assembly do establish Beach Tomlinson to be Captain of the Seventh Company or trainband in the 14th regiment in this Colony."—(Colonial Records, vol. XV., 343.)

He was in the Revolutionary War, according to the following record taken from the Adjutant General's report of *Connecticut men:*

"Capt. Beach Tomlinson's Company at Peekskill in October, 1777—

| | | | | | |
|---|---|---|---|---|---|
| Capt. Beach Tomlinson | entered service Oct. | 5; | disch. | Oct. 22. |
| Lieut. Ephraim Curtiss | " | " | Oct. 15; | " | Oct. 27. |
| Ens. John Judson | " | " | Oct. 5; | " | Oct. 15. |
| Sergt. Silas Wheeler | " | " | Oct. 5; | " | Oct. 15. |
| Sergt. Agur Judson | " | " | Oct. 5; | " | Oct. 27. |
| David Wells | " | " | Oct. 5; | " | Oct. 27. |
| Henry Tomlinson | " | " | Oct. 5; | " | Oct. 27. |
| Curtiss Mills | " | " | Oct. 5; | " | Oct. 27. |
| James Hawley | " | " | Oct. 5; | " | Oct. 27." |

It is probable he was in the war several times with his militia company, or several men selected from it for the occasion, as were needed.

Capt. Beach Tomlinson's will was dated June 18, 1811, and proved Dec. 2, 1817. In it he first gives to his children as "advanced portion," sufficient to amount to $4,000 to each son, and $2,000 to each daughter, and then directs that the remainder shall be distributed in the proportion of five dollars to

each son to two dollars to each daughter. These
portions included large quantities of lands in the
townships of Fairfield, Berkshire and East Haven,
Vermont, and "Toby's Farm," in Waterbury, Ct.,
to Victory, houses and lands in Huntington, Ct.,
and shares in the Derby turnpike and in the Phœnix
Bank. In the final distribution, each of the five
sons living, or their heirs, received $10,167.59;
and each of the daughters, or their heirs, received
$4,111.68; the whole amount being $73,896.35.

The accompanying engravings of Capt. Beach and
Charity Tomlinson are made from oil paintings (still
most carefully preserved in the old homestead),
which are now (1890) about one hundred years old,
and although they are considerably faded, it is a
great pleasure to many that they are so well preserved, and that copies have been secured which so
definitely represent the characters of these remarkable persons. In the year eighteen hundred, it is
quite doubtful if there was a farmer in Fairfield
County more noted for industry, enterprise and
success than Beach Tomlinson, of Huntington, Ct.

*Children of Capt. Beach and Charity Tomlinson :*

141    I. Josiah,[5] born July 29, 1753.+

142    II. Henry,[5] born Mar. 1, 1755.+

143    III. Agur,[5] born Dec. 1, 1756.+

144    IV. Eunice,[5] born Oct. 24, 1758; married Ebenezer **Birdseye**,
son of Rev. Nathan Birdseye, of Stratford. They had :

I. Victory Birdseye.⁶
II. Hannah Birdseye.⁶
III. Eunice Birdseye.⁵
IV. Charlotte Birdseye.⁶
V. Eben Birdseye.⁶
VI. Ezra Birdseye.⁶
VII. Ketchel Birdseye.⁶
VIII. Ezekiel Birdseye.⁶
IX. John Birdseye.⁶

145   V. VICTORY,⁵ born Sept. 12, 1760. +

146   VI. MARY,⁵ born Mar. 6, 1762; married David Beard, a farmer in Huntington, Ct. She died July 28, 1793. He married (2d) —— Beard, his cousin. *Their children were:*

    I. Linson Beard,⁶ died aged 11 years.

    II. Beach Beard,⁶ removed to Pompey, N. Y., and had a large family.

147   VII. HANNAH,⁵ born Mar. 28, 1764; married Othniel DeForest, of Huntington, July 18, 1784. She died Sept. 1, 1803, aged 39 years. He died Feb. 21, 1811, aged 50 years.

*Their children were:*

    I. Linson DeForest,⁶ born Mar. 1, 1784; died an infant.

    II. Nancy DeForest,⁶ born May 31, 1786; married Rev. Jason Allen, of Woodbridge, Conn., and had:

        I. Catharine Allen,⁷ married Rev. Mr. Wright, of Alabama. He removed to Texas and died at Matagorda.

        II. Maria Allen,⁷ married Mr. Sayre and died in Montgomery, Ala. No children.

III. Elizabeth **Allen**,¹ lives in Matagorda, Texas, is married, and had 4 children.

III. Linson **DeForest**,⁶ born Aug. 13, 1787; married Sept. 8, 1807, Jane, daughter of Cyrus **Hawley**, of Monroe, Ct. She was born Aug. 22, 1797 (?) and died Feb. 21, 1849, aged 51 (?) years. Linson De Forest died May, 1823, aged 36 years. They had:

    I. Mary Jane **DeForest**,⁷ married Edward N. **Shelton**, of Birmingham, Ct.

    II. Charles **DeForest**.⁷

IV. Sidney **DeForest**,⁶ born Mar. 22, 1789; died unmarried.

V. Maria **DeForest**,⁶ born April 8, 1790; married Hezekiah **Rudd**, of Huntington. He was a teacher and fitted young men for college, but died aged only 37 years. They had:

    I. Abigail **Rudd**,⁷ married Wellington **Shelton**. She died Mar. 1, 1838, and he married (2d) Mrs. Cornelia Curtis **Shelton**.

    II. Mary **Rudd**,⁷ married Jason **Allen**, a professor in Oberlin College, and had a son Charles, who resides in Brooklyn, N. Y.

VI. Charles **DeForest**,⁶ born Mar. 1, 1794; married Katharine **Burlock**, of New York.

148 VIII. Charity,⁵ born Mar. 22, 1766; married John **Morris**, of East Haven, Ct., who made some useful inventions. She died in Derby in 1838, aged 90 years. He died in Ohio.

149 IX. Zechariah,⁵ + ⎫ twins, born May 14, 1768; Elizabeth died
150 X. Elizabeth,⁵ ⎭     April 21, 1772.

151 XI. Gideon,⁵ born May 2, 1770; died Dec. 1, 1772.

152 XII. ELIZABETH,⁵ born Oct. 1, 1772; married Col. William French, of Southbury, Ct., removed to Ohio and died in 1853.

153 XIII. GIDEON,⁵ born July 19, 1774.+

154 XIV. DAVID JOSEPH NICHOLS,⁵ born May 22, 1779.+

**52. ZACHARIAH TOMLINSON,** 2d, son of *Zechariah*,³ (*Agur*,² *Henry*,¹) and Hannah (Beach) Tomlinson, married Amy, daughter of John and Hannah (Beach) *Lewis*. She was born Aug. 19, 1732. They lived in that part of Huntington which is now the town of Monroe, in 1762. After Zachariah Tomlinson, 2d, died, his widow Amy married William Pixlee, who kept a hotel at Old Mill Green, in Stratford, Ct. Her death is recorded in the family Bible, Sept. 24, 1800, as Emma Pixlee. William Pixlee died in the year 1800.

*Children of Zachariah and Amy Tomlinson:*

155. I. SARAH,³ born Oct. 8, 1753; married Dea. Elihu Curtiss, of New Stratford Society, March 14, 1769. She died and he married (2d) Sarah, widow of Robert Lewis, who was daughter of John Morse. She died Dec. 13, 1840, aged 98 years. He died Nov. 2, 1804, aged 55 years.

*Children by the first wife were:*

I. Amy Curtiss,⁶ born Feb. 19, 1771.

II. Zachariah Tomlinson Curtiss,⁶ born May 10, 1774.

III. Isaac Curtiss,⁶ born Oct. 12, 1777.

*Children by second wife were:*

IV. Rosaillae Curtiss,⁶ born Aug. 16, 1781; died Oct. 17, 1791.

V. Polly **Curtiss**,⁶ born Jan. 1, 1786.

VI. William **Curtiss**, born July 12, 1789; died Dec. 30, 1791.

156 II. ANNE,⁴ born June 26, 1757; married (1st) Capt. Henry **Curtiss**, April 14, 1774. He died Jan. 11, 1796, and she married (2d) as second wife, the Rev. David **Ely**, D. D., of Huntington, Ct., and died Jan. 31, 1849, aged 91 years and 7 months. The Rev. David Ely, D. D., Mrs. Anna Tomlinson's second husband, was born at Lyme, Ct., July 7, 1749, graduated at Yale College in 1769, ordained pastor at Huntington, Oct. 27, 1773, and died at that place Feb. 16, 1816, in the 67th year of his age, and the 42d year of his ministry. He was a successful and quite celebrated minister of the gospel. He had no children by his second wife.

*Her children by Capt. Henry Curtiss were:*

I. William Pixlee **Curtiss**,⁵ born May 29, 1778.

II. Sarah Ann **Curtiss**,⁵ born May 27, 1780; married Gideon **Beardsley**, M. D.

III. Lydia **Curtiss**,⁵ born May 20, 1785; married Youngs **Hawley**.

IV. Lucius **Curtiss**,⁵ born April 6, 1787; married Polly Ann, daughter of Elnathan **Bostwick**, Oct. 12, 1809.

V. Elouise Ann **Curtiss**,⁵ born Dec. 29, 1790.

VI. Hiram **Curtiss**,⁵ born June 6, 1793.

VII. Henry Tomlinson **Curtiss**,⁵ born Sept. 21, 1796; died July, 1876.

157 III. JEMIMA,⁵ born May 10, 1764; married, in 1780, Edmund **Darrow**, by whom she had two sons. He died in 1784, and she married William **Peet**, Esq., of Bridgeport, Nov. 25, 1785. This William Peet was son of William and Beula (Nichols) Peet, and grandson of Dea. Thomas Peet, the "Post Rider of Stratford, Ct." She died aged 93 years.

## Line of Henry Tomlinson.

*Children of Edmund and Jemima Darrow:*

I. Pearce[6] **Darrow**, married and had:

    I. Frances,[7] who married **Wilmot**. II. Minerva, who married a **Wilmot**. III. Maria, not married. IV. Frank, and another son.

II. Edmund[6] **Darrow**; married and had Elizabeth, Mary Ann, Rosella, Caroline, Sarah, Edmund.

*Children of Wm. and Jemima Peet were:*

III. Catherine[6] **Peet**, born Sept. 24, 1786; married Charles **Bostwick**, and had:

    I. Jane[7] **Bostwick**, married Henry W. **Hubbell**.

    II. Charles[7] **Bostwick**, died unmarried.

    III. Charlotte[7] **Bostwick**, married George E. **Thrall**.

    IV. John R.[7] **Bostwick**, married Helen **Menard**.

    V. Henry[7] **Bostwick**, died unmarried.

    VI. Sarah[7] **Bostwick**, died unmarried.

IV. Maria[6] **Peet**, born July 7, 1788; married Thomas **Longworth**; had Frederick W., and died January 11, 1854.

V. George[6] **Peet**, born Oct. 15, 1790, and died April 16, 1830.

VI. Eleazer[6] **Peet**, born Mar. 3, 1793; married Maria, daughter of Barrett **Ames**, and had:

    I. Mary[7] **Peet**.

    II. William E.[7] **Peet**.

    III. Laura[7] **Peet**, died.

    IV. Charles B.[7] **Peet**.

    V. Frederick[7] **Peet**, died.

VII. Minerva[6] Peet, born December 3, 1795; married Hon. William Wright, and died March 2, 1882. They had:
    I. Catherine[7] Wright, married Baron Gevers.
    II. Edward H.[7] Wright, married Dora Mason.
    III. Frederick V.[7] Wright, died.

VIII. William Henry[6] Peet, born July 13, 1797; married 1st Abby, daughter of Capt. Stephen Somers, March, 1822, and died. They had:
    I. Susan[7] Peet, who died.
    II. Mary[7] Peet, married Gilead A. Smith.
    He married (2d) Margaret ———.

IX. Frederick Tomlinson[6] Peet, born Dec. 20, 1799; married Elizabeth, daughter of Lambert and Elizabeth (Roe) Lockwood, March, 1822, and died Dec. 17, 1866. They had:
    I. William[7] Peet, born Dec. 4, 1822; married Martha Isabell, daughter of James T. Homans, July 17, 1851, and had:
        I. Frederick[8] Tomlinson Peet, born June 17, 1852; married Oct. 9, 1877, Lizzie, daughter of Samuel S. and Anna N. (Booth) Knox. She died July 30, 1884, and he married Charlotte White Hinsdell, widow of L. H. Hinsdell, daughter of Clinton T. and Janet Rindge, of Cortland, N. Y., Sept. 3, 1885.
        *Children by first wife:*
            I. William[9] Peet, born July 27, 1878.
            II. David Knox[9] Peet, born May 16, 1880.
            III. Amy Isabel[9] Peet, born Feb. 26, 1882.

## Line of Henry Tomlinson.

  IV. Frederick Tomlinson⁹ **Peet**, born June 15, 1883; died Nov. 29, 1888.

  V. Lizzie Knox⁹ **Peet**, born July 1, 1884.

  *Children by second wife:*

  VI. Elsie Janet⁹ **Peet**, born May 16, 1887; died in 1889.

  VII. Majorie⁹ **Peet**, born Oct. —, 1889.

II. Edward Homans⁸ **Peet**, born June 17, 1852; died Nov. 25, 1886.

III. William⁸ **Peet**, born June 30, 1856.

IV. Harry Homans⁸ **Peet**, born June 19, 1857; died Oct. 18, 1859.

V. Rebecca Lockwood⁸ **Peet**, born Jan. 27, 1860; died Aug. 17, 1860.

VI. Isabel Homans⁸ **Peet**, born March 25, 1863.

VII. Lambert Lockwood⁸ **Peet**, born April 28, 1865; died Sept. 7, 1865.

VIII. Torrance Lord⁸ **Peet**, born Dec. 1, 1866; died Sept. 22, 1867.

IX. Charles Livingston⁸ **Peet**, born June 10, 1868; died Aug. 16, 1868.

X. James Homans⁸ **Peet**, born July 27, 1871; died July 28, 1871.

XI. Robert Augustin⁸ **Peet**, born Sept. 11, 1872.

II. Rebekah Lockwood⁷ **Peet**, born Oct. 27, 1824.

III. Elizabeth Roe Lockwood⁷ **Peet**, born Oct. 4, 1826.

IV. Robert Barfe⁷ **Peet**, born Jan. 18, 1829; died Mar. 23, 1829.

V. Robert Barré[5] Peet, born Jan. 9, 1831.
VI. Maria[7] Peet, born Dec. 14, 1832; died an infant.
VII. Julia Maria[7] Peet, born Feb. 27, 1834.
VIII. Sarah Creighton[7] Peet, born June 13, 1837.
IX. Harriet Cutler[7] Peet, born July 20, 1839.
X. Frederick Tomlinson[7] Peet, born Aug. 7, 1841.

X. Francis[6] Peet, born Aug. 4, 1801; married Maria Mead, Nov. 21, 1826, and had:
    I. Francis[7] Peet, married.
    II. Munson[7] Peet.
    III. Bythinia[7] Peet, married Rev. —— Willes.
    IV. Minerva[7] Peet, married —— Schwangler.

XI. Edward William[6] Peet, D.D., born Feb. 19, 1804; married Sarah, daughter of William Creighton, June 30, 1831.
    I. William Creighton[7] Peet, married.
    II. Charles B.[7] Peet, married.
    III. George Jones[7] Peet.
    IV. Joseph D.[7] Peet, married.
    V. Frederick T.[7] Peet, died.
    VI. Henry D.[7] Peet, married.

XII. Sarah Ann[6] Peet, born March 5, 1806; married Henry K. Harral, and died Dec. 17, 1867.
    I. William W.[7] Harral.
    II. Henry[7] Harral.
    III. George[7] Harral.
    IV. Frederick[7] Harral, died.
    V. Helen[7] Harral.
    VI. Edward W.[7] Harral.

XIII. Elizabeth,[6] died an infant.

# THOMAS FITCH, Esq;

Colony of Connecticut. } Captain General and Governor in Chief in and over His Majesty's English Colony of Connecticut in New England, in America.

*to* GIDEON TOMLINSON, Esq<sup>r</sup> ——— *Greeting :*

**BY** Virtue of the power and Authority to me given, in and by the Royal Charter to the Governor and Company of the said Colony, under the Great Seal of England, I do, by these Presents reposing especial Trusts and Confidence in your Loyalty, Courage and good Conduct, constitute and appoint you the said Gideon Tomlinson ——— to be Captain ——— of the Sixth ——— Company in a Regiment of Foot, raised within this Colony to proceed and co-operate with a body of the King's British Forces, and under the Supreme Command of his Majesty's Commander in Chief in America, against Canada, in order to reduce Montreal and all other Posts of the French in those parts, and further to annoy the Enemy in such manner as his Majesty Commander in Chief shall judge pourable, of which Regiment ——— David Wooster——— Esq<sup>r</sup>, Is Colonel. You are therefore carefully and diligently to discharge the Duty of a Captain——— in leading, ordering and exercising said Company in Arms, both Inferior Officers and Soldiers, in the service aforesaid, and to keep them in good order and discipline hereby commanding them to obey you as their Captain ——— and yourself to observe and follow such orders and Instructions as you shall from time to time receive from me or the Commander in Chief, of the said Colony, for the time being, or other your Superior Officers, according to the rules and disciplines of War, pursuant to the Trusts reposed in you.

*GIVEN* Under my hand and the Publick Seal of the said Colony, at ——— Norwalk ——— the twenty fourth ——— Day of March ——— in the 33<sup>d</sup> ——— year of the Reign of his Majesty King GEORGE the second Annoque Domini, 1760.

*By his honors command,*
GEORGE WYLLYS FAREL.

THOMAS FITCH.

**53. CAPT. GIDEON¹ TOMLINSON,** son of *Zachariah³ (Agur,² Henry,¹)* and Hannah (Beach) Tomlinson, married Mary, widow of David *Welles*, Oct. 9, 1757. She was the daughter of Dea. John Thompson, of Stratford, and died June 6, 1758, in childbed, aged 26 years. He married (2d) Hannah, daughter of Col. Jabez Huntington, of Windham, Ct., Jan. 17, 1760, and lived on the homestead at Oronoke, in Stratford, given him by his father, where he died Jan. 19, 1766, aged 35 years. She died in 1762, aged 27 years.

Capt. Gideon Tomlinson was an officer in the French War under Col. David Wooster.

"In March, 1756, Gideon Tomlinson was appointed First Lieutenant in the Seventh Company, in the Fourth regiment, in the forces ordered to be raised in the Colony for the French War. The captain of his company, David Lacey, died, and Tomlinson succeeded him as captain. (Col. Records, X. 473.) He was appointed Captain by the Legislature March, 1758, for the French War; also in March, 1759, and March, 1760.

In May, 1759, the Rev. Izrahiah Wetmore, of Stratford, preached a sermon to Captain Tomlinson and his company, on their departure for the northern campaign which resulted in the taking of Quebec. The sermon is still preserved by his descendants, also the Captain's chessboard, presented to him by

General Wooster, on which they had often played together, they living near neighbors.

The inscriptions of their grave-stones in Stratford burying place are as follows:

"In memory of Capt. Gideon Tomlinson, who departed this life January 19$^{th}$ 1766, in y$^e$ 35$^{th}$ Year of His age.

"He was an officer in y$^e$ Army and fought in y$^e$ battle at y$^e$ Narrows; was at y$^e$ taking Ticonderoga, Crown Point, La Collette and Montreal.

"In memory of Mrs. Mary Tomlinson, who departed this life June y$^e$ 7$^h$, 1758, in y$^e$ 26$^{th}$ Year of Her Age.

"In memory of Mrs. Hannah Tomlinson and Daut$^r$ of Colo. Jabez Huntington, of Windham, Who departed this Life December y$^e$ 26, 1762, in y$^e$ 27$^{th}$ Year of Her Age."

*The Will of Capt. Gideon Tomlinson, dated in 1765.*

"In the Name of God Amen, I Gideon Tomlinson, of Stratford, in the County of Fairfield and Colony of Connecticut in New England, being under great weakness and bodily infirmity, but of sound mind and memory, thanks be to God therefor, Do make this my last Will and Testament in the first I give and recommend my Soul into the Arms of the Almighty God who gave it, in hope of Everlasting Life in and through Christ Jesus, my exalted Redeemer And my Body to be Buried in the Earth in a Decent Christian Burial at the Discretion of my Executors hereafter named And as to what worldly estate it hath pleased God to Bless me with I Give and Dispose of the Same in the following Manner, that after my Just Debts and Funeral Charges are first paid and Satisfied:

*Item.* I Give and Bequeath unto my loving Son Jabiz Huntington Tomlinson, the whole of my Estate both Real and Personal, to be his own forever—Excepting the legacies hereafter mentioned.

*Item.*—I Give unto Mary Welles, Daughter to Nathan Welles, one set of stone jewels that was my first wife's.

*Item.*—I Give unto my Sister Mary Tomlinson, one Brown Silk Gown.

*Item.*—I Give unto Hannah Tomlinson, Daughter to my brother Joseph Tomlinson, one string of Gold beads.

*N. B.*—My Will further is and my Executors are hereby Desired and impowered to Sell my land in Town that I Bought of Capt. Nechols, Situated near the Ferry-bridge creek, to sell it in small building lots or otherwise as may be most advantageous, if there be opportunity, and my said executors think best and the money be put to use for my said son.

My will further is, that if so be that Providence should so order that my said son Jabiz should be taken away by Death before he should arrive at the Age of twenty one Years and should leave no surviving heirs of his body, That then I give unto the Rev$^d$ Mr. Izrahiah Wetmore and his Heirs, the sum of fifty pounds lawfull money.

My Will further is that if so be that my son Jabiz should be taken away by Death before he should arrive to the age of twenty one Years and should leave no surviving heir of his Body as aforesaid, that then I Give and Bequeath unto Nathan Welles and Stephen Welles, both of Stratford, equally to Divide Between them, my lot of land at James Farm, so called, containing about seven acres, Bounded west upon Highway, north and part east upon land of Stiles Curtiss and south and part east upon land of Daniel Booth.

My Will further is y$^t$ my said son Jabiz have a public or College education (left to the discretion of my executors hereafter named, whether he be disposed for education of a public kind), that is to say y$^t$ if my said executors find my said son prove likely and disposed for learning, that he do then have a college education.

*Item.*—I give unto Hannah Huntington, daughter of Mrs. Jabiz Huntington, of Windham, one pair of stone jewels that was my last wife's.

And I do constitute and appoint my Hond$^d$ Father Mr. Zechariah Tomlinson, and my brother Joseph Tomlinson, and the Rev. Mr.

Izrahiah Wetmore to be executors of this my last will and testament, hereby Revoking all other wills, Declaring this and this only to be my last Will and Testament, in Confirmation thereof I have hereunto set my hand and seal in Stratford this 28th day of December, A. Dom., 1765.

GIDEON TOMLINSON.

Published, pronounced
and declared by the
testator to be his
last will and testament;
In presence of us :

    JOSEPH BIRDSEY,

    ELIHU CURTIS,

    SILAS CLARK."

The child of Capt. Gideon and Hannah (Huntington) Tomlinson was: 158 I. JABEZ HUNTINGTON,⁵ born Dec. 24, 1760.+

**54. ABRAHAM⁴ TOMLINSON**, son of *Zachariah*,³ (*Agur*,² *Henry*,¹) and Hannah (Beach) Tomlinson, married (1st) Rebecca, daughter of Hezekiah *Gold*, Dec. 1754. She died in 1774, aged 39 years. He married (2d) Anne, daughter of Samuel *Folsom*, Oct. 11, 1777. She was born August 19, 1740, died in 1827, aged 85 years, and was an elder sister of Gloriana Folsom, who married the son of Lord Stirling of Scotland. Abraham Tomlinson was a lawyer, a communicant in the Episcopal Church, and a strong Tory in the Revolution. A number of his children, it is said, were patriots, and the conflict on this subject was sometimes a little animated, although good harmony otherwise prevailed. After the death of his father-in-law, Gold, Abraham's

father purchased of the heirs the homestead on the corner of Main street and the highway leading to the Congregational burying-place, in Stratford, where he resided until his decease in 1821, aged 88 years.

*Inscriptions on Tombstones in Stratford, Ct.:*

"Abraham Tomlinson died April 1821, aged 88 years.

"Here lies Hid in this Grave the Body of Mrs. Rebekah, the amiable Consort of Abraham Tomlinson, Esq., who Departed this life on the first day of Novem$^{br}$, 1774, in the 39$^{th}$ year of her age.

> "I have been what thou art now, and are what
>   thou shalt shortly be.
> "How Loved tho' valued once, avail me not; to whom
>   Related or by whom forgot, a heap of
>   Drift alone
> "Remains of me, 'tis all I am, and all that
>   you must be."

"Anna Tomlinson, relict of Abraham Tomlinson, died May 5, 1827, Aged 85."

"In memory of Anna Tomlinson, daughter Abraham and Anna Tomlinson, who died July 28, 1790, aged 17 years.

"In memory of Sarah Tomlinson, daughter of Abraham and Rebecca Tomlinson, who died March 24, 1813, in the 53 year of her age."

## Line of Henry Tomlinson.

*Children by the first wife:*

159  I. JERUSHA,⁵ born Mar. 1756, married as second wife Abijah McEwen, and for their children, see under the name Katee, daughter of Doct. Agur Tomlinson—(No. 48.)
160  II. ALEXANDER,⁵ born Jan. 1759; died in 1759.
161  III. SARAH,⁵ born May, 1760; married Samuel Peet Mills (?) in 1787.
162  IV. REBECCA,⁵ born Aug. 1762; married —— Pyncheon, of Guilford.
163  V. HULDAH,⁵ born May, 1766; died unmarried in 1844.
164  VI. HENRY ABRAHAM,⁵ born in 1768; died in 1785, in the West Indies.
165  VII. DAVID,⁵ born Nov. 1769, in Stratford.+
166  VIII. MARY,⁵ born Jan., 1772; died unmarried, Dec. 19, 1861, aged 89 years. It was through her memory that much history of the Tomlinson family was preserved. She lived with her father 55 years, and he with his father Zechariah, who had the coat-of-arms, 85 years; therefore an unbroken chain of history by three persons was continued from 1693 to 1861.
167  IX. CHARLES,⁵ born Sept., 1774.+

*Children by the second wife:*

168  X. ELIZABETH,⁵ born Jan. 8, 1778; married Nathan Peck.
169  XI. ANNE,⁵ born Aug., 1782; died in 1790.

**60. DOCT. ABRAHAM TOMLINSON,** son of Jonah,⁴ (Abraham,³ Jonas,² Henry,¹) and Mary (Moss) Tomlinson, married Abigail Gibson, daughter of David Gibson, of Milford and Woodbury, Nov. 11, 1760. She was born in 1738 and died Mar. 10, 1807. He married (2d) Esther Benjamin

Dec. 28, 1808, who died in 1831. He resided some years in Judea Society, then settled as a physician in Milford, Ct., where he died Dec. 29, 1816.

170   I. WILLIAM,⁶ born Nov. 9, 1761.
171   II. ABRAHAM,⁶ born April 1, 1763.+
172   III. DAVID,⁶ born Jan. 25, 1767.+
173   IV. JOHN G.,⁶ born June 14, 1769; died Aug. 26, 1773.
174   V. CALEB,⁶ born Sept 29, 1771; died at sea, N. lat. 23, Aug. 2, 1794, "after 4 days' illness of bilious fever."
175   VI. JOHN GIBSON,⁶ born June 24, 1774; died Jan. 20, 1838, at Oswego, N. Y.+
176   VII. MARY,⁶ born Oct. 1, 1777; married Daniel Merwin, and had:
        I. Calena Merwin.
177 VIII. ABIGAIL,⁶ born Nov. 23, 1779; died Dec. 28, 1802.

**65. *CALEB TOMLINSON,*** son of *Jonah*¹ (*Abraham,*³ *Jonas,*² *Henry,*¹) and Mary (Moss) Tomlinson, was born in 1749, and is supposed to have been the young man of whom the following story is told:

Caleb Tomlinson, of Huntington, being a soldier in the Revolution, was sent by General Wooster with a dispatch to General Washington. Being from the same neighborhood as General Wooster, young Tomlinson was selected because the General knew him to be a plucky Yankee, although a little uncultivated in his manners, but one to be trusted for the discharge of duty.

Arriving at headquarters he asked to see General Washington, to which the guard replied: "You cannot see him." "But I must, I have a dispatch for him from General Wooster." The guard reported to Washington, and he was admitted to the presence of the General, who was seated at a rude table writing, when Tomlinson handed the dispatch, and Washington on reading it nodded assent and asked, "Anything more?" "Nothing," said Tomlinson, "but an answer from you." "Do you presume to tell me what I must do?" inquired the General. "No, General, but I'll be darned if I leave these quarters without something to show that I have discharged my duty as a soldier." Rising from his seat Washington remarked, "you are from Connecticut, I perceive." "I am, sir," was the reply. Tapping him on the shoulder, the General said, "Young man, I wish to the God of battles I had more such soldiers as you. You shall be granted your request."

**70. JOSEPH² TOMLINSON**, son of Agur,⁴ (Abraham,³ Jonas,² Henry,¹) and Sarah (Bowers) Tomlinson, married Bethia *Glover*, of Newtown, Ct., Oct. 27, 1763. He died Sept. 23, 1813, in the 73ᵈ year of his age. Bethiah, his wife, died Nov. 1, 1799, in the 57ᵗʰ year of her age. Both are buried in Brookfield, Conn. After the death of his first wife, Bethia, Joseph Tomlinson married Jedida Wakelee, the widow of Jeremiah Hawley, of Brookfield, an aunt of Mrs. Daniel Tomlinson.

Joseph Tomlinson was a man of wealth and position, especially noted for his benevolence. He offered his four sons a collegiate education; David and Daniel availed themselves of the offer, and Agur spent two years in college.

178  I. Joseph Bowers,⁶ born in 1764.+

179  II. David,⁶ born —— —— +

180  III. Daniel,⁶ born Oct. 17, 1776.+

181  IV. Agur,⁶ born Dec. 20, 1778.+

**71. WEBB⁵ TOMLINSON**, son of Agur,⁴ (Abraham,³ Jonas,² Henry,¹) married Jerusha *Beers*, of Newtown, Ct., Dec. 11, 1768.

182  1. Sarah, born Mar. 1, 1772.

*Line of Henry Tomlinson.* 71

**72. SERGT. DAVID⁵ TOMLINSON**, son of *Agur*,⁴ (*Abraham*,³ *Jonas*,² *Henry*.¹) and Sarah (Bowers) Tomlinson, married Ruth *Hawkins*, of Derby. She was probably daughter of Zechariah Hawkins and born June 22, 1754.

*From the Adjutant General's "Connecticut Men."*

"David Tomlinson enlisted May 15, 1775; discharged Dec. 23, 1775. His company served at the siege of Boston. Ensign David Tomlinson, of Derby, was appointed Ensign Dec. 26, 1776, commissioned Jan. 1, 1777, in the Sixth Regiment of Conn.; retired by arrangement of officers Nov. 15, 1778.

He was Sergeant in Capt. Johnson's company in 1776, in the Fifth Battalion Wadsworth's Brigade.

*Children of David and Ruth Tomlinson:*

183  I. DAVID,⁶ born Feb. 15, 1778.+
184  II. AGUR.⁶
185  III. NANCY,⁶ born Feb. 21, 1782, in Derby; married Feb. 5, 1807, Thomas G. Knies, who was born July 26, 1778, in Salisbury, Ct. They resided in Lenox, Madison Co., N. Y. He was a farmer, and held the office of Justice of the Peace. He died April 15, 1854, aged 75 years. His widow Nancy, died April 6, 1857, aged 75 years. They had:

    I. Mary Knies, born Dec. 8, 1807; married Horace H. Hall.
    II. Betsey Knies, born Mar. 29, 1810; died Aug. 1, 1856.
    III. Emma Jane Knies, born Aug. 15, 1815; married Jonathan Goffe.

186  IV. BETSEY,⁶ born April 15, 1784; married Abijah Tomlinson. (No. 233).

**85. CAPT. JOHN L.⁵ TOMLINSON,** son of Capt. John,⁴ (John,³ Jonas,² Henry,¹) and Deborah (Bassett) Tomlinson, resided in Derby, Ct. The History of Derby, Ct., has the following:

"John L. Tomlinson was born in Derby, Ct., and read law with Josiah Dudley. His office was in one of the chambers of the ancient house, now [1880] occupied by Miss Rachel Smith and her two sisters. He succeeded Mr. Dudley; the latter, as near as can be ascertained, was the first educated lawyer located in Derby Narrows. Mr. Tomlinson was well read, and of a discriminating mind, but was not a very successful advocate at the bar. The latter years of his life were under the shadow of a great cloud, by his unfortunate connection with the Derby Bank, he being its president, which failed in 1825 through the legerdemain of Wall street brokers. The popular belief awards Mr. Tomlinson the credit of being honest in his transactions with the bank."

He was in the war of 1812, serving at New London, Ct., as lieutenant under Col. Elihu Sanford from Sept. 8, 1814 to Sept. 20, 1814, and during that time was in command of his company. About 1826 he became a Congregational clergyman, went west, where he died, aged about 70 years.

*Children of Capt. John L. Tomlinson:*
194   I. John Lewis.⁶+
195   II. Samuel.⁶+

196   III.  LEWIS,⁶ born July 30, 1791, in Derby, Ct.+

197   IV.   LEVI.⁶+

198   V.    SARAH,⁶ married Russell Hawkins.

199   VI.   LUTHENIA,⁶ married Waterman Eels.

200   VII.  BETSEY,⁶ married Philo Lum.

**86. REV. DANIEL⁵ TOMLINSON,** son of *Capt. John⁴ (John,³ Jonas,² Henry,¹)* and Deborah (Bassett) Tomlinson, was graduated at Yale College in 1781 and died in 1842. "He was long the pastor of the church at Oakham, Mass., and was a man of distinguished excellence. His voice and manner in the desk were very peculiar. They were his own and inimitable. He always preached with black gloves on his hands, and I well remember that my pastor, sometimes noticing that there was smiling about the house when Mr. Tomlinson officiated, would rise from his seat and in a dignified and solemn way, request that there should be no levity in the house of God."[10]

201   I.   "DAUGHTER,⁶ who never married."

**93. ISAAC⁵ TOMLINSON,** 3d, son of *Capt. Isaac,⁴ (Sergt. Isaac,³ Jonas,² Henry,¹)* and Sibyl (Russell) Tomlinson, married Mary *Hawkins*, of Oxford, Ct., Dec. 19, 1775.

---

[10] History of Derby, Ct., 299.

*Their children were:*

202  I. SILAS,⁶ born Sept. 19, 1776.
203  II. ISAAC,⁶ born April 2, 1778.
204  III. TRUMAN,⁶ born July 7, 1780.+
204½ IV. MARY,⁶ born March 17, 1782.
205  V. AMMON,⁶ born July 23, 1784.
205½ VI. ZACHARIAH,⁶ born Aug. 16, 1767; died Aug. 1, 1789.

*94. RUSSELL⁵ TOMLINSON*, Esq., son of Capt. Isaac,⁴ (Sergt. Isaac,³ Jonas,² Henry,¹) and Sibyl (Russell) Tomlinson, married Agnes Cortelyou, of New Utrecht, L. I., April 26, 1779. She was born March 10, 1764, and died Feb. 10, 1843. He died June 22, 1809, aged 54 years. He resided in Derby and Woodbury.

*Their children were:*

206   I. SARAH,⁶ born March 14, 1780; married David Tomlinson, of Derby, Ct. (See No. 178.)
207   II. ISAAC,⁶ born May 26, 1782.+
207½ III. PETER,⁶ born Nov. 18, 1784; married Esther Holbrook, and died June 11, 1842.
208  IV. SIMON,⁶ born May 22, 1787.+
209   V. JAMES,⁶ born Aug. 18, 1789; died April 22, 1804.
210  VI. BETSEY,⁶ born April 29, 1792; married Charles Bacon; no children.
211 VII. RUSSELL,⁶ born Mar. 27, 1801.+
212 VIII. JAMES C.,⁶ born Mar. 4, 1806.+

**95. TIMOTHY[5] TOMLINSON**, son of *Capt. Isaac*,[4] (*Sergt. Isaac*,[3] *Jonas*,[2] *Henry*,[1]) and Sibyl (Russell) Tomlinson, married Eunice *Booth*, who was born in Roxbury, Ct., March 24, 1771.

Timothy Tomlinson died Jan. 2, 1821, aged 62 years. His widow Eunice died Nov. 25, 1821, aged nearly fifty years.

*Their children were:*

213  I. TIMOTHY,[6] born Mar. 19, 1792.+
214  II. SAMUEL,[6] born Nov. 28, 1796.+
215  III. JOSEPH,[6] born Sept. 12, 1798.+
216  IV. ISAAC,[6] born Mar. 27, 1803; died aged 26 years, probably not married.
217  V. NATHANIEL,[6] born Aug. 8, 1807.+

**97. HON. DAVID[5] TOMLINSON**, son of *Capt. Isaac*,[4] (*Sergt. Isaac*,[3] *Jonas*,[2] *Henry*,[1]) and Sibyl (Russell) Tomlinson, married Lovena, daughter of Jabez *Bacon*, a merchant of Woodbury.

Hon. David Tomlinson was born and bred in Woodbury, settled as a merchant and farmer at Quaker's Farm, in Oxford, Ct., and through the aid of his father-in-law became wealthy in following his mercantile business.

He was a Justice of the Peace many years; a Representative and a State Senator. He died March 24, 1822, aged 56 years. His widow Lovena, died October 25, 1837, aged 71 years.

*Their children were:*

218    I. CHARLES,[6] born June 19, 1785.+
219    II. DAVID,[6] born July 11, 1787; died March 4, 1788.
220    III. MARIA THERESA,[6] born Aug. 1, 1789; married Edwin E. Lewis,[9] son of the Rev. John and Eunice Lewis, of Wethersfield, Ct., March 23, 1815. He was born Nov. 9, 1799. They had:

    I. Maria Augusta Lewis,[7] born June 18, 1816.

    II. Mary Eliza Lewis,[7] born June 3, 1818; married Samuel J. Lewis, of Naugatuck, Ct., Oct. 30, 1839, and had: George Albert Lewis; married Emma F. Lewis and had Tracey Samuel Lewis, born Feb. 11, 1843; Edwin Augustus Lewis, born Oct. 5, 1847; married Eunice S. Tuttle, June 17, 1875 and had Edwin Tuttle Lewis, and Marion Etelka Lewis; Samuel Hilo Lewis, born May 21, 1850.

    III. Elizabeth Scott Lewis,[7] born Feb. 26, 1821; died Jan. 22, 1857.

    IV. Jane Caroline Lewis,[7] born Dec. 20, 1823; died July 31, 1854.

    V. Edwin Augustus Lewis,[7] born May 21, 1829; died June 19, 1829.

221    IV. DAVID,[6] born Aug. 1, 1791; died Sept. 22, 1814.
222    V. LOVENA,[6] born August 4, 1793; died Mar. 8, 1826. She married Samuel Meigs. They had:

    I. Sarah Meigs,[7] who married Charles Deck.

    II. Jane Meigs,[7] who married George Lum.

    III. David Meigs,[7] who married James Brush.

    IV. Charles Meigs,[7] who married Bernice Riggs and had Samuel Meigs and Mary Meigs.

## Line of Henry Tomlinson.

223    VI. LYDIA AUGUSTA,⁶ born Sept. 25, 1795; married William C. DeForest, of Humphreysville and New Haven, Oct. 25, 1824. She died Nov. 6, 1858. He was born Sept. 21, 1796, and died June 10, 1877.

*Their children were:*

I. Jane Caroline DeForest,⁷ born April 12, 1826.

II. Mary Augusta DeForest,⁷ born Mar. 3, 1828; married David T. Hotchkiss, and had Mary DeForest Hotchkiss, born Sept. 25, 1857; David Tomlinson Hotchkiss, born May 28, 1861, who died Dec. 26, 1862.

III. William Augustus DeForest,⁷ born Dec. 12, 1829; died Aug. 7, 1851.

IV. Charles Tomlinson DeForest,⁷ born Dec. 22, 1831; married Ellen Goodyear, Jan. 1, 1857.

V. George Albert DeForest,⁷ born Jan. 4, 1834; died May 15, 1854.

VI. Henry Porter DeForest,⁷ born April 11, 1836; died April 20, 1841.

223½ VII. JANE CAROLINE,⁶ born June 30, 1797; died April 24, 1821.

224  VIII. BENNETT BENEDICT,⁶ born May 5, 1799; died Sept. 4, 1822.

225    IX. MARY ANN,⁶ born Mar. 10, 1801; died Mar. 21, 1832.

226     X. JENNETTE ADELAIDE,⁶ born July 6, 1803, was a twin with George; married Dec. 25, 1823, William Scott Hotchkiss, Jr., of New Haven, born May 17, 1798. He died August 16, 1835. She died April 13, 1847.

*Their children were:*

I. Louisa Augusta Hotchkiss,⁷ born April 12, 1825; married Frederick A. Candee, of Oxford, Ct., Oct. 7, 1845, and had:

  I. David Candee,² born Sept. 22, 1846, who died Oct. 16, 1869.
  II. Jennett Adeline Candee,⁸ born May 30, 1848.
  III. Louisa Elizabeth Candee,⁸ born April 11, 1850.
  IV. Mary Henrietta Candee,⁸ born Sept 29, 1851.
  V. Frederick Catlin Candee,⁸ born Aug. 15, 1854.
  VI. Hannah Augusta Candee,⁸ born June 9, 1856.
  VII. George Augustus Candee,⁸ born April 12, 1858, died May 31, 1859.

II. William Augustus Hotchkiss,⁷ born May 29, 1827; married Jan. 1, 1852, Henrietta Wiggins, of Williamsburg.

III. Bennett Benedict Hotchkiss,⁷ born Aug. 15, 1829; married Mar. 15, 1860, Ann Amelia Darcey, of New Orleans, La., and had :
  I. James Darcey Hotchkiss,⁸ born July 18, 1862.
  II. Robert Usher Hotchkiss,⁸ born Mar. 15, 1866; died Sept. 23, 1870.
  III. Jennett Amelia Hotchkiss,⁸ born Aug. 25, 1871.
  IV. William Bennett Hotchkiss,⁸ born Nov. 7, 1874; died Nov. 9, 1874.

IV. Henrietta Maria Hotchkiss,⁷ born Nov. 5, 1831; married Henry E. Hawkins, of Derby. Ct., Dec. 31, 1857, and had :
  I. Henry Abijah Hawkins,⁸ born May 27, 1864.
  II. Jennett Tomlinson Hawkins,⁸ born June 8, 1868.

227 XI. GEORGE ALBERT,⁶ born July 6, 1863, a twin brother of Jennett Adelaide.—

## Line of Henry Tomlinson.

228 XII. ELIZA CATHERINE,[6] born May 29, 1805; married Isaac T. Hotchkiss, Nov. 7, 1827. She died Feb. 21, 1881. He was born Feb. 9, 1804, and died Sept. 20, 1870. They had:

    I. David Tomlinson Hotchkiss,[7] born Aug. 15, 1829; married Mary A. DeForest, Dec. 15, 1856.

    II. Mary Ann Hotchkiss,[7] born Jan. 12, 1832; married Joseph A. Welch, May 19, 1857.

    III. Edwin Augustus Hotchkiss,[7] born Mar. 20, 1834, died Oct. 22, 1835.

    IV. Edwin Augustus Hotchkiss,[7] born Dec. 4, 1835, and died Dec.16, 1883. He married Caroline M. Backus, Nov. 25, 1858, and had Edwin Augustus Hotchkiss, born Sept. 28, 1859; Caroline Mulford Hotchkiss, born July 31, 1866; died Dec. 18, 1868; Howard Backus Hotchkiss, born April 1, 1870.

    V. Amelia Caroline Hotchkiss,[7] born April 16, 1838; married Edward W. Hotchkiss, Dec. 14, 1859, and had: Russell Hotchkiss, born May 18, 1861; Eliza Hotchkiss, born June 5, 1863; Helen Louisa Hotchkiss, born June 18, 1866; Edward Wadsworth Hotchkiss, born Jan. 4, 1869.

    VI. Isaac Thompson Hotchkiss,[7] born Oct. 23, 1840; died April 4, 1843.

    VII. Isaac Thompson Hotchkiss,[7] born April 23, 1844; died May 18, 1876. He married Ella G. Stafford, Aug. 23, 1871, and had Mabel Stafford, born July 1, 1873.

229 XIII. HENRIETTA LOUISA,[6] born Sept. 13, 1807; died Aug. 14, 1829.

230 XIV. WILLIAM AUGUSTUS,[6] born Sept. 15, 1809.

80    *Tomlinsons in America.*

***101. DAN⁵ TOMLINSON,*** son of *Noah,*[4] (*Isaac,*[3] *Jonas,*[2] *Henry,*[1]) and Abigail (Beers) Tomlinson, married Susanna, daughter of Dea. Eliphalet *Hotchkiss,* June 3, 1774. She died aged 96 years. Their residence was in Derby, Ct.

*Their children were:*

231   I. SUSAN,[6] born June 11, 1776; died young.

232   II. PHILO,[6] born May 15, 1778.+

233   III. ABIJAH,[6] born June 2, 1780.+

234   IV. DAN,[6] born June 4, 1785.+

235   V. SUSAN,[6] born May 3, 1787; married Christopher **Allyn.** He was born Feb. 28, 1792, in Groton, Ct. They resided in New Preston, Ct., until 1829, then removed to Beverly, N. Y. Mr. Allyn died in 1872, aged 79 years. Mrs. Allyn died in 1857, aged 70 years. They died at Delta, Ontario Co., N. Y.

*Their children were:*

   I. Cyrus[7] **Allyn,** born May 23, 1815.

   II. Sherman[7] **Allyn,** born ——, died.

   III. Susan[7] **Allyn.**

   IV. Christopher[7] **Allyn.**

   V. Henrietta[7] **Allyn.**

   VI. Sherman[7] **Allyn,** 2d.

   VII. Lucretia[7] **Allyn.**

236   V. ELIPHALET,[6] born June 10, 1789.+

*Line of Henry Tomlinson.*

**104. BEERS⁵ TOMLINSON,** son of *Noah,⁴ (Isaac,³ Jonas,² Henry,¹)* and Abigail (Beers) Tomlinson, married Sarah, daughter of Samuel *Bassett*, Jr., of Great Hill, in Derby, Ct., Mar. 1, 1781. She was born Feb. 14, 1761. This is all that has been learned of him.

**106. NATHAN⁵ TOMLINSON,** son of *Noah⁴ (Isaac,³ Jonas,² Henry,¹)* and Abigail (Beers) Tomlinson, married Zervia (?) *Bassett*, of Oxford, Ct., March 6, 1783, and resided at first on Great Hill, in Derby, Ct. No more has been learned of him.

**115. HENRY⁵ TOMLINSON,** Jr., son of *Henry,⁴ (Samuel,³ Jonas,² Henry,¹)* and Patience (Tomlinson) Tomlinson, married Sarah *Davis*. He was a farmer on Great Hill, in Derby, Ct.

237    I. WILLIAM,⁶ born Oct. 27, 1773, in Southbury, Ct.+

238    II. PERMELIA,⁶ married Joseph Tucker.

239    III. SHELDON,⁶ married Rhoda Farrington, of Boston, Mass.; was captain of a vessel and was lost at sea.

240    IV. MARK,⁶ married Polly Rider. He died and she married (2d) Agur Tomlinson (No.   )

241    V. CHARLES.⁶

242    VI. LEWIS,⁶ who lived in New York City, married and had a son Seymour.

243    VII. RUSSELL,⁶ died unmarried.

**123. DOCT. HEZEKIAH⁵ TOMLINSON**, son of *Doct. Agur,*⁴ (*Zachariah,*³ *Agur,*² *Henry,*¹) and Mary (Gold) Tomlinson, married Sarah, daughter of Joseph *Lewis*, Jr. No children. He died and she married the Rev. Elisha Rexford, of Monroe, Ct., and had a daughter who died young.

The grave-stone in Stratford old cemetery reads:

"In memory of Dr. Hez. Tomlinson, A.M., a learned and eminent Physician, who departed this Life on the 12th day of May, A.D. 1781, in the 34th year of his Age.

"He lived much esteemed and died greatly lamented. Vain World, farewell to you; Heaven is my native Air, I bid my friends a short Adieu, Impatient to be there."

**131. DOCT. WILLIAM A.⁵ TOMLINSON**, son of *Doct. Agur,*⁴ (*Zachariah,*³ *Agur,*² *Henry,*¹) and Mary (Gold) Tomlinson, married Phebe, daughter of Joseph *Lewis*, Jr., of Stratford, November, 1786. His grave-stone says: "William Agur Tomlinson, an eminent Physician who departed this Life on the 20th day of August, A.D. 1789, in the 27th Year of his Age. He lived much esteemed and died greatly lamented." His widow, Phebe, died March 11, 1842, aged 76 years.

244  I. CATHERINE, born Oct. 9, 1787; died June 2, 1835. She married Hon. David Plant, Dec. 5, 1810. He was born March 29, 1783, and died Oct. 18, 1851. David Plant was graduated at Yale College in 1804, studied at Litchfield Law School. In 1819 and 1820 he was Speaker of the House of Representatives, in his own State, and in 1821 was elected to the State Senate, and twice re-elected. He was Lieutenant-Governor of the State from 1823 to 1827, and from 1827 to 1829 he was a member of the Congress of the United States and was one of the most influential men in political circles in his day in the State of Connecticut.

*The children of David and Catharine Plant were:*

    I. William Agur Plant, who is living at Syracuse.

    II. Catharine Tomlinson Plant, who married Capt. John W. Sterling, of Stratford, where she still resides. Capt. Sterling was a well-known sea captain. They had several children.

    III. Sarah Elizabeth Plant, married Lauren Beach.

    IV. Henry Plant is living at Minneapolis, Minn.

    V. John David Plant, died at Anthony's Falls, Minn., Feb. 29, 1860.

245  II. WILLIAM AGUR, born December, 1789.+

**135.  *CURTISS*[5] *TOMLINSON*,** son of *Capt. Joseph,*[4] (*Zachariah,*[3] *Agur,*[2] *Henry,*[1]) and Elizabeth (Curtiss) Tomlinson, married Mrs. Lucy (Atwood) *Martin.*

"Curtiss Tomlinson, Corporal, marched with a company of Light Dragoons in July, 1779, to New

Haven, thence to Fairfield and thence to Norwalk, at the time that Col. Tryon invaded the coast localities." He served from July 5 until July 16. He probably served at other times, as many did, for he was a Revolutionary pensioner in Connecticut in 1832.

*The children of Curtiss and Lucy Tomlinson were:*

246     I. STEPHEN,[6] born Nov. 4, 1791.+

247     II. JOHN A.,[6] born ——.÷

248     III. MARY A.,[6] born ——; married Doct. Charles Beardsley, and removed to Pennsylvania.

249     IV. LUCY,[6] born ——; married Wakeman Burritt.

250     V. CAROLINE,[6] born ——; married Dr. Martin B. Bassett, and had:

       I. Elizabeth S.[7] Bassett.

       II. Sallie[7] Bassett.

       III. Fannie[7] Bassett.

       IV. Frederick[7] Bassett.

       V. Emily[7] Bassett.

250½    VI. THOMAS JEFFERSON,[6] died young.

251     VII. CHARLES,[6] born ——.+

**136. JOSEPH[5] TOMLINSON**, Jr., son of Capt. Joseph[4] (Zachariah,[3] Agur,[2] Henry[1]) and Elizabeth (Curtiss) Tomlinson, married Sally Curtiss, March 20, 1790.

"Joseph Tomlinson, of Derby, Ct., was in the Connecticut Line, Capt. Humphrey's Company. Enlisted Nov. 26, 1776, for the war."

*Line of Henry Tomlinson.* 85

*Their children were :*

252   I. JOSEPH,⁶ born ———.+

253   II. LUCIUS, not married.

254   III. HENRY, died young.

255   IV. MARY, married Burr Hotchkiss, and had two children, names not known.

256   V. ELIZABETH, not married.

**141. *JOSIAH⁵ TOMLINSON*,** son of *Capt. Beach⁴* (*Zachariah,³ Agur.² Henry¹*) and Charity (Shelton) Tomlinson, married Anna, daughter of Samuel *Shelton,* a cousin of his mother, Jan. 7, 1773. She died in May, 1836. He died in 1841. He was a farmer and resided in Newtown, about two miles from Zoar Bridge.

*Their only child was :*

257   I. BEACH,⁶ born May 4, 1777; married Anna, daughter of Cyrenus and Phebe (Camp) Hard, and had :

258     I. JOSIAH SHELTON HARD⁷ (Tomlinson), born Feb. 24, 1804; married Harriet, daughter of Amasa Goodyear. He died in Central America while in search of crude rubber for his brother-in-law, Charles Goodyear, of India rubber fame.

259   II. ISAAC,⁶ born Dec. 31, 1781.+

259½   III. ZECHARIAH,⁶ born May 5, 1784; not married.

259¾   IV. ABIGAIL ELIZABETH,⁶ born Oct. 29, 1789; married Elijah Sanford, of Newtown, Ct., born in 1787, and died Oct. 26, 1840. She died Feb. 3, 1855. *They had :*

I. David⁷ **Sanford**, born Aug. 1, 1806; married Emily, daughter of Isaac and Phebe (Atwater) **Townsend**, of New Haven, Ct. He died Feb. 6, 1875. *They had:*

    I. John⁸ **Sanford**, born Sept. 5, 1832; married Hattie, daughter of Isaac **Mills**, Sept. 5, 1841.

    II. William⁸ **Sanford**, born Mar. 2, 1834; married ——

    III. Jane⁸ **Sanford**, born Mar. 8, 1836; married Rev. William Moore.

    IV. George Morton⁸ **Sanford**, born Dec. 18, 1841.

    V. Grace⁸ **Sanford**, born Oct. 10, 18—.

    VI. Julia⁸ **Sanford**, died.

    VII. Julia⁸ **Sanford**, born May 3, 1844; died ——.

    VIII. Paul⁸ **Sanford**, born Oct. 1, 1846.

II. Juliette⁷ **Sanford**, born ——; married George, son of Isaac **Townsend**, of New Haven, Ct.

III. Elizabeth⁷ **Sanford**, born ——; married Edmund **Gibson**.

*142.* *HENRY⁵ TOMLINSON*, son of *Capt. Beach*,¹ (*Zachariah*,³ *Agur*,² *Henry*,¹) and Charity (Shelton) Tomlinson, married Abigail, daughter of David *Welles*, of Huntington, now Monroe, a farmer residing near Zoar Bridge. He was one of the old fashioned farmers, with his house always open to a large circle of relatives and friends. One of the Tomlinson family says of his home: "I have seen the wide fire-place in the kitchen with a quar-

ter of a cord of wood blazing in it, and old Samson turning the turkeys and geese hung before it on a string, to grace the table of my grandfather Henry, on Thanksgiving day, when the children and grandchildren were happily seated around it." His wife Abigail died May 2, 1836, aged 72 years. He died June 13, 1843, aged 88 years.

"Henry Tomlinson was in Capt. Beach Tomlinson's Company from Oct. 5 to Oct. 27, 1777, at Fishkill, N. Y.

"Ensign Henry Tomlinson, of Derby, was in Col. Canfield's Militia Regiment at West Point, Sept., 1781."

260 I. CHARITY, born Mar. 6, 1786; married in 1808, Andrew Bartholomew, who was born in Plymouth, Ct., became a merchant in New Haven, and afterwards removed to Wyoming Co., Pa., where he died. She married (2d) Elias Cock, of Waterbury.

*Her children by her first husband were two:*

I. Jane Bartholomew, born Sept. 5, 1809; married Benjamin Franklin Leavenworth, of Waterbury, Ct. He was engaged as a merchant in Philadelphia, and as a manufacturer in Waterbury. He went to California in 1850, where he died by the hand of an assassin, at Angel's Camp, on Carson Creek, in October, 1850, leaving no children. She resides in New Haven.

II. ——— ———.

261 II. DAVID,[6] born Feb. 28, 1788.+

262 III. ELOISA,[6] born May —, 1789; married Wait Lewis, son of William, Aug. 11, 1814. He was a farmer, removed to Canandaigua, N. Y., and thence to Old Hickory County, Ohio, where he had a large farm.

*Their children were:*

    I. Nelson[7] Lewis, born Jan. —, 1812; married and had Diantha, who married and had several children.

    II. Sarah Peck[7] Lewis, born Oct. 8, 1814; died unmarried.

    III. Henrietta Abigail[7] Lewis, born April ——, 1816; married and had two sons living with her in Ohio.

    IV. Henry Tomlinson[7] Lewis, born Feb. ——, 1819; married and lives in Jackson, Ohio, and is a large farmer; no children but an adopted daughter.

    V. George Lewis,[7] went to California in 1862, returned, married and died leaving no heirs.

263 IV. LUCIUS,[6] born April 17, 17—; married Charlotte Laborie; removed to Ohio, where he had a fine farm. Left no children.

264 V. HENRY,[6] born April 17, 1794; went to Golconda, Ill., in 1826, in company with his cousin Elisha Mills, a lawyer, where he married Jane Chitwood. He died in June, 1832. They had one child, GUY R.,[7] who died in 1831, aged 2 years.

## Line of Henry Tomlinson.

265   VI. MARY,[6] born June 3, 1799; lived with and devoted to her parents, especially her father, who survived his wife many years; then lived a number of years with her youngest sister, in care of the sister's children. She resided a time in New Haven, and furnished a considerable history of the Tomlinson family. A true Christian, beloved by all who knew her, died June 3, 1881.

266   VII. ABIGAIL AURELIA,[6] born in 1803; was a successful teacher and a sincere Christian, but died of five days' intermittent fever, Feb. 1, 1838, in Brooklyn, N. Y., unmarried.

267   VIII. ANN REBECCA,[6] married George C. **Peck**, Mar. 4, 1838. He was son of Abner Peck, of Newtown, Conn.

*Their children were:*

I. John F.[7] **Peck**, born Jan. 30, 1839; married Nellie S. Ackley, Dec. 29, 1869. He is a salesman, resides in Chicago, and had a son, Ira John, born Nov. 25, 1870.

II. Gideon[7] **Peck**, born April 16, 1841.

III. Homer Abner[7] **Peck**, born Dec. 31, 1842; married Mary Ann **Tuthill**, of Utica, N. Y.; and had Georgiana E., born Oct. 29, 1871, and Nettie Louisa, born in 1873.

IV. Cornelius B.[7] **Peck**, born Jan. 10, 1846.

V. Abbie L.[7] **Peck**, born April 9, 1850.

VI. Hattie M.[7] **Peck**, born April 21, 1852.

**143. AGUR TOMLINSON,** son of *Capt. Beach,*[4] (*Zachariah,*[3] *Agur,*[2] *Henry,*[1]) and Charity (Shelton) Tomlinson, married Sarah *Curtiss,* May 20, 1781. He was a farmer in Upper White Hills, in Huntington, Ct., and was in the Revolutionary War with his father. He died Oct. 31, 1843, aged 87 years.

Agur Tomlinson enlisted May 14, 1775, in 8th Company, Continental Regiment, discharged Dec. 9, 1775. The Regiment marched to New York and thence north, and was at the siege of St. John in October of that year.

He was a pensioner of New Haven Co., in 1832.

He was a pensioner in Huntington, Conn., in 1840, aged 84 years.

*Their children were:*

268    I. Sarah,[6] married Richard **Hubbell**, of Bridgeport, Ct., in 1804. He was lost at sea in 1811. They had:

         1. Agur Tomlinson[7] **Hubbell**, born June 7, 1805; married Emily Coles, in 1830, and had:

            I. Charles Sidney[8] **Hubbell**.

            II. Josephine[8] **Hubbell**.

            III. Walter Bennet[8] **Hubbell**.

            IV. Sarah Ann[8] **Hubbell**.

         II. Charles Richard[7] **Hubbell**, born July 31, 1806; died in New York in 1830.

## Line of Henry Tomlinson.

III. Sidney Algernon⁷ **Hubbell**, born Feb. 14, 1808, lived in New Haven.

IV. Fenelon⁷ **Hubbell**, born July 25, 1810; married Harriet Stillman, Sept. 12, 1833, and had:

    I. Sarah Tomlinson⁸ **Hubbell**.
    II. Anna Stillman⁸ **Hubbell**.
    III. Pierson Mortimer⁸ **Hubbell**.
    IV. Theodore Fenelon⁸ **Hubbell**.
    V. Caroline A.⁸ **Hubbell**.
    VI. Priscilla A.⁸ **Hubbell**.

V. Mortimer⁷ **Hubbell**, born July 25, 1810; married Rebecca Barnett, of New Haven, Oct. 10, 1848, and had:

    I. Anna Reese⁸ **Hubbell**.
    II. Mortimer Barnett⁸ **Hubbell**.
    III. Fenelon Sidney⁸ **Hubbell**.

269  II. NANCY⁶; married Josiah Morse, of Monroe; lived in New Haven, where he was Sheriff in 1817. They removed to Edgartown, South Carolina. They had:

    I. Sarah Morse,⁷ married and had four children.

    II. Agur Morse.⁷

    III. Sophia Morse,⁷ married John **Hubbell**, of Brookfield, Ct., where she lived until they removed to Davenport, Iowa, with her son George, who graduated at Yale College. He married Mary Pease, of New Haven, and had three children.

    IV. Cyrus Morse,⁷ who went to Chicago.

    V. John Morse,⁷ who went to South Carolina.

270   III. John,⁵+

271   IV. Betsey,⁶ married Josias Gunn, of Waterbury, Feb. 14,
      1813, who died, and she married (2d) David Gunn, and
      had two sons who died young. She removed to Pough-
      keepsie, N. Y.

272   V. Charles,⁶ born Feb. 20, 1788.+

273   VI. Sophia,⁶ married —— Reese, who went to South Carolina,
      was a planter and had :

      I. Ann Reese,⁷ married, and had Rebecca.

      II. Emily Reese,⁷ married —— Stone, and removed to
      Colorado.

**145. VICTORY⁵ TOMLINSON,** son of *Capt. Beach⁴* (*Zachariah,³ Agur,² Henry¹*) and Charity (Shelton) Tomlinson, married Eunice Dunbar, of Plymouth, Ct., where he settled and became a wealthy farmer, his estate having been estimated at $150,000. He owned, it is said, in its prosperous days "nearly all the turnpike," from New Haven to Litchfield.

He was Ensign in the Revolutionary War, being only sixteen years of age when the war began ; was made nearly deaf by the explosions of cannon shot, and was sometime a prisoner of war.

His wife, Eunice, died Dec. 23, 1791, and he married (2d) Martha Warner.

The following is given as the explanation of the occasion which gave him the name of " Victory."

He was born Sept. 12, 1760. Four days before this, or on the 8th of the same month, "Montreal, Detroit, Michilimackinac, and all other places within the government of Canada were surrendered to his "Brittanic Majesty," and thus the French war came to an end.

"On a Sunday morning soon after, as this infant was being carried to the church for baptism, to receive some name that had been borne by the older members of the family, a courier from the back settlements on the Hudson, came riding up, waving a white flag and shouting Victory! Victory! Victory! For a moment he drew rein at the steps of the church, while he told the pastor and people the story of the fall of Montreal and all Canada, and the great victory of the English. To every one who heard it, the tidings seemed as if from death to life.

When the courier had vanished, the congregation gathered in the church for worship and thanksgiving, but before these could proceed the child must be baptized. The minister, an aged man,[11] dipping his hand into the water and placing it on the forehead of the child, apparently forgetting the family name it was intended he should bear, said, 'Victory, I baptize thee,' and thus the name came into the family, and it was perpetuated in several relative branches for many years."

---

[11] The Rev. Jedidiah Mills, who died in 1776, aged 78 years.

94   *Tomlinsons in America.*

Victory Tomlinson was in the "Connecticut Line" in Capt. Stoddard's Company in the Revolutionary War. He enlisted April 30, 1778, and served eight months, being discharged Jan. 1, 1779."[12]

*Children of Victory and Eunice Tomlinson:*

274   I. EUNICE,[6] born April 27, 1788; married the Rev. Joseph Davis Welton, an Episcopal clergyman of Waterbury, May 11, 1808. He preached in Woodbury, Ct., and died in Waterbury, Ct., Jan. 16, 1825, aged 42 years. She died Feb. 20, 1832, and he married (2d) Martha Warner. His children were:

    I. Julia M.[7] Welton, born July 15, 1809; married George Warner. Three children.

    II. Hobart Victory[7] Welton, born Oct. 28, 1811; married Adaline, daughter of Luther Richards, of Vermont. Their residence was in the eastern part of the city of Waterbury, and they had:

        I. Edwin D.[8] Welton.

        II. Sarah C.[8] Welton.

        III. Harriet A.[8] Welton.

    III. Joseph[7] Welton, born May 15, 1814; married Mary, daughter of Seabury Pierpont. Their residence was in Waterbury, Ct., and they had:

        I. Homer Heber[8] Welton, born Feb. 22, 1837; married Ellen J. Garrigus, April 26, 1868, and had, Julia,[9] Joseph D.[9] and Edith J.[9]

        II. Eunice[8] Welton, born Oct. 7, 1839.

        III. Lucy A.[8] Welton, born Nov. 14, 1841.

---

[12] Men in the Revolution.

## Line of Henry Tomlinson. 95

  IV. Henry Beach[5] **Welton,** born Sept. 27, 1824; died Feb. 9, 1876.

275 II. Zechariah.[6]

276 III. Beach.[6]

**149. ZACHARIAH[5] TOMLINSON,** son of Capt. Beach[4], (Zachariah[3], Agur[2], Henry,[1]) and Charity (Shelton) Tomlinson, was graduated at Yale College in 1788, became a lawyer in practice in Lansingburg, N. Y., and is said to have been a man of very fine character. Who he married is not known.

*The child of Zachariah Tomlinson:*

277 I. Antoinett, who married as second wife the Rev. Sheldon **Dibble,** a missionary to the Hawaiian Islands. (See under No. 153, Gideon Tomlinson's daughter Maria.) She died leaving one daughter; who married Mr. **Pierpont,** went to California, had three daughters, and is still living there, (1884).

**153. GIDEON[5] TOMLINSON,** son of Capt. Beach,[4] (Zachariah,[3] Agur,[2] Henry,[1]) and Charity (Shelton) Tomlinson, studied law with Judge Asa Chapman, of Newtown, and became quite noted in his profession. He married Barbary, daughter of William McManus, of Troy, N. Y., at 14 years of age.

*They had one child:*

278 I. Maria,[6] born in 1808; married the Rev. Sheldon **Dibble,** Oct. 31, 1831, of Skaneateles, N. Y. They went as missionaries to the Hawaiian Islands, and she was

reported as one of the most efficient workers of the American Board. She died of heart disease, leaving a son, who died young, and a daughter:

 I. Maria[7] **Dibble**, who married the Rev. —— ——, **Pierpont**, who is pastor of one of the largest churches in San Francisco, Cal. Mrs. Pierpont died leaving two daughters. The Rev. Sheldon Dibble married (2d) Antoinett, daughter of Zechariah **Tomlinson**, of Newtown and Lansingburg, N. Y., a cousin to his first wife. The had :

  I. Seymour[7] **Dibble**, who is an engineer and resides in Washington, D. C.

  II. Clara[7] **Dibble**, who married Lieut. Philip **Inch**, U. S. Navy, and resides in Washington, D. C. They had Agnes **Inch** and Robert **Inch**.

**154. *DAVID J. N.*[5] *TOMLINSON*,** son of Capt. *Beach*,[4] (*Zachariah*,[3] *Agur*,[2] *Henry*,[1]) and Charity (Shelton) Tomlinson, married Elizabeth Ann, daughter of Joseph *Beardsley*. They lived at the White Hills, in Huntington, where they had a large dairy farm.

*Their children were:*

279 I. Nancy,[6] born in March, 1812; married Daniel Alonzo **Nichols**. She died May 25, 1852, and he married (2d) Elizabeth **Clark**, widow of William Clark, and daughter of Henry **Lewis**, of Monroe. There was a son by the first marriage, born May 24, 1852; died in Nov., 1854.

280 II. Gould,[6] born Nov. —, 1816.+

281 III. MARY ELIZABETH,[6] born July 4, 1820; married Wright Drew in 1840. He was a farmer in Huntington, Conn.

    I. Elizabeth[7] Drew, born in 1841; married Sept. 4, 1867, Sylvester Roundsleve, of Shelton, Conn.

    II. Martha[7] Drew, born in 1843; married Burr Hawley, of Monroe.

    III. Mary L.[7] Drew, born in 1845; married Reuben Parrott, and resides in Farmer's Mills, N. Y.

    IV. George W.[7] Drew, born in 1847; married Cornelia Brooks, of Huntington, Conn.

    V. Ellen[7] Drew, born in 1849; married Louis Wheeler.

    VI. Emily Estelle[7] Drew, born in 1851; married Andrew Leavenworth, of Monroe, Conn.

    VII. Loretta Maria[7] Drew, born in 1854; married Edward Wheeler, of Huntington, Conn.

    VIII. Tilla Theresa[7] Drew, born in 1859.

    IX. Charles Roundsleve[7] Drew, born in 1867; resides in Dakota.

**158. JABEZ HUNTINGTON[5] TOMLINSON**, son of *Capt. Gideon*,[4] (*Zachariah*,[3] *Agur*,[2] *Henry*,[1]) and Hannah (Huntington) Tomlinson, married Rebecca, daughter of Joseph *Lewis*, of Old Mill, in Stratford, in January, 1780. He was a graduate of Yale college in 1780. Being left an orphan at an early age, he was reared by his grandfather Zachariah and his aunt Mary Kellogg. It is said that he had a complete genealogy of the Tomlinson family,

but it is not preserved, so far as known. He had a remarkable memory, and was noted for discriminating judgment and practical sense. He had a farm at Oronoke, in Stratford. A copy of the coat-of-arms, painted in colors, has been preserved by him and his son, Governor Gideon Tomlinson, and is in a fine state of preservation. The grandfather of Jabez H. had the original, which has come down to the present day well preserved, through the family of Abraham, the uncle of Jabez H. There can be no doubt but that Jabez H. knew whether this coat-of-arms was brought to this country by Henry Tomlinson or not, for his grandfather, Zachariah, by whom he was brought up, was the grandson of Henry, the first settler here, and it is silly to suppose all these families of honorable standing have imposed on themselves a fiction or delusion, for two hundred years, for the sake of pretense.

A paper is preserved in the handwriting of Jabez H. Tomlinson, which says, "Henry Tomlinson came from Derby in England, to this country.

His grave-stone inscription says: "Jabez H. Tomlinson, Esqr., who died January 14. 1849. Æ 89. He was highly respected as a patriotic officer of the revolutionary army and an experienced, able and upright legislator and magistrate ; and deservedly honored and beloved as a friend, husband, father and Christian."

The inscription for his wife's grave-stone was most probably prepared by himself, and is a model of propriety as well as elegance:

"Rebecca Tomlinson, the wife of Jabez H. Tomlinson, who was born on the 3 day of Dec., 1761, and died on the 1 day of Jan., 1823, deeply and justly lamented by her afflicted husband and bereaved children.

"Let those who delight to cherish the remembrance of her unwearied and constant affection, imitate the pious example of one whose active and unshaken faith in the divine Redeemer affords just ground of confidence that she has gone to possess an inheritance incorruptable and eternal in the heavens."

"Ensign Jabez H. Tomlinson was in the army under Capt. Joseph Walker of Stratford, in the 'Connecticut Line,' and continued as Ensign from 1777 until his resignation May 1, 1781.

"He was a pensioner in New Haven County (?) in 1832, and also a pensioner residing at Stratford, Ct., in 1840, aged then 79 years."[13]

---

[13] **Record of Service of Connecticut Men in the Revolution**, 332.

## Jabez H. Tomlinson as Guard to Major Andre.

NEW HAVEN, August 8, 1832.

To JEREMIAH DAY, D. D., President of Yale College.

*Dear Sir:*—It affords me pleasure, as the agent of Jabez H. Tomlinson, Esq. of Stratford (the father of our late Governor), and of Nathan Beers, Esq. of this city, to request your acceptance of the accompanying miniature of Major John Andre, Adjutant General of the British army during the Revolutionary war. The melancholy fate of that accomplished gentleman exerted such universal grief in the hearts of his countrymen, and such undisguised sympathy in the hearts of his foes, that it is presumed this memorial may be viewed with interest, and be deemed worthy of preservation among the historical collections of the college. Although the gift, without some explanation, might appear to be trivial, yet it possesses an *incidental value* that renders it truly interesting.

It is the likeness of Major Andre, seated at a table in his guard room, drawn by himself with a pen, on the morning of the day fixed for his execution. Mr. Tomlinson informs me that a respite was granted until the next day, and that this miniature was in the meantime presented to him (then acting as officer of the guard) by Major Andre himself. Mr. Tomlinson was present when the sketch was made, and says it was drawn without the aid of a glass.

The sketch subsequently passed into the hands of Deacon Beers, a fellow officer of Mr. Tomlinson on the station, and from thence was transferred to me. It has been in my possession several years.

While the high character of the officers who have preserved since the Revolution this interesting memorial of a lamented victim to the necessary usages of war, places its genuineness beyond doubt, it may be remarked that its accuracy as a likeness is rendered probable from the circumstance that Major Andre was accustomed to delineate as an amusement, the outlines of his face and person.

The London edition of Joshua Smith's narrative of Arnold's treason, and of his personal connection with Andre in his attempt to escape, has a frontispiece exhibiting the likeness of Major Andre. It is noted by the engraver as a copy from a portrait by Major Andre himself now (or then) in the possession of his relatives in England. I have compared the sketch with that engraving and thought I could discern in the outlines a striking similarity.

Mr. Tomlinson and Mr. Beers were officers in the regular line of the army at the time of Major Andre's execution. I believe they severally held the rank of Lieutenant.

With great respect,
Your friend and obedient servant,
EBENEZER BALDWIN."

*Children of John H. and Rebecca Tomlinson were:*

282   I. GIDEON⁵ (the Governor), born Dec. 31, 1780.+
283   II. HANNAH,⁶ born Jan. 10, 1784; died April 2, 1827, unmarried.
284   III. ANN⁶ (Nancy), born Jan. 23, 1785; married Feb. 27, 1808, George Kneeland Nichols, born Dec. 26, 1771. They had:
     I. Philip⁷ Nichols.
     II. Charles Mansfield⁷ Nichols, died unmarried.
285   IV. SARAH LEWIS,⁶ born Feb. 25, 1789; married Feb. 27, 1808, Charles Theophilus Nichols, born July 21, 1771. They had:
     I. Ann Eliza⁷ Nichols, born Dec., 1813; married William Sumner Johnson.
     II. George Huntington⁷ Nichols, D.D., an Episcopal clergyman, of Hoosac Falls, N. Y.
286   V. HUNTINGTON.⁶+

**165. DAVID⁵ TOMLINSON,** son of *Abraham,⁴ (Zachariah,³ Agur,² Henry,¹)* and Rebecca (Gold) Tomlinson, married Sept. 22, 1799, Phebe, daughter of Charles *Miller*, of Schenectady, who was a native of Yorkshire, England. David Tomlinson died Oct 1, 1856, aged 86 years and 11 months. His wife Phebe, died Sept. 12, 1845, aged 73 years. Both were buried in St. George's Church-yard in Schenectady, N. Y.

*Their children were:*

287   I. MARY JANE,⁶ married as second wife the Rt. Rev. Horatio Potter, D.D., LL.D., of New York City, and died aged 43 years.
288   II. CHARLES HENRY,⁶ born in 1802.+

## Line of Henry Tomlinson.

**167. DOCT. CHARLES TOMLINSON,** son of *Abraham,*[4] (*Zachariah,*[3] *Agur,*[2] *Henry,*[1]) and Rebecca (Gold) Tomlinson, married Susan *Hill*, of Guilford. He was a physician in Stratford, Ct., his home being the northern part of his father's homestead on Main street, next the Congregational Church. This place was purchased by the late Capt. John W. Sterling, and is now owned by his heirs, who are descendants of Zachariah Tomlinson, and upon it in 1886, they erected a beautiful mansion of modern style, with enlarged lawns all round it, making it a most substantial and beautiful home.

*Their children were:*

289  I. Mary Ann,[6] married the Rev. John **Mitchell**.
290  II. Henry,[6] a physician, married Maria, daughter of Dr. Levi **Ives**, of New Haven.
290½ III. Charles,[6] married Susan **Hedden**.

**170. WILLIAM⁶ TOMLINSON,** son of *Doct. Abraham,*[5] (*Jonah,*[4] *Abraham,*[3] *Jonas,*[2] *Henry,*[1]) and Abigail (Gibson) Tomlinson, married Jane *Treat*, Nov. 1, 1787. She died Sept. 9, 1799. He died Sept. 29, 1807.

*Their children were:*

291  I. Maria,[7] born June 11, 1789; married Elisha **Tibbals** Oct. 1806, and died Dec. 1862.
292  II. Martha,[7] born Aug. 3, 1792, died ——.
293  III. Jeannette,[7] married Elisha **Johnson**, in 1816; died in 1818.
294  IV. William,[7] married Amy, daughter of Isaac **Briscoe**, Aug. 30, 1819.
295  V. Caleb,[7] born Oct. 25, 1797. +

**171. ABRAHAM⁶ TOMLINSON, M. D.,** son of *Doct. Abraham,⁵ (Jonah,⁴ Abraham,³ Jonas,² Henry,¹)* and Abigail (Gibson) Tomlinson, married ———— ————. They lived in Milford, Ct., and all of his children named below received legacies from their grandfather, Doctor Abraham Tomlinson.

*Their children were:*

| | | |
|---|---|---|
| 296 | I. | WILLIAM.⁷ |
| 297 | II. | CALEB.⁷ |
| 298 | III. | MARIA.⁷ |
| 299 | IV. | MARTHA.⁷ |
| 300 | V. | JENETTE.⁷ |

**172. DAVID⁶ TOMLINSON,** son of *Doct. Abraham,⁵ (Jonah,⁴ Abraham,³ Jonas,² Henry,¹)* and Abigail (Gibson) Tomlinson, married Anna, daughter of David and Mehitable *Camp*, of Milford, Ct., Nov. 6, 1791. He was a farmer and his residence in Milford, Ct. He died Nov. 17, 1825. She was born June 9, 1774, and died Aug. 17, 1859, aged 85 years.

*Their children were:*

301    I. ANNA,⁷ born Aug. 25, 1792; married Benjamin Lot Lambert, of Milford, Ct., and died Jan. 22, 1815, leaving a daughter.

        I. Anna Tomlinson **Lambert**, who married Edwin Woodruff, M. D., in 1839, and they removed to Tallmadge, Ohio.

302    II. POLLY,⁷ born May 20, 1794; married ———— **Baldwin,** and died April 29, 1852, leaving Mark Baldwin, David Baldwin, and Dennis Baldwin.

## Line of Henry Tomlinson. 105

303   III.  MEHETABLE,⁷ born Oct. 22, 1796; died unmarried, in Milford, Jan. 27, 1869.

304   IV.  DAVID GIBSON⁷ (Rev.), born Jan. 14, 1799.+

305   V.  LOUISA,⁷ born June 18, 1801; married Nehemiah **Smith**, of Milford and had :
- I. Susan **Smith**.⁸
- II. Theron G. **Smith**.⁸

306   VI.  ABIGAIL,⁷ born Sept. 28, 1803; died Jan. 28, 1847, unmarried.

307   VII.  JULIA,⁷ born Jan. 19, 1806; died Jan. 31, 1850, unmarried.

308   VIII.  MARTHA,⁷ born Sept. 22, 1809; married Bela Clark, of Milford, Ct., and died Sept. 1, 1849, leaving two children :
- I. Eliza⁸ **Clark**.
- II. Marshall⁸ **Clark**.

309   IX.  CHARLES LAMBERT,⁷ born July 14, 1811.+

310   X.  NATHAN CAMP,⁷ born Nov. 21, 1813.+

311   XI.  ANNA,⁷ born Dec. 8, 1816; married Samuel L. **Burns**, Sept. 30, 1835. *Their children were:*
- I. Maria Antoinett **Burns**,⁸ born June 29, 1836.
- II. Augusta Harrington **Burns**,⁸ born Aug. 5, 1838.
- III. Alonzo Wellington **Burns**,⁸ born Oct. 16, 1840.
- IV. Anna Tomlinson **Burns**,⁸ born Oct. 14, 1844; died Sept. 14, 1845.
- V. Mary Frances **Burns**,⁸ born Jan. 21, 1850.
- VI. Isabell Louisa **Burns**,⁸ born May 7, 1852; died April 22, 1861.
- VII. Elliot Judson **Burns**,⁸ born Mar. 17, 1854.
- VIII. Edith Thornton **Burns**,⁸ born Jan. 17, 1857.
- IX. DeWitt Clinton **Burns**,⁸ born Mar. 28, 1861.

**175. JOHN G.⁶ TOMLINSON**, son of *Doct. Abraham,⁵ (Jonah,⁴ Abraham,³ Jonas,² Henry,¹)* and Abigail (Gibson) Tomlinson, married —— ——. He died Jan. 29, 1838, at Oswego, N. Y.

312    I. CELIA,⁷ married "Penette" Hawley, and died without heirs at the age of 61 years.

**178. JOSEPH B.⁶ TOMLINSON**, son of *Joseph,⁵ (Agur,⁴ Abraham,³ Jonas,² Henry,¹)* and Bethiah (Glover) Tomlinson, married Susannah Mead, of Bridgewater, Ct. He died Aug. 18, 1839.

313    I. OLIVER MEAD.⁷-|.

314    II. ELIZA,⁷ married a Mr. **Stringham**, and had three daughters and six sons, the youngest of whom is a professor in a college in Ca'ifornia. She died Aug. 30, 1881, in Topeka, Kansas.

315    III. ANNA MARIA,⁷ born in 1804, married Chauncey **Ray**, and had eight children.

316    IV. HANNAH,⁷ married Cyrenius **Mallett**, and died in Fairport, N. Y., in 1844.

317    V. CATHARINE,⁷ married Wolcott A. **Chappell**, and had ten children, one of whom married Judge **Ellis**, of Green Bay, Wis., and left an interesting family. She died July 1, 1881, in Ill.

318    VI. SALLY,⁷ married Abijah **Blakeman**, of Oronoque, in Stratford, Conn., and had Louise, who married Charles Crawford, of Ch'cago.

319    VII. SUSAN,⁷ who died in Albany, N. Y., aged 18 years.

320    VIII. SON,⁷ who died in infancy.

**179. DAVID⁶ TOMLINSON, A. M., M. D.,** son of *Joseph,*⁵ (*Agur,*¹ *Abraham,*³ *Jonas,*² *Henry.*¹) and Bethia (Glover) Tomlinson, was born at Derby, Connecticut, in August, 1772. He entered the classical department of Williams College, and was graduated in the year 1798, receiving the degree of Bachelor of Arts. Subsequently he studied medicine and surgery under the celebrated Dr. Wheeler, of Red Hook, Dutchess County, New York, and was licensed to practice medicine and surgery by the Connecticut State Medical Society on November 24, 1802, of which Society Dr. James Potter was then President. Doctor Tomlinson began the practice of his profession at Rhinebeck, New York. He rose rapidly into prominence, numbering among his patients the most distinguished residents of that County, among whom may be mentioned, Chancellor Livingston and General John Armstrong. He was elected and served for a number of years as President of the Dutchess County Medical Society, a position only tendered to physicians of great eminence in the County.

In 1812 he was appointed by Governor Tompkins, Surgeon to the Second Regiment, and acted as such for a few years.

In the year 1819 he was elected to the Legislature of the State, as a member of Assembly from Dutchess County.

In 1825 he removed to the City of New York in order to advance the educational interests of his children. His fame in his profession had preceded him and he at once took the rank his acquirements justified.

He became an intimate personal friend and professional associate of Dr. Hoosack, Dr. Francis and the elder Dr. Mott, and while in active practice he was regarded as one of the ablest physicians in that city.

Dr. Tomlinson was a man of great learning and stood very high as a classical scholar.

In 1810 he was married at Rhinebeck, to Cornelia Adams, a granddaughter of Chief Justice Andrew Adams of the State of Connecticut, and of the Hon. John Canfield, a member of the Continental Congress.

*They had the following children:*

321    I. HENRY TALMAGE,[1] born Feb. ——, 1816; adopted his father's profession, married Christina Adams, of Coxsackie, N. Y., and died in his 34th year. No children.

322    II. THEODORE EDWIN,[1] born Dec. 25, 1817.+

323    III. CORNELIA L.,[1] born July 4, 1819; married in 1837, Harvey A. Weed, a lawyer, son of Nathaniel Weed, a prominent merchant of New York City. He was a graduate of Columbia College and valedictorian of his class.

*Line of Henry Tomlinson.*

*Their children were:*

I. Caroline Laura³ Weed, married (1st) Harry Blow, of Virginia, who died, and she married (2d) Mr. Beaten, of Brooklyn, N. Y.

II. Louisa³ Weed, died in infancy.

III. Harvey Nathaniel³ Weed, married Mrs. Nellie Queen.

324  IV. MARIA A,⁷ born April 3, 1821; married Abraham C. Dayton, the accomplished author of "Last Days of Knickerbocker Life in New York."

*Their children were:*

I. Charles Willoughby⁸ Dayton, married Laura A. Newman, of New York. He is a distinguished lawyer, and was elected to cast his vote in the electoral college for President Cleveland.

II. Laura C. S.⁸ Dayton, married Benjamin Arthur Fessenden.

III. William Adams Dayton, married Miss Sampson, daughter of the Rev. Dr. Sampson, of New York City. He is a practicing physician in that city, his specialty being diseases of the ear and throat.

IV. Harold C.⁸ Dayton, is with the B. and M. Elevator Co. of Burlington, Iowa.

325  V. JULIA CAROLINE,⁷ married Richard Burleigh Kimball, of New Hampshire, April 17, 1844, and died July 24, 1879. He was a lawyer, but devoted much of his life to literary pursuits, and is the author of "St. Leger Papers," "Under Currents of Wall Street," and several other works.

*Their children were:*

I. Richard⁶ **Kimball**, a practicing lawyer at Kimball, Texas, who married Nannie Aurelia Ogden, of Texas, in 1881, and had Richard Huntington **Kimball** and Mary **Kimball**.

II. Julia⁶ **Kimball**, died Sept. 29, 1861.

III. Cornelia⁶ **Kimball**.

IV. Eunice Marsh⁶ **Kimball**.

V. Daniel⁶ **Kimball**.

326  VI. Ellen Adams,⁷ married Henry A. **Warren**, grandson of Dr. John Warren, of Boston, and grand-nephew of General Warren, of Bunker Hill fame. They had:

I. Henry Tomlinson⁸ **Warren**.

***180. DANIEL⁶ TOMLINSON***, son of *Joseph⁵* (*Agur,⁴ Abraham,³ Jonas,² Henry,¹*) and Bethia (Glover) Tomlinson, married Mrs. Lucia R. Holman, Sept. 13, 1835. He died Dec. 11, 1863, aged 87 years. Her maiden name was Ruggles and she married Thomas Holman, M.D., October 23, 1819, and sailed with the first missionary company sent by the American Board to the Sandwich, now Hawaiian Islands, arriving at their destination April 11, 1820. After two years' service there, Doctor Holman and family returned to Connecticut, where he died in 1826. She died in 1886, aged nearly 93 years.

Daniel Tomlinson was graduated at Williams' College, studied law with Chancellor Livingston at

Rhinebeck, N. Y., and was admitted to the Bar, but shortly afterwards he turned his attention to mechanical pursuits and certain numerous inventions, for which he had a peculiar genius, and which with other enterprises engrossed his efforts during his long life. A description of one of Mr. Tomlinson's inventions, was given by F. J. French, in the Bridgeport *Standard*, Dec. 14, 1863, as follows:

"Sixty years ago the only knife used among curriers, for shaving leather, was the old 'Co—knife' of England, manufactured and stamped with the crown and arms of Great Britain. It was made of one piece of iron with the steel welded upon each edge, and of course after wear and repeated sharpening, the steel wore away and the tool was useless. Mr. Tomlinson's invention consisted in making the body of the knife in two pieces of iron, screwed together. Between the lips of the two edges was inserted a thin blade of steel forming the cutting edge, and as these wore away new ones could be obtained at a small price, so that the body of the knife with ordinary care, would last a century. It is appreciated by the trade, is simple, cheap and so perfect that it has never been improved, and is the only knife used, except splitting machines, in the United States, Great Britain, France and most other countries. Honor therefore to the memory of the man who was among the first to take the lead in that inventive march in

this country, which in its progress has beaten the English all the way from a currier's knife to a monitor."

The obituary notice of Daniel Tomlinson says:

"He was always a loyal citizen and served his town in both houses of the Legislature, and lived respected by all who knew him. His many acts of unostentatious benevolence will be known in the great day when all will receive their reward."

181. AGUR⁶ TOMLINSON, son of *Joseph*⁵ (*Agur*,⁴ *Abraham*,³ *Jonas*,² *Henry*¹) and Bethia (Glover) Tomlinson, married Mary, daughter of Peter and Mary (Lockwood) *Fairchild*. Agur Tomlinson entered Williams College, where he remained two years, then he studied medicine with Doct. Eli Perry, of Ridgefield, Conn., was graduated and commenced practice in Brookfield, Conn., but soon relinquished it and engaged in farming, which he continued through life.

Peter Fairchild, father of Mary, was a Tory in the Revolutionary War, as most of the members of the Church of England were in those days, and he fought for the mother country, dying at his post on Long Island of a fever, shortly after the birth of Mary. At the time of her birth the house was surrounded for several days by soldiers who hoped for the return of the father so as to capture him. This

house was standing in Redding, some years ago, time worn and pierced with bullets. Agur Tomlinson died June 7, 1840, aged 62 years. Mary, his widow, died Mar. 24, 1861, aged 84 years.

The children of Agur and Mary Tomlinson were born in Brookfield as follows:

327   I. MELINDA,[7] born Aug. 5, 1802; married Oct. 6, 1823, Philo Hurd, son of Jabez Hurd, of Brookfield, Ct. She died at Bridgeport, Ct., Oct. 29, 1882. Philo Hurd was engaged many years in constructing railroads and operating them, residing at Bridgeport, Ct. He died Aug. 14, 1885, aged 90 years.

*Their children were:*

   I. Philo Melancthon[8] Hurd, died in infancy.

   II. Melancthon Montgomery[8] Hurd, who married Clara Hatch, daughter of Daniel Hatch, of Bridgeport, Ct.

   III. Mary Justine[8] Hurd, who married James E. Dunham, of Bridgeport, Ct.

   IV. Caroline M.[8] Hurd, who married William Mecker, of Bridgeport, Ct.

   V. Eugene Augustus[8] Hurd, married Sarah Case, of Montrose, Pa., and died June 10, 1864, of yellow fever, at Morehead City, N. C., while engaged in the service of his country during the war of the Rebellion.

328   II. JULIA,[7] born Sept. 12, 1804; married Samuel Ferris Hurd, brother of Philo Hurd, on Christmas eve, 1824, and died Jan. 28, 1877. They had:

  I. Catherine Sophia⁵ Hurd, born 1825.

  II. Samuel Henry⁸ Hurd, born 1828.

  III. Theodore Augustus⁸ Hurd, died in 1831.

  IV. Julia Caroline⁸ Hurd, died April 17, 1850.

329 III. JOSEPH,⁷ born in February, 1806; died Aug. 7, 1839.

330 IV. MARY,⁷ born Aug. 8, 1808; married Capt. Lockwood N. DeForest, and died Sept. 29, 1879.

331 V. JANE,⁷ born July 31, 1810; married George Keeler, of Brookfield, in 1835, and had:

  I. David Henry⁸ Keeler, died Oct. 3, 1839.

  II. Theodore Augustus⁸ Keeler, died ——.

  III. George Henry⁸ Keeler, died June 7, 1844.

332 VI. CORNELIA,⁷ born Dec. 10, 1813; married Edward Thorp, a civil engineer, and died at Hyde Park, Pa., Sept. 23, 1882. They had:

  I. Mary⁸ Thorp.

  II. Caroline⁸ Thorp.

333 VII. CAROLINE,⁷ born Dec. 4, 1815; married Lucius C. Northrop, of Brookfield, Conn., and had:

  I. Lucius⁸ Northrop.

  II. Edward⁸ Northrop, a physician, and who died in 1885.

334 VIII. DAVID,⁷ born Dec. 25, 1821; died at White Hall, Alabama, Aug. 9, 1837.

*Line of Henry Tomlinson.*

**183. DAVID⁶ TOMLINSON**, son of *David*,⁵ (*Agur*,⁴ *Abraham*,³ *Jonas*,² *Henry*,¹) and Ruth (Hawkins) Tomlinson, married Sarah, daughter of Russell (No. 94) and Agnes (Cortelyou) Tomlinson, Sept. 26, 1799. Their residence was Derby, Conn.

*Their children were:*

335  I. ELIZA,⁷ born May 4, 1801; married Elijah Baldwin, Jan. 6, 1820. She died June 4, 1822, aged 21 years. He married (2d) Ruth Ann Tomlinson, Mar. 13, 1823. She was born Jan. 6, 1808, and died Sept. 30, 1840, aged 33 years, and was the daughter of Abijah Tomlinson (No. 233). He died April 30, 1838, aged 45 years. Their residence was in New Preston, Ct. Their children were:

    I. Eliza Aurelia⁸ Baldwin, born Jan. 4, 1824; married George Washington Coyswell, Jan. 4, 1853. Residence, Marbledale, New Preston, Ct.

    II. Julia Maria⁸ Baldwin, born Feb. 8, 1826; married Sept. 26, 1849, Henry S. Wheaton, and resided in her father's homestead in New Preston, Litchfield Co., Conn.

    III. Betsey Tomlinson⁸ Baldwin, born Oct. 5, 1827; married William Hoag.

    IV. Jerome Wales⁸ Baldwin, born June 14, 1829; died Mar. 21, 1834.

    V. Elijah Wheeler⁸ Baldwin, born Jan. 9, 1831; resides in Milwaukee, Wis.

    VI. Abiel Sherman⁸ Baldwin, born March 11, 1833; resides in Iowa.

    VII. Jerome Edward⁸ Baldwin, born June 13, 1835, died Aug. 15, 1861.

336　II. Mary,⁷ born Mar. 5, 1803; died Oct. 14, 1803.
337　III. David,⁷ born Sept. 1, 1804; married Nancy Hayes, Sept. 24, 1825. He died Oct. 20, 1878, aged 74 years.
338　IV. Augustus,⁷ born Nov. 12, 1806; married Dorcas English, April 17, 1830.
339　V. Jane,⁷ born Nov. 7, 1808; married (1st) John Lane, Nov. 24, 1831. She married (2d) Roger Newton Whittelsey, Aug. 19, 1838, and (3d) Samuel Camp, May 15, 1843. She died April 29, 1877.
340　VI. Charles,⁷ born Nov. 6, 1810; married Jane Canfield, Nov. 10, 1831. He died July 18, 1839.
341　VII. Betsey,⁷ born Sept. 21, 1812; married Samuel Russell, April 21, 1833.
342　VIII. Sarah,⁷ born Dec. 5, 1814; married John Clark Hull, July 25, 1830. Their children were:

  I. Mary Eliza⁸ Hull, born Oct. 2, 1831; married Egbert Cogswell, Feb. 21, 1858, and had Frederick Hull Cogswell, born Mar. 11, 1859; Sarah Rosa Cogswell, born Nov. 16, 1861; Arthur Grant Cogswell, born Feb. 18, 1866.

  II. Isaac⁸ Hull, born March 29, 1834.

  III. Charles⁸ Hull, born June 5, 1835; married Isora Taylor, in Portland, Oregon, Dec. 27, 1864. He married (2d) Lilly Davis, Oct. 2, 1873, and had:

    I. Dewitt Clinton⁹ Hull, born May 22, 1866.
    II. Charles⁹ Hull, born Jan. 10, 1868.
    III. Alfred James⁹ Hull, born June 10, 1875.
    IV. Mary Agnes⁹ Hull, born April 12, 1878.
    V. John Clark⁹ Hull, born Mar. 9, 1883.

343　IX. Isaac,⁷ born May 24, 1817; married Eliza Baylis, Oct. 15, 1839.
344　X. Simon,⁷ born April 11, 1820; married Maria Lewis, April 23, 1843.

*194. REV. JOHN L.⁶ TOMLINSON*, son of *Capt. John L.⁵ (Capt. John,⁴ John,³ Jonas,² Henry¹)*, and —— (——) Tomlinson, was graduated at Yale College, in 1807, in the class with Alexander H. Stephens, the famous statesman of Georgia. He studied law for a time, then turned his attention to theology; was licensed to preach by the New Haven Central Association in 1854, and continued a Congregational minister until the close of life, at Adrian, Michigan.

345    I. Daughter,⁷ married —— Bliss, and resided at Stamford, Conn.

*195. SAMUEL⁶ TOMLINSON*, son of *Capt. John L.⁵ (Capt. John,⁴ John,³ Jonas,² Henry,¹)* and —— (——) Tomlinson, married Hannah *Wheeler* when he was well advanced in life. They resided at Kirtland, Ohio, where they both died.

*They had one child:*

346    I. Nathan,⁷ who removed to Illinois, in Carroll county, and removed thence to Waterloo, Iowa, where he died unmarried.

*196. LEWIS⁶ TOMLINSON*, son of *Capt. John L.⁵ (Capt. John,⁴ John,³ Jonas,² Henry,¹)* and —— (——) Tomlinson, married Hannah *Hawkins*, of Derby, April 18, 1813.

In early life he was engaged in the coasting trade between northern and southern ports, and on one

occasion his vessel was dismasted and driven by a violent storm into mid-ocean and it was three weeks over-due when it reached port. His last work on the sea was to command a vessel owned by Lyman Osborn, of New York City. Relinquishing that he took an interest in a market, first in Stratford and afterwards in Bridgeport, Ct., during which he engaged also in buying and driving cattle to New York City.

About 1828 he removed to Kirtland, Lake County, Ohio, which was then known as the Western Reserve, or New Connecticut. Here he remained but a short time, for the Mormons had become quite numerous and were quite quarrelsome towards those who differed from them in religious belief, and he removed to Rockport, Cuyahoga County, Ohio. Soon afterward he, in connection with others, opened a market in Cleveland, and for a few years divided his time between his farm in Rockport, the market in Cleveland and buying stock for a Cleveland packing house.

In 1843 a severe drouth prevailed in Northern Ohio, and he was employed by the farmers to drive their stock to the State of New York and sell it, a commission he executed to their satisfaction.

On his return trip from New York in November, instead of taking a boat from Buffalo as he intended, he traveled in the stage to Cleveland, to avoid the dangers of the Lake. His fears were well founded,

for a gale of great severity swept over Lake Erie, wrecking many vessels and destroying many lives. His family and friends suffered great anxiety for his safety, which was happily relieved by his safe return.

In 1841, he and his wife visited Connecticut, leaving his family at home except his son, Lyman Osborn, who was safely housed at his uncle Levi Tomlinson's at Ridgeville, a neighboring township, and after a few weeks among old friends in the East they returned to Ohio, bringing with them his wife's mother, an aged lady, who after two or three years, died at the age of 84 years, and the remains were buried at Rockport.

In 1846 he went to Northern Illinois, visiting his daughter, Jane H. Andrews, in Stephenson County, and his son, John L., in Carroll County, and brought back a drove of cattle to market at Cleveland, and then in 1847 entered a partnership with General Orson M. Oviatt, of Cleveland, to deal in live stock, and returned to Illinois, delivering that year two droves in Cleveland, and with a third he started for New York, but becoming sick on the way, his son Albert took charge and successfully marketed them in New York City, there being over three hundred head, many of them driven from west of the Mississippi River.

In 1848 he delivered another drove in Cleveland from Illinois.

The next Spring, his daughter Jane H., and sons John L. and George, being residents of Illinois, and his daughters Laura C. and Sarah A., having died, he with his wife, and sons Albert D. and Lyman O., went by steamer from Cleveland to Detroit, Michigan, thence by railroad to Battle Creek, the terminus then of the Michigan Central, thence by stage to New Buffalo, thence by steamer to Chicago, and thence to Freeport, Illinois. His wife's health having been failing for some years, the journey proved too severe for her and she died at her daughter's home May 12, 1849.

In 1850 he removed to Carroll County and the following Spring built a house on his tract of land near Mount Carroll, where he resided with his son Albert D., until 1856, joining with his sons John L., and Lyman O., in dealing in and marketing stock.

While still enjoying full vigor of intellect, although somewhat infirm in body, he took a severe cold on January 1, 1864, while a wave of severe cold passed over the Northwest, which developed into pneumonia, which all skill and devotion could not relieve, and he died January 17, 1864, aged 72 years, six months and thirteen days.

Lewis Tomlinson was of medium height, with a strong, symmetrical frame, and had black eyes and abundant black hair, and maintained an erect carriage to the close of life.

Politically, he was an old time whig, then in 1844 he voted for the Liberty party, and in 1848 the Free-Soil party, and in 1856 became a Republican with energy and activity. While in Ohio his home was one of the stations of the "under-ground railroad," and scores of slaves were aided on their way to Canada.

He was a member of the Congregational Church in Rockport, and an officer in the Sunday School, and maintained his Christian life to the last.

*Children of Lewis and Hannah Tomlinson:*

347  I. JANE H.,[1] born Dec. 21, 1813, in Derby, Ct., removed with her father's family to Kirtland, O., in 1828, thence to Rockport, near Cleveland, where she taught school until she married, Nov. 5, 1838, William Y. **Andrews**. They removed to Howardsville, Stephenson County, Illinois, where they soon became prosperous farmers. In person she was below medium height, erect and symmetrical, with dark hair and eyes, and having good health, she was energetic, genial and enjoyed a happy life. Although a Congregationalist, yet she united with the Presbyterian Church in her vicinity, there being none of the former there, in whose communion she died Oct. 10, 1872. Their children were:

    I. Daughter,[2] died in infancy.
    II. Daughter, ———;[3] married Harvey **Bailey**.
    III. Daughter, ———;[4] married James **Perry**, and is residing in Nebraska.
    IV. ——— ———.[5]
    V. Lewis B.[6] **Andrews**; married and is a banker in Kansas.

348    II. John Lewi,[7] born Dec. 20, 1816.+

349    III. George Hawkins,[7] born March 30, 1819, in Derby, Ct.+

349½   IV. Lewis Swift,[7] born Nov. 8, 1821; died in infancy.

350    V. Sarah Ann,[7] born July 9, 1824; married Homer F. Bassett, in 1847, and died Aug. 7, 1848.

351    VI. Albert DeForest,[7] born Dec. 11, 1827, in Stratford, Ct.+

352    VII. Laura Caroline,[7] born Nov. 6, 1830, in Kirtland, Ohio, and died in infancy.

353    VIII. Lyman Osborn,[7] born Jan. 6, 1835, at Rockport, Ohio.-|-

*197. LEVI[6] TOMLINSON*, son of *Capt. John L.*[5] (*Capt. John*,[4] *John*,[3] *Jonas*,[2] *Henry*.[1]) and Deborah (Bassett) Tomlinson, married Amelia Beard, Dec. 29, 1774. She was a widow Wordin. Some time in the year 1792 he removed with his family to Ridgeville, Ohio.

*Their children were:*

354    I. Betty,[7] born Nov. 30, 1775.

354⅓   II. Amelia,[7] born Dec. 3, 1777; died Sept. 29, 1794.

354⅓   III. Ruth,[7] born Mar. 11, 1780.

354⅗   IV. Deborah,[7] born Nov. 20, 1782.

354⅝   V. Levi,[7] b ——, 1785; died Sept. 22, 1794.

354¾   VI. Phebe,[7] born July ——, 1790; died May 11, 1794.

354⅞   VII. Urania,[7] born Nov. ——, 1792; died Oct. 1, 1794.

*Line of Henry Tomlinson.* 123

**204. TRUMAN⁴ TOMLINSON,** son of *Isaac,⁵ (Capt. Isaac,⁴ Sergt. Isaac,³ Jonas,² Henry,¹)* and Mary (Hawkins) Tomlinson, married in June, 1806, Nancy, daughter of Yelverton *Perry.* She was born Oct. 1, 1783, and died Nov. 8, 1841. Truman Tomlinson died Dec. 25, 1846.

*Their children were:*

355   I. Ransom,⁷ born April 29, 1808.+

356   II. Mary,⁷ born Jan. 16, 1810; married June 25, 1837, Joel R. Chatfield, of Derby, Ct. They reside in Seymour, Ct.

*They had:*

    I. John⁸ Chatfield.

    II. Edwin⁸ Chatfield.

    III. Ransom⁸ Chatfield.

    IV. Hiram⁸ Chatfield.

    V. Mary Tomlinson⁸ Chatfield.

    VI. Joel⁸ Chatfield.

    VII. Charlotte Frances⁸ Chatfield.

    VIII. Hattie Minerva⁸ Chatfield, died Nov. 24, 1879.

357   III. Emily,⁷ born Jan. 24, 1812; married Capt. Philo Holbrook, of Derby, Ct., now Seymour, Ct. She died Nov. 24, 1859.

*Their children were:*

    I. Frederick⁸ Holbrook.

    II. Andrew⁸ Holbrook.

    III. Julia⁸ Holbrook.

IV. Philo⁸ Holbrook. ⎫
                      ⎬ twins.
V. Emily⁸ Holbrook. ⎭

VI. Royal⁸ Holbrook.

VII. Daniel Tomlinson⁸ Holbrook.

VIII. Herman⁸ Holbrook.

IX. Charles N.⁸ Holbrook.

358 IV. HARRISON,⁷ born April 25, 1814.+

359 V. LAURA,⁷ born Aug. 4, 1816; married George Bassett, of Seymour, Ct. They resided in Meriden, Conn. She died March 21, 1855.

*Their children were:*

    I. Bernard G.⁸ Bassett; died.

    II. Minerva M.⁸ Bassett; married J. W. Page, of Syracuse, N. Y.

    III. Laura Elizabeth⁸ Bassett; died.

360 VI. MINERVA,⁷ born Dec. 7, 1818; married Benjamin Nichols, of Oxford, Ct. They reside in West Ansonia, Ct.

*Their children were:*

    I. Nancy E.⁸ Nichols.

    II. Arthur⁸ Nichols; died.

361 VII. JOHN G., born Mar. 23, 1821; married and resides in Portland, Ore.

*Line of Henry Tomlinson.* 125

**207. ISAAC⁶ TOMLINSON,** son of *Russell,*⁵ (*Capt. Isaac,*⁴ *Sergt. Isaac,*³ *Jonas,*² *Henry,*¹) and Agnes (Cortelyou) Tomlinson, married Grace *Lum*, of Derby, where they resided.

362   I. SALLY J.,⁷ married Roger S. Prescott.
363   II. JAMES ;⁷ married Milly Miles, of Derby, Ct.
364   III. MARY ANN ;⁷ married Anson T. Colt, of New Haven, Ct., and had eight children.
365   IV. PETER CORTELYOU ;⁷ married Charlotte Canfeld, of Derby, Ct.
366   V. BETSEY ;⁷ married Albert Wilcoxson, and had :
    I. Isaac F.⁸ Wilcoxson.
    II. Crawford C.⁸ Wilcoxson.
367   VI. WILLIAM SHERMAN ;⁷ died young.
368   VII. GRACE C. ;⁷ married Henry A. Cunningham.

**208. SIMON⁶ TOMLINSON,** son of *Russell,*⁵ (*Capt. Isaac,*⁴ *Sergt. Isaac,*³ *Jonas,*² *Henry,*¹) and Agnes (Cortelyou) Tomlinson, married Charity Hurd.

*Their children were:*

369   I. CHARLES ;⁷ married (1st) Esther Smith; (2d) —— Smith.
370   II. GEORGE ;⁷ married Delia Skeels.
371   III. WILLIAM RUSSELL ;⁷ married Phebe Bassett.
372   IV. MARIETTA ;⁷ married (1st) —— Johnson; (2d) Legrand Bennett.
373   V. SARAH ;⁷ married —— Benton.
374   VI. AGNES ;⁷ married George Wagner.
375   VII. CATHERINE ;⁷ married William Shelton.

**211. RUSSELL⁶ TOMLINSON**, son of *Russell⁵ (Capt. Isaac,⁴ Sergt. Isaac,³ Jonas,² Henry¹)* and Agnes (Cortelyou) Tomlinson, married Sarah *Burwell*, of Brookfield, Ct.

*Their child was:*
376 I. Mary Burwell.

**212. JAMES C.⁶ TOMLINSON**, son of *Russell⁵ (Capt. Isaac,⁴ Sergt. Isaac,³ Jonas,² Henry¹)* and Agnes (Cortelyou) Tomlinson, married Laura, youngest daughter of John and Deborah Tomlinson, of Derby, Ct., (No. —).

*Their children were:*

377   I. John Russell,⁷ born Oct. 20, 1825.+
378   II. Sarah Elizabeth,⁷ born ——; married Rev. E. N. Crossman, and had:
    I. Ella M.⁸ Crossman, born Feb. 3, 1850; married Orris Beers.
    II. Ida B.⁸ Crossman, born Jan. —, 1853.
379   III. Agnes Cortelyou ;⁷ died young.
380   IV. Mary Ann,⁷ born Jan. 9, 1832; married (1st) Smith Riggs; (2d) Frank Breck, and had:
    I. Edward F. Riggs,⁸ born Feb. 14, 1857.
*By second husband:*
    II. Mattie Breck,⁸ born July —, 1873.
    III. Willie Breck,⁸ born April —, 1875.
381   V. James Willard,⁷ born Jan. ——, 1834.+
382   VI. Edward Delavan,⁷ born Nov. 17, 1836.+
383   VII. Isaac Cornell,⁷ born Dec. 24, 1838.+
384   VIII. Laura Cornelia,⁷ born Oct. 21, 1841; died April 11, 1867.

## Line of Henry Tomlinson.

**213. TIMOTHY⁶ TOMLINSON**, Jr., son of Timothy⁵ (Capt. Isaac,⁴ Sergt. Isaac,³ Jonas,² Henry¹) and Eunice (Booth) Tomlinson, married Nancy Hibbard. He died June 27, 1827.

385  I. NELSON,⁷ "went west when a young man, and that is all we know of him."

386  II. HORACE,⁷ " married and left one son."

387  III. MARY ANN,⁷ married —— **Taylor**, and had :
    I. Ambrose **Taylor**.
    II. George **Taylor**.

388  IV. JULIA ; married —— **Peck** and had children, "all of whom lived in Fairfield County, Ct."

**214. SAMUEL⁶ TOMLINSON**, son of Timothy⁵ (Capt. Isaac,⁴ Sergt. Isaac,³ Jonas,² Henry¹) and Eunice (Booth) Tomlinson, married Jennette, daughter of Elisha *Patterson* and his wife, Betsey *Leavenworth*, Nov. 8, 1827, in Roxbury, Ct. Samuel Tomlinson died Dec. 10, 1860, aged 64 years. His widow, Jennette, died March 29, 1874, aged 67 years.

389  I. SARAH JANE,⁷ born Sept. 9, 1828 ; married Robert C. **Partree**, Jan. 5, 1848, and had :
    I. Mary⁸ **Partree**, born Nov. 27, 1848, who married William Minor **Staples**, of Bridgeport, Ct., May 30, 1871.
    II. Fred H.⁸ **Partree**, born Sept. 8, 1854 ; died April 26, 1874.
    III. Samuel R.⁸ **Partree**, born Aug. 21, 1857.

IV. Julia Welton⁸ Partree, born Oct. 10, 1859; married Frank Cone, April 6, 1880.

V. Robert C.⁸ Partree, born Feb. 10, 1862; married Mary Fowler, Jan. 20, 1885.

VI. Homer T.⁸ Partree, born Dec. 1, 1865, graduate of Yale University in 1887.

390 II. Betsey Jennette,⁷ born Jan. 20, 1830; married John W. Judson, and died May 15, 1885, aged 55 years. She had children:

I. Nellie M.⁸ Judson, born Feb. 6, 1865.

II. Fletcher C.⁸ Judson, born Mar. 7, 1868.

391 III. Elisha Patterson,⁷ born Aug. 2, 1832, in Woodbury.+

392 IV. Homer S.,⁷ born Sept. 29, 1835.+

393 V. Ellen A.,⁷ born May 17, 1845; died Feb. 3, 1860.

**215. JOSEPH⁶ TOMLINSON**, son of *Timothy*⁵(*Capt. Isaac*,⁴ *Sergt. Isaac*,³ *Jonas*,² *Henry*¹) and Eunice (Booth) Tomlinson, married Alma Partree (?) He died in Ohio, Nov. 8, 1857, and was brought to Woodbury for interment.

394 I. John Darius,⁷ died Jan. 20, 1854, a member of the class of 1855 of Yale College.

395 II. George ———,⁷ who died in Boston, of fever, in June, 1869.

**217. NATHANIEL⁶ TOMLINSON**, son of *Timothy*⁵(*Capt. Isaac*,⁴ *Sergt. Isaac*,³ *Jonas*,² *Henry*¹) and Eunice (Booth) Tomlinson, married Elizabeth *Davis*, Sept. 1, 1830. He settled in Michigan, where he died July 10, 1845.

## Line of Henry Tomlinson.

*Their children were:*

396  I. SARAH ELIZABETH,[7] born July 15, 1834, at Rockland, N. Y.

397  II. LUCINDA,[7] born at Liberty, N. Y.

398  III. CHARILLA,[7] born at Superior, Mich.

399  IV. MATILDA,[7] born at Brighton, Mich.

400  V. ALVA DAVIS,[7] born May 16, 1844, at Howell, Mich.+

401  VI. GEORGE,[7] died young.

402  VII JENNETT,[7] died young.

403  VIII. JAMES HENRY,[7] died young.

**218. *CHARLES*[6] *TOMLINSON*,** son of *Hon. David*[5] *(Capt. Isaac,*[4] *Sergt. Isaac,*[3] *Jonas,*[2] *Henry*[1]) and Lovena (Bacon) Tomlinson, married Esther Candee, Oct. 26, 1811. She was born in Oxford, Ct., June 27, 1789, and died Mar. 10, 1857. He died April 4, 1879, aged 94 years.

404  I. CHARLES AUGUSTUS, born Feb. 27, 1813.+

405  II. DAVID AUSTIN, born July 15, 1816; died Oct. 24, 1834.

406  III. HORACE ELISHA, born Aug. 22, 1819.+

407  IV. SARAH ANN, born Nov. 30, 1821; married George Bunnell, Feb. 14, 1845.

**227. GEORGE A.[6] TOMLINSON**, son of Hon. David,[5] (Capt. Isaac,[4] Sergt. Isaac,[3] Jonas,[2] Henry,[1]) and Lovena (Bacon) Tomlinson, married Feb. 14, 1830, Eliza Antoinette Judson, who was born July 14, 1807, and died Oct. 4, 1841. He married (2d) May 15, 1842, Ellen Candee, born May 31, 1819. He died Dec. 9, 1860.

*Their children were:*

408    I. George Albert,[7] born Jan. 7, 1832; married Nancy E. Nichols, Oct. 1, 1862.

409    II. David Welles,[7] born Jan. 27, 1835; died April 27, 1854.

410    III. Maria Antoinette,[7] born March 7, 1838; married Hon. Smith P. Glover, born Sept. 30, 1861, and had:

     I. William Tomlinson[8] Glover, born Oct. 13, 1862; died Sept. 5, 1863.

     II. Lovena Tomlinson[8] Glover, born May 6, 1863.

     III. Infant son[8] Glover, born Jan. 5, 1867; died Jan 10, 1867.

     IV. Harriet Peck[8] Glover, born May 30, 1870.

411    IV. Ellen Candee,[7] born May 31, 1839; married George A. Tomlinson, May 15, 1842, and had:

     I. Eliza[8] Tomlinson, born Feb. 28, 1842; died Nov. 11, 1867.

     II. Jane Caroline[8] Tomlinson, born March 16, 1845.

*Line of Henry Tomlinson.*

**230. WILLIAM A.⁶ TOMLINSON**, son of Hon. *David*,⁵ (*Capt. Isaac*,⁴ *Srgt. Isaac*,³ *Jonas*,² *Henry*,¹) and Lovena (Bacon) Tomlinson, married Susan ——.

412   I. SUSAN,⁷ married George Montague, and had George, Mary and Frank.

413   II. LOVENA,⁷ married (1st) George Sheldon, (2d) Charles Downs.

414   III. ALICE.⁷

415   IV. FRANK.⁷

**232. PHILO⁶ TOMLINSON**, son of *Dan*,⁵ (*Noah*,⁴ *Isaac*,³ *Jonas*,² *Henry*,¹) and Susanna (Hotchkiss) Tomlinson, married Harriet *Atwell*, Feb. 5, 1820. She was born June 25, 1781, in Durham, Ct. Philo Tomlinson died Mar. 22, 1830, aged 52 years, in Sharon, Ct. His widow, Harriet, died Aug. 4, 1846, aged 65 years, at Springfield, Mass. Their residence was in New Preston, Ct.

[14] "About the year 1800, Philo Tomlinson, of Derby, and Samuel Bassett, of New Preston, opened a quarry on land of the latter a short distance northeast of the rectory in Marbledale, and built a mill where the mill of the late George W. Cogswell now stands, said to have been the first stone sawmill erected in the State of Connecticut.

---

[14] History of New Milford, Ct., 342.

Philo Tomlinson was the inventor of the automatic feeder, by which sand and water were applied to aid or facilitate the sawing.

Mr. Tomlinson, with his sons Abijah and Eliphalet, soon after removed to New Preston and opened a marble quarry on land belonging to Orange Wheaton, in company with Christopher Allen. Sylvester S. Wheaton had a quarry connected with the Tomlinson quarry, and the Tomlinson-Wheaton and Goodsell quarries were more extensively worked than any others."

*Children of Philo and Harriet Tomlinson:*

416   I. MINERVA,[7] born July 16, 1803; married John Bolles, of New Preston, Ct., Mar. 27, 1822. She died in Randolph, Wis., Dec. 6, 1879. He was born Nov. 14, 1794, and died at Randolph, Wis., Dec. 6, 1864.

    I. Charlotte R.[8] Bolles, born Mar. 31, 1823.

    II. Horace T.[8] Bolles, born Feb. 12, 1824; married Caroline Putnam, Dec. 19, 1850.

    III. Theodore W.[8] Bolles, born Dec. 11, 1825; married Mary E. Davis, June 22, 1853.

    IV. Edgar W.[8] Bolles, born Sept. 27, 1827; married Elizabeth Paulding, Oct. 3, 1854; died April 21, 1870.

    V. Sarah[8] Bolles ) born Sept. 22, 1829; married Nathan
       [twins]     }    H. Ellis, Sept. 24, 1867.
    VI. Mary[8] Bolles )

    VII. Betsey M.[8] Bolles, born April 22, 1831; married Ezra H. Alley, Oct. 16, 1853.

VIII. Frederick O.⁸ **Bolles**, born Sept. 29, 1833 ; married Emma Pierce, Dec. 30, 1876.

IX. Julia A.⁸ **Bolles**, born Mar. 22, 1835; married Daniel **Emmerson**, Mar. 5, 1876.

X. Frances A.⁸ **Bolles**, born Sept. 29, 1838 ; married S. R. **Emerson**, Jan. 26, 1876.

XI. William H.⁸ **Bolles**, born Nov. 30, 1840 ; married Maggie **Bradley**, Sept. 21, 1873.

XII. Happy Lonie B.⁸ **Bolles**, born Aug. 26, 1844 ; married Edward **Stark**, Dec. 3, 1869.

417    II. ABIJAH,⁷ born Feb. 14, 1806,-|-  }
418    III. SHELDON,⁷ born Feb. 14, 1806,  } twins.

419    IV. CHARLES,⁷ born July 5, 1813. Residence in Norwich, Ct.

420    V. CAROLINE,⁷ born Sept. 17, 1816.

**233.** *ABIJAH⁶ TOMLINSON,* son of *Dan,⁵ (Noah,⁴ Isaac,³ Jonas,² Henry,¹)* and Susanna (Hotchkiss) Tomlinson, married Betsey (No. 186), daughter of David (and Ruth Hawkins) *Tomlinson,* April 29, 1805. They resided at Great Hill, Derby, until in 1808, when they removed to Marbledale, New Preston, Ct., where he pursued the business of marble dealer. He died Jan. 11, 1862, aged 81 years. She died Jan. 18, 1876, aged 91 years.

421    I. GEORGE⁷ (Rev.), born Feb. 5, 1806.+

422    II. RUTH ANN,⁷ born Jan. 6, 1808; married Elijah **Baldwin**, Sept. 30, 1840. (See No. 335.)

423   III. GILES HAWKINS,¹ born Sept. 22, 1809 ; married Eunice A. Ensign, June, 1842.

424   IV. ELIZA,¹ born July 17, 1812; married Horatio G. **Sperry**, Oct. 20, 1834, and died April 16, 1884.

425   V. DANIEL,¹ born Mar. 21, 1814; died Feb. 21, 1878.

426   VI. CHARLES,¹ born Oct. 10, 1820; died Sept. 8, 1862.

427   VII. AGNES CHARLOTTE,¹ born April 24, 1822 ; married Walter D. **Sperry**, April 28, 1841; died May 4, 1849.

428   VIII. NANCY SOPHIA,¹ born Sept. 9, 1825; married George **Sperry**, June 6, 1849.

**234. DAN⁶ TOMLINSON**, son of *Dan*,⁵ (*Noah*,⁴ *Isaac*,³ *Jonas*,² *Henry*,¹) and Susanna (Hotchkiss) Tomlinson, married Lydia, daughter of Matthew *Judd* (and his wife Lydia Morris Judd), Jan. 5, 1818. She was born April 17, 1794, in Kent, Litchfield County, Conn., and died Feb. 16, 1845, aged 50 years. Mr. Tomlinson died Jan. 10, 1850, aged 64 years. Their residence was at East Bloomfield, N. Y.

429   I. MARY,¹ born Feb. 9, 1820; married Moses **Stevens**, May 31, 1848. He was born March 1, 1819, and died Aug. 28, 1867.

430   II. MARTHA,¹ born Nov. 15, 1824; died Aug. 20, 1826.

*Line of Henry Tomlinson.* 135

**236. ELIPHALET⁶ TOMLINSON**, son of *Dan.⁵* (*Noah,⁴ Isaac,³ Jonas,² Henry¹*) and Susanna Hotchkiss) Tomlinson, married, Oct. 12, 1824, Polly, daughter of Johnson and Susanna (Ford) *Logan*. She was born at Washington, Ct., June 5, 1795. Their residence was in New Preston, Ct., where he was a marble dealer. He died April 15, 1839, aged 50 years. She died Sept. 15, 1850, aged 55 years.

431    I. Johnson Logan⁷ (Rev.), born May 1, 1826; married Hannah M. Hazelton, Sept. 7, 1869.

432    II. Remus,⁷ born Dec. 8, 1827;    ) died Aug. 28, 1833.
[twins]
433    III. Romulus,⁷ born Dec. 8, 1827.+ )

**237. WILLIAM C.⁵ TOMLINSON**, son of *Henry,⁵ Jr.*, (*Henry,⁴ Samuel,³ Jonas,² Henry¹*) and Sarah (Davis) Tomlinson, married Amy, daughter of Stephen *Curtiss*, of Southbury, Ct. They resided in Oxford, Ct. He died Nov. 13, 1819, and she married (2d) Oct. 26, 1823, Edmund Leavenworth, who was born in Huntington, Ct., Dec. 14, 1766, and died in Derby, Jan. 20, 1857, greatly beloved by his step-children. His wife Amy was born Feb. 8, 1774, and died April 30, 1849.

434    I. Sally,⁷ born Oct. 2, 1796, and died Jan. 22, 1887. She married Cyrus, son of Deacon Bestwick, of Southbury, Ct., where they always resided. She was the eldest child and only daughter of the family of ten children, and was remarkable for her strength of character and

many Christian virtues. She died of paralysis at the advanced age of 90 years, in full possession of her mental faculties, tenderly nursed by her devoted daughter, Mrs. Harriet Hunt. He died Mar. 20, 1876.

*Their children were:*

I. Hannah Bostwick,[8] born Oct. 11, 1818, married John E. Smith, Oct. 23, 1837, and died July 3, 1841.

II. Harriet Bostwick,[8] born Mar. 21, 1821; married Hanibal H. Hunt, Oct. 26, 1846.

III. Augusta Bostwick,[8] born Nov. 11, 1822; died Jan. 11, 1846, unmarried.

IV. George Bostwick,[8] born Feb. 29, 1824; married Clara E. Judson, Feb. 22, 1856.

V. Sarah Bostwick,[8] born May 3, 1826; died Nov. 30, 1847.

435   II. CURTIS,[7] born Feb. 3, 1798. He left home in 1823 on a business tour when about 22 years of age, an active, promising young man; went to Elizabeth, N. J., and from there to New York City, where all traces of him were lost.

436   III. CLARK,[7] born May 30, 1799.+

437   IV. WILLIAM HENRY[7] (called Harry), born Mar. 17, 1801.+

438.   V. STEPHEN,[7] born July 29, 1803.+

439   VI. CYRUS BURTON,[7] born June 6, 1806.+

440   VII. RUSSELL,[7] born April 5, 1807.+

441   VIII. CHARLES,[7] born July 6, 1809; died June 11, 1842, unmarried.

442   IX. BENNETT,[7] born May 1, 1811.+

443   X. WILLIAM,[7] born Feb. 1, 1813.+

*Line of Henry Tomlinson.*

**245. WILLIAM A.⁵ TOMLINSON**, 2d., son of *Doct. William A.,⁵ (Doct. Agur,⁴ Zachariah,³ Agur,² Henry,¹)* and Phebe (Lewis) Tomlinson, married Susan, daughter of Gen'l Joseph *Walker*, May 12, 1818.

444   I. WILLIAM AGUR, born May ——, 1819.+

445   II. SUSAN, born Sept. ——, 1821; died in 1822.

**246. STEPHEN⁶ TOMLINSON**, son of *Capt. Joseph,⁴ (Zachariah,³ Agur,² Henry,¹)* and Lucy (Atwood) Tomlinson, married Caroline *Hawkins*, Jan. 14, 1813. She died Jan. 13, 1872.

*Their children were:*

446   I. MARIA,⁷ born June 2, 1816; married Dr. William A. Palmer, and they resided on the homestead at Oronoke, and had:

    I. Emma⁸ Palmer.

    II. Fannie⁸ Palmer.

    III. Frederic⁸ Palmer.

    IV. Carrie⁸ Palmer.

    V. Isabel⁸ Palmer.

    VI. Stephen⁸ Palmer, who married Hattie E. Blakeman, and had:

        I. Bessie L.⁹

        II. Maria T.⁹

        III. William G.⁹

        IV. Myra B.⁹

447    II. ELIZABETH,⁷ born Sept. 16, 1817; married Rev. Ralph Perry, Aug. 31, 1843, and died Mar. 23, 1846.

448    III. CURTISS WILLIAM,⁷ born Mar. 2, 1819.

449    IV. STEPHEN MARTIN,⁷ born December 7, 1820; died young.

**247. JOHN A.⁶ TOMLINSON**, M. D., son of *Curtiss*,⁵ (*Capt. Joseph*,⁴ *Zachariah*,³ *Agur*,² *Henry*,¹) and Lucy (Atwood) Tomlinson, married Eliza *Thompson* and settled in Harrodsburg, Ky., where he practiced his profession as a physician.

*Their children were:*

450  I. SALLY.⁷

451  II. JAMES.⁷

452  III. JOHN.⁷

453  IV. CARRIE,⁷ who married W. W. **Belknap**, Secretary of War, U. S. A.

454  V. WILLIAM,⁷ a physician, now in Chicago, Ill.

455  VI. ANNIE,⁷ married Wm. **Gosrenor**, of Cincinnati, O.

**251. CHARLES C.⁶ TOMLINSON**, son of *Curtiss*,⁵ (*Capt. Joseph*,⁴ *Zachariah*,³ *Agur*,² *Henry*,¹) and Lucy (Atwood) Tomlinson, married Nancy *Wakeley*.

456  I. LYDIA J.⁷

457  II. MARY.⁷

458  III. FRANCELIA.⁷

459  IV. SOPHIA.⁷

460  V. HENRIETTA.⁷

*Line of Henry Tomlinson.*

**252. JOSEPH⁶ TOMLINSON**, 3d, son of *Joseph*, 2d,⁵ (*Joseph*,⁴ *Zachariah*,³ *Agur*,² *Henry*,¹) and Sally (Curtiss) Tomlinson, married Sally E. Bennett.

*Their children were:*

461　I. JOSEPH⁷ 4th, born Dec. 27, 1828.+

462　II. ISAAC,⁷ born in　　1830; died in 1832.

463　III. SARAH E.,⁷ born Mar. 6, 1833; married Henry L. Downs in 1867.

**259. CAPT. ISAAC TOMLINSON**, son of *Josiah*,⁵ (*Capt. Beach*,⁴ *Zechariah*,³ *Agur*,² *Henry*,¹) and Anna (Shelton) Tomlinson, married Polly, daughter of Solomon and Esther (Holbrook) *Curtis*, Oct. 28, 1799. He was a large hearted and enterprising citizen.

464　I. SARAH,⁷ born Mar. 6, 1801; married Charles, son of Hon. Asa Chapman, of Newtown, and New Haven, Ct. Charles Chapman is a lawyer of Hartford, Ct.

*Their children were:*

I. Frances Ann⁸ Chapman, married Edward, son of Horace and Thyrza (Thorpe) Filley, of East Windsor, Ct. Their children were:

I. Charles Chapman⁹ Filley, born Oct. 15, 1843.

II. Charlotte⁹ Filley, born Jan. 31, 1848; married Henry Kip, and resides in Buffalo, N. Y.

III. Edward Tomlinson⁹ Filley, born Nov. 17, 1850; married Adele, a French lady, and resides in Brooklyn, N. Y.

II. Charles⁵ **Chapman**, married Mrs. Harriet Thomas, daughter of Rt. Rev. Bishop Brownell, of Connecticut. Mr. Chapman is a lawyer of Hartford, Ct., and has been several years Mayor of of that city, and also postmaster of the city for a number of years. They had:

    I. Lillie⁹ **Chapman**.

    II. William⁹ **Chapman**.

III. Charlotte⁸ **Chapman**, born ———. ———; married Samuel **McLane**, of Brooklyn, N. Y., a merchant of New York City. Their children were:

    I. Annie⁹ **McLane**, born Sept. 28, 1847; married John **Buckingham**, of Waterbury, Ct.; reside in Brooklyn, N. Y., and had: I. Schoville McLane¹⁰ **Buckingham**, and II. Charles Benedict¹⁰ **Buckingham**.

    II. Thomas⁹ **McLane**, married Harriet Halsey **Creighton**.

**261. *DAVID⁶ TOMLINSON*,** son of *Henry,⁵ (Capt. Beach,⁴ Zechariah,³ Agur,² Henry,¹)* and Abigail (Welles) Tomlinson, married Betsey, daughter of Elnathan *Bostwick*, May 1, 1807. She was born in 1790, and died March 11, 1813. He married (2d) Rhoda *Alderman*. They lived in Monroe, Ct.

## Line of Henry Tomlinson. 141

*Their children were:*

465   I. EDWIN,[7] born Feb. 28, 1809; died.

466   II. PHILO BOSTWICK,[7] born July 20, 1811; went to South Africa, where he was engaged in trade; was interpreter of the Spanish language. He died there of fever in 1840.

*Children by second wife:*

467   III. HENRY WARREN,[7] born Nov. 1, 1825.+

468   IV. NATHAN WELLES,[7] born June 6, 1827.+

469   V. OSCAR WATSON,[7] born Jan. 22, 1830.

470   VI. ELIZABETH MARIA,[7] born Feb. 3, 1835.

**270. DOCT. JOHN[6] TOMLINSON**, son of *Agur*,[5] (*Capt. Beach*,[4] *Zachariah*,[3] *Agur*,[2] *Henry*.[1]) and Sarah (Curtiss) Tomlinson, married (1st) Anna Maria, daughter of Samuel L. and Anna Davidson *Perry*. She died Feb. 6, 1821, and he married Charlotte *Perry*, sister of his first wife. She died May 9, 1833. He died in Huntington, Ct., March 20, 1837.

*Their children were:*

471   I. SAMUEL PERRY,[7] married Mary A. **Blakeman**, of Stratford, Ct., and resides in Vineland, N. J.

472   II. JOHN BRAINARD.[7] He was a soldier in the late war.

473   III. ANN MARIA,[7] married Birdseye Blakeman, of Stratford, Ct. Residence in New York City; publisher.

*Their children were:*

    I. Frederick Tomlinson[8] Blakeman, born Nov. 30, 1850; died Nov. 5, 1873.

    II. Marianna[8] Blakeman, born Mar. 15, 1852; married John V. B. Lewis, June 21, 1881, and had Anna Blakeman[9] Lewis, born Feb. 2, 1883, and Birdseye Blakeman[9] Lewis, born Feb. 23, 1888.

    III. Theodore[8] Blakeman, born Aug. 26, 1856; died Oct. 22, 1856.

    IV. Louis Henry[8] Blakeman, born May 30, 1858; married Eleanor Leal Greenleaf, Oct. 4, 1881, and had:

        I. Frederic Tomlinson[9] Blakeman, born July 25, 1883.

        II. Thomas Greenleaf[9] Blakeman, born Oct. 23, 1887.

    V. Emily Morrison[8] Blakeman, born Oct. 6, 1863; died Mar. 8, 1868.

474   IV. BETSEY,[7] married (1st) Josiah Gunn, and (2d) David Gunn, both of Waterbury, Ct., and had two sons.

475   V. CHARLES.[7]+

476   VI. SOPHIA,[7] married a Rose, and lived and died in South Carolina, and had two daughters.

**272. CHARLES⁵ TOMLINSON**, son of Agur,⁵ (*Beach,*⁴ *Zachariah,*³ *Agur,*² *Henry,*¹) and Sarah (Curtiss) Tomlinson, married Anna *Pearce* of Southbury, Ct., April 26, 1818. She died March 3, 1881, aged 92 years. He died May 10, 1879, aged 91 years.

*Their children were:*

477   I. NELSON,¹ born Jan. 20, 1819.+

478   II. WILLIAM,¹ born May 7, 1821.+

479   III. ANN MARIE,¹ born Feb. 25, 1824; married Jan. 28, 1844, John Hull, of Oxford, Ct. He was born Jan. 12, 1819, and died Dec. 21, 1871. They had:

    I. Augusta⁸ Hull, born Nov. 11, 1844; married Oct. 19, 1873, Royal Holbrook, and had Carrie M.⁹ Holbrook, born May 10, 1875.

    II. Albert E.⁸ Hull, born April 23, 1846; married Nov. 20, 1883, Lucy Seeley, and had Florence E.⁹ Hull, born Oct. 17, 1885, and Bernice⁹ Hull, born Sept. —, 1889.

    III. Caroline⁸ Hull, born May 4, 1848; died Feb. 28, 1849.

    IV. Cyrus John⁸ Hull, born Oct. 30, 1851.

480   IV. AVICE CAROLINE,¹ born Jan. 1, 1829; married Jan. —, 1851, John Sherman, son of Zera, of Newtown, Ct., and had Leroy Sherman.⁸

    V. MARY EMILY,¹ born April 27, 1833; married Legrand L. Stone, of Orange, Ct. They reside in Smith County, Kansas.

**280. GOULD TOMLINSON**, son of *David J. N.[3] (Capt. Beach,[4] Zachariah,[3] Agur,[2] Henry,[1])* and Elizabeth A. (Beardsley) Tomlinson, married Sarah Ann *Judson*, of Huntington, Ct., in 1841. She died in 1865. He is a farmer.

*Their children were:*

481   I. SARAH LOUISA,[7] born Mar. 12, 1843; married Charles F. Wheeler, of Huntington, Ct. They reside in Bridgeport, Ct., and have:

  I. Jennie Louisa[8] Wheeler, born June 20, 1865.

  II. Anna Maria[8] Wheeler, born July 21, 1870; married June 17, 1890, Frank L. Schubert.

482   II. FREDERICK DAVID,[7] born Feb. 26, 1845; is a dentist in New York City.

483   III. ALONZO WALTER,[7] born Mar. 22, 1846; died in 1884.

484   IV. ANN MARIA,[7] born March 10, 1848.

485   V. MILLARD GOULD,[7] born April 30, 1850; married Oct. 13, 1883, Mary E. Durand, and had Wesley Wheeler[8] (Tomlinson,) born June 1, 1890.

485½   VI. JOHN VICTORY,[7] born June 4, 1853; died June 5, 1874.

486   VII. EMILY REBECCA,[7] born Sept. 25, 1856.

487   VIII. WILBUR BEACH,[7] born Mar. 28, 1859.

488   IX. LEMUEL ETHERIDGE,[7] born Aug. 23, 1861.

489   X. ELMER,[7] born Sept. 2, 1863; married Nov., 1888, Anna Burr. They reside in Stockton, Cal.

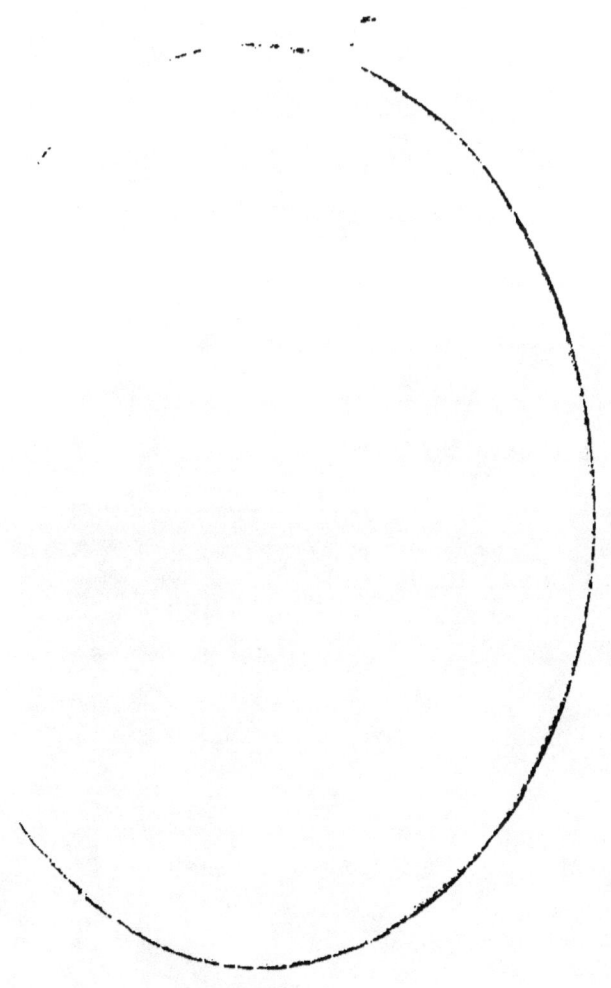

GOV. TOMLINSON.

From a painting by Prof. S. F. B. Morse.

**282. GOVERNOR GIDEON⁶ TOMLINSON**, son of *Jabez H.*⁵ (*Capt. Gideon,*⁴ *Zechariah,*³ *Agur,*² *Henry.*¹) and Rebecca (Lewis) Tomlinson, was graduated at Yale College in 1802. He married Sarah *Bradley*, of Greenfield Hill, in Fairfield county, Ct., where he resided. He was elected a member of the House of Representatives in his state for May, 1817, and the next October was chosen Clerk of the same, and the next May was made Speaker of the House, which position he held two sessions. He was then, in 1819, elected member of the House of Representatives of the United States for two years, and re-elected in 1821, 1823 and 1825, serving eight years in that body, being Speaker of the House a part of the time.

In 1827 he was elected Governor of the State of Connecticut, which office he held until he was elected by the Legislature in 1831 a Senator of the United States, where he remained six years, until 1837.

In 1836 he was elected first President of the Housatonic Railroad, and served several months.

The portrait of Governor Tomlinson was painted while he was Senator in Washington, and is now in possession of the Corcoran Gallery in Washington, D. C.

The prints of that portrait, inserted herewith in this volume, were executed in Washington for this

purpose, and it is a matter of much pleasure that they have been secured, and that the painting is preserved.

*Governor Tomlinson's only child was:*

490 I. JABEZ HUNTINGTON,⁷ baptized Sept. 27, 1818; entered Yale College in 1835; was dismissed in 1836, because of ill health, and died in New York, aged 20 years.

**286. HUNTINGTON⁶ TOMLINSON,** son of *Jabez H.⁵ (Capt. Gideon,⁴ Zechariah,³ Agur,² Henry,¹)* and Rebecca (Lewis) Tomlinson, married Eliza Tomlinson, daughter of Samuel Peet Mills. He resided on the old homestead at Oronoque, in Stratford, where he died Feb. 5, 1839, in his 48th year. His widow, Eliza, died June 22, 1873, aged 81 years.

491 I. GIDEON M.,⁷ born ——.+

492 II. SARAH, married Charles Henry Tomlinson, of Schenectady, N. Y. (No. 288.)

**288. CHARLES H.⁶ TOMLINSON,** son of *David,⁵ (Abraham,⁴ Zechariah,³ Agur,² Henry,¹)* and Phebe (Miller) Tomlinson, married Sarah, daughter of Huntington *Tomlinson,* of Oronoke, in Stratford, Ct. (No. 492). He died Jan. 8, 1856, aged 54 years. Sarah, his wife, died Jan. 14, 1853, in her 37th year.

*Their children were:*

493 I. MARY,⁷ married Mr. Moore, "an artist" of Cambridge, Mass., and had two children.

494 II. DAVID,⁷ unmarried, and spends much time in Europe.

**295. CALEB TOMLINSON,** son of *Abraham,⁶ Jr., M. D. (Doct. Abraham,⁵ Jonah,⁴ Abraham,³ Jonas,² Henry,¹)* and ——— (———) Tomlinson, married in 1862, Susan, daughter of Peter and Anna (Wheeler) *Meeker*. She was born Dec. 27, 1798. Their grave-stones say: "Caleb Tomlinson, Died Aug. 12, 1848; Æ 50 years, 10 mo." "Susan M., wife of Caleb Tomlinson, Died Oct. 27, 1862; Æ 63 years and 10 mo."

*Their children were:*

495    I. WILLIAM,⁸ married Mary Estelle ———; had a son and a daughter.
496    II. HENRY T.⁸+

***304. REV. DAVID GIBSON⁷ TOMLINSON,*** son of *David,⁶ (Doct. Abraham,⁵ Jonah,⁴ Abraham,³ Jonas,² Henry,¹)* and Anna (Camp) Tomlinson, was ordained Deacon in the Episcopal Church by Bishop Brownell, at Bridgeport, Ct., Nov. 17, 1831, and Priest, Jan. 17, 1833, at Watertown, Ct., by the same Bishop. He married Mary Frances Whitman *Fenn*, of Milford, Ct., March 28, 1826. She was born June 10, 1802, at Milford. He died at the parsonage at Emmanuel Church in Weston, Ct., Nov. 3, 1864.

497    I. EDWARD RUTLEDGE,⁸ born April 10, 1832; died a member of Trinity College, Hartford, Ct., July 15, 1856, and was buried at Milford, July 17, 1856, the day his college class was graduated.

**310. NATHAN CAMP[7] TOMLINSON**, son of *David*,[6] (*Doct. Abraham*,[5] *Jonah*,[4] *Abraham*,[3] *Jonas*,[2] *Henry*,[1]) and Anna (Camp) Tomlinson, married on Oct. 27, 1835, Susan Catharine, daughter of Hezekiah *Baldwin*, of Milford, where he resided until his decease, Nov. 21, 1885, being 72 years of age. He was a farmer, and a prominent citizen in civil, political and religious matters. His residence was in Milford village at the northwestern corner of the public green. His wife, Susan Catharine, was born Sept. 20, 1816, and died May 5, 1884.

498    I. Susan Catharine,[8] married (1st) Andrew **Isbell**, who died, and she married (2d) Henry **Platt**, and had Sarah[9] **Platt**.

499    II. Mary Gibson,[8] married Charles **Smith**, of Orange, Ct., and had Susie[9] **Smith** and Minnie[9] **Smith**.

500    III. Anna,[8] resides on her father's homestead.

501    IV. William Walter,[8] died young.

502    V. Charles Abraham.[8]+

503    VI. Celia Hawley,[8] is a school teacher, and resides on the old homestead.

504    VII. David Gibson,[8] died young.

505    VIII. Isabell Andrew,[8] died young.

506    IX. Jessie Alzena,[8] is a school teacher and elocutionist, resides at the old home.

**313. OLIVER MEAD⁶ TOMLINSON**, son of *Joseph B.*⁶ (*Joseph,*⁵ *Agur,*⁴ *Abraham,*³ *Jonas,*² *Henry,*¹) and Susannah (Mead) Tomlinson, married Ann *Staples*. He died at Buffalo, N. Y., aged 62 years.

507   I. VICTORY LEANDER,⁷ who resides in Fairport, N. Y.; unmarried.

508   II. ANN ELIZA,⁷ married Anson S. Cobb, of Buffalo, N. Y.

509   III. STATIRA.⁷ married Theodore Maltman, a banker in California, who was killed in a riot of miners.

**322. HON. THEODORE E.⁷ TOMLINSON**, son of *David,*⁶ (*Joseph,*⁵ *Agur,*⁴ *Abraham,*³ *Jonas,*² *Henry,*¹) and Cornelia (Adams) Tomlinson, the second son of Dr. David Tomlinson, was born at Rhinebeck, Dutchess County, New York, on the 25th day of December, 1817. His early studies were pursued at Rhinebeck, where he had as schoolmates, Augustus, Robert and Edward Schell. He entered the University of the City of New York, and was graduated from that college in the year 1836, receiving the degree of Bachelor of Arts. Subsequently he studied law at the Law School of Yale College, and was admitted to the bar in the year 1839, and at once began the practice of his profession in the city of New York.

In 1850 he was appointed Attorney to the Corporation of the City of New York, and filled the

office with signal ability. He acquired great prominence in his profession, and while in active practice was regarded as one of the leaders of the bar of that state. He was an intimate friend and associate of Charles O'Connor, James T. Brady, William Curtis Noyes and David Graham, ranking with them, and universally regarded as one of the most able lawyers of his day.

In politics, he was one of the most brilliant and influential representatives of the old Whig Party in that State. From 1850 to 1855 he was Chairman of the Whig State Committee, and active in all the work of that party. He was intimately associated with Henry Clay, Horace Greeley, and the prominent men of their period. His fame as an orator was national, being regarded by the Whigs of that State as second only to Henry Clay. His address upon graduating from college on "Genius and Perseverance," attracted wide attention, and gave promise of the great fame he subsequently acquired. Perhaps his speech that will be most remembered was his reply to the toast of "Woman," delivered at the New York Historical Society in 1854, which for purity of diction, delicacy of thought, and beauty of simile has few equals in specimens of American eloquence.

In 1859, Mr. Tomlinson was elected a member of the Assembly of the State of New York, and was

regarded as by far the most brilliant and able debater in either House. His active interest in politics ceased with the dissolution of the Whig Party, although he followed public affairs with great interest up to the time of his death in 1888.

In 1844 Mr. Tomlinson was married to Abbey Esther Walden, of New York City, by whom he had five children.

*Their children were:*

510  I. DAVID,⁸ born Oct. 1, 1846.+

511  II. HENRY TALLMADGE,⁸ born Jan. 11, 1848; died Dec. 6, 1871.

512  III. THEODORE EDWIN,⁸ born July 20, 1851.

513  IV. ESTHER WALDEN,⁸ born May 15, 1853; married McPherson **Kennedy**, Feb. 19, 1878, and had the following children:

    I. McPherson⁹ **Kennedy**, born Dec. 7, 1878; died Dec. 9, 1878.

    II. McPherson⁹ **Kennedy**, born Aug. 24, 1880.

    III. Esther Walden⁹ **Kennedy**, born Nov. 5, 1881.

    IV. John Wagner⁹ **Kennedy**, born Dec. 10, 1882.

514  V. JOHN CANFIELD,⁸ born Dec. 28, 1856.+

**348. JOHN L. TOMLINSON,**—See p 185.

**349. GEORGE H. TOMLINSON**, son of Lewis[6] (Capt. John L.,[5] Capt. John,[4] John,[3] Jonas,[2] Henry,[1]) and Hannah (Hawkins) Tomlinson, was born in Derby, Ct., March 30, 1819. Removed with his father's family to Ohio in 1828, and worked with his brothers in opening up a farm near Cleveland. In 1841 he accompanied his brother John on his return to Illinois, where he was employed by his father and brothers as a drover most of the time until the war of 1861, when he enlisted in the 92d Regiment of Illinois (the "Lead Mine") and served until near the close of the war, when he became almost blind.

After his discharge from the army, he married and settled in Freeport, Stephenson County, Illinois, where he still resides, receiving a pension from the government.

In person, he was below medium height, broad shoulders, erect, had dark hair and eyes, ruddy complexion, and usually the picture of health. Being of a roving disposition, the exposure and hardships of a drover's life he thought fully compensated by its freedom, variety of scenery and adventure.

351. ALBERT DeF.⁷ TOMLINSON, son of *Lewis*,⁶ (*Capt. John L.*,⁵ *Capt. John*,⁴ *John*,³ *Jonas*,² *Henry*,¹) and Hannah (Hawkins) Tomlinson, was born in Stratford, Ct., Dec. 11, 1827, and the following year the family removed to Ohio, where he grew to early manhood, working on his father's farm and attending the district school until 1845, when he attended the academy at Berea, and afterwards the college at Oberlin.

In 1848 he took a trip with his father to Illinois, but becoming ill, returned by Chicago, and a steamer to Cleveland, while his father and younger brother returned by land with a drove of cattle.

In 1849 he removed with the family to Carroll County, Illinois, and spent the early part of that summer in assisting in buying cattle and driving them to New York City to market. Returning to Illinois, he built a house in the spring of 1851, went to Cleveland and married Harriet Rockell, and returned to his home, where he continued in raising and dealing in cattle until 1858, when he removed to Mount Carroll, and thence in 1863 to Chicago, where he carried on a grain commission business until 1870, and then removed to Belindere, Boone County, Illinois, where he was teller in a banking house until his decease, September 15, 1879, the remains being buried in the Belindere graveyard.

He was of medium height, slight build, with a little stoop at the shoulders. He had black hair and eyes, a brownish beard, a kindly face, the paleness of which indicated a lack of that robust vitality possessed by his brother.

He was passionately fond of music, and had a heavy but musical bass voice, which led him to join musical societies wherever he resided.

He united with the Congregational Church at Rockfort, Ohio, but in Illinois united with and was an officer in the Presbyterian Church.

*Children of Albert D. F. Tomlinson:*

 I. CLARA H.,[8] died in infancy.

 II. ALBERT D.,[8] born in 1867 in Chicago; is now (1891) employed in the drug business in Elgin, Ill.

**354. *LYMAN O. TOMLINSON.*—See p 185.**

**355. *RANSOM*[7] *TOMLINSON*,** son of *Truman*,[6] (*Isaac*,[5] *Capt. Isaac*,[4] *Sergt. Isaac*,[3] *Jonas*,[2] *Henry*,[1]) and Nancy (Perry) Tomlinson, married Nancy *Bates*, of Oxford, Ct. They reside in Seymour, Ct.

*Their children were:*

525 I. MARTHA BATES.[8]
526 II. RANSOM PERRY BATES.[8]
527 III. NANCY MARIAN BATES.[8]

*Line of Henry Tomlinson.* 155

**358. HARRISON[7] TOMLINSON**, son of *Truman[6]* (*Isaac,[5] Capt. Isaac,[4] Sergt. Isaac,[3] Jonas,[2] Henry[1]*) and Nancy (Perry) Tomlinson, married, Jan. 10, 1841, Emeret, daughter of Truman *Davis*, of Naugatuck, Ct. Harrison Tomlinson died Nov. 25, 1855. Emeret Tomlinson died Oct. 2, 1881.

*Their children were:*

528   I. MARY,[8] born May 19, 1842.

529   II. EMMA S.,[8] born Sept. 5, 1847.

530   III. HARRIET,[8] born April 18, 1850; married, Jan. 1, 1878, Horace G. Chatfield, of Birmingham, Ct. They had:
  I. Maud Tomlinson[9] Chatfield, born Dec. 6, 1878.

531   IV. CLARISSA,[8] born Mar. 9, 1852; died June 7, 1853.

532   V. HENRY HARRISON,[8] born Nov. 28, 1855; died Dec. 29, 1856.

**377. JOHN R.[7] TOMLINSON**, son of *James C.[6]* (*Russell,[5] Capt. Isaac,[4] Sergt. Isaac,[3] Jonas,[2] Henry,[1]*) and Laura (Tomlinson) Tomlinson, married (1st) Lydia Perkins *Davis*, (2d) Mariett *Botsford*.

*Their children were:*

533   I. JULIA,[8] born Oct. 15, 1845; married Stanley Botsford, and had:
  I. Roland S.[9] Botsford.

534　II. Lucy,[7] born Oct. 1, 1847; married Capt. Wells Allis, and had :

 I. Lucy[9] Allis, born June 18, 1870.

 II. Florence[9] Allis, born June 6, 1872.

 III. Frank W.[9] Allis, born Nov. 25, 1874.

535　III. Agnes C.,[8] born Oct. 17, 1849; married Alfred M. Briscoe, and had :

 I. Jennie[9] Briscoe, born Nov. 26, 1870.

 II. Louis T.[9] Briscoe, born May 26, 1877.

536　IV. Carrie,[8] born May 30, 1857; married Alfred R. Briscoe, and had :

 I. Florence[9] Briscoe, born Jan. —, 1878.

 II. Howard[9] Briscoe, born May —, 1879.

537　V. Robert S.,[8] born Aug. 27, 1864; married Hattie C. Crofut.

538　VI. John L.,[8] born Oct. 17, 1866; married Lina Platt.

**381. JAMES W.[7] TOMLINSON**, son of James C.[6] (*Russell,[5] Capt. Isaac,[4] Sergt. Isaac,[3] Jonas,[2] Henry,[1]*) and Laura (Tomlinson) Tomlinson, married Frances *Wooster*.

*Their children were :*

539　I. Arthur,[8] born Nov. —, 1865; married Nellie Candee, and has :

 I. Rowland,[9] born Jan. —, 1890.

540　II. Laura,[8] born April 16, 1867; married Edward Leavenworth.

*Line of Henry Tomlinson.*

**382. EDWARD D. TOMLINSON,**[7] son of *James C.*[6] (*Russell,*[5] *Capt. Isaac,*[4] *Sergt. Isaac,*[3] *Jonas,*[2] *Henry,*[1]) and Laura (Tomlinson) Tomlinson, married Hattie C. *Lum.*

*Their children were:*

541    I. WILLARD L.,[8] born May 25, 1858.

542    II. EDWARD G.,[8] born Dec. 6, 1863; married Clara M. Wilcox.

543    III. JAMES T.,[8] born Aug. 14, 1866.

544    IV. HENRY S.,[8] born Aug. 1, 1869.

**383. ISAAC C.**[7] **TOMLINSON,** son of *James C.*[6] (*Russell,*[5] *Capt. Isaac,*[4] *Sergt. Isaac,*[3] *Jonas,*[2] *Henry,*[1]) and Laura (Tomlinson) Tomlinson, married Frances *Smith.*

*Their children were:*

545    I. FRED,[8] born in 1871.

546    II. ALICE,[8] born in 1874.

**391. ELISHA PATTERSON**[7] **TOMLINSON,** son of *Samuel,*[6] (*Timothy,*[5] *Isaac,*[4] *Isaac,*[3] *Jonas,*[2] *Henry,*[1]) and Jennette (Patterson) Tomlinson, married Della A., daughter of William *Reading*, in Delaware township, Hunterdon County, N. J. The following is taken from the "History of Hunterdon County, N. J.":

"Mr. Tomlinson combines the three branches of farming, dairying, grain and stock-raising, and fruit. He is a progressive, wide-awake farmer and has devoted much attention to the subject, both theoretically and practically. Of late he has taken a deep interest in promoting agriculture by assisting in establishing an analysis and experiment station for the practical development of the resources of the soil, destined to be of great benefit to the State. He has been some time a member of the State Horticultural Society. He has been an active member of the Patrons of Husbandry, and during his first two years therein held the office of lecturer and afterward filled the office of Master and Secretary."

392. *HOMER S.[5] TOMLINSON,* son of Samuel,[6] (*Timothy,*[5] *Isaac,*[4] *Isaac,*[3] *Jonas,*[2] *Henry,*[1]) and Jennette (Patterson) Tomlinson, married Emeline A. *Curtiss,* June 1, 1872, and resides in Woodbury, Conn.

547 I. SAMUEL C.,[8] born Jan. 4, 1875.

548 II. EMELINE C.,[8] born April 27, 1877.

549 III. FANNIE E.,[8] born April 12, 1879.

*Line of Henry Tomlinson.* 159

**400. ALVA D.⁷ TOMLINSON**, son of Nathaniel,⁶ (Timothy,⁵ Isaac,⁴ Isaac,³ Jonas,² Henry,¹) and Elizabeth (Davis) Tomlinson, married —— Cole, of Sheawasser County, Michigan, Oct. 22, 1876.

Their child is:

 I. Alva,⁸ born June 15, 1876, in Howell, Livingston Co., Mich.

**404. CHARLES A.⁷ TOMLINSON**, son of Charles,⁶ (Hon. David,⁵ Capt. Isaac,⁴ Sergt. Isaac,³ Jonas,² Henry,¹) and Esther (Candee) Tomlinson, married Julia M. Clark. She died March 25, 1841. He married (2d) Eliza Chatfield, who died Dec. 28, 1878. He died Dec. 22, 1870.

Their child was:

550 I. Willard,⁸ born in 1844.

**406. HORACE E.⁷ TOMLINSON**, son of Charles,⁶ (Hon. David,⁵ Capt. Isaac,⁴ Sergt. Isaac,³ Jonas,² Henry,¹) and Esther (Candee) Tomlinson, married Mary Candee, Nov. 22, 1858.

551 I. Esther Candee,⁸ born Jan. 28, 1860.

552 II. Andrew Kidston,⁸ born Sept. 9, 1862; died Sept. 22, 1864.

553 III. Edward Kidston,⁸ born Aug. 11, 1866.

554 IV. George Wallace,⁸ born June 5, 1869.

**417. ABIJAH⁷ TOMLINSON,** son of Philo,⁶ (Dan,⁵ Noah,⁴ Isaac,³ Jonas,² Henry,¹) and Harriet (Atwell) Tomlinson, married Marian *Wright,* at Stonington. Conn., Feb. 23, 1832. He died Oct. 19, 1878, at Gainesville, Florida. She died in June, 1880, at Chicago.

*Their children were :*

555    I. JOSEPH,⁸ born Sept. 17, 1834; died Mar. 16, 1854.

556    II. EDWARD H.,⁸ born Sept. 29, 1836.+

557    III. EVERETT S.,⁸ born Dec. 24, 1838.+

558    IV. LUCRETIA W.,⁸ born Dec. 29, 1842; died Nov. 12, 1844.

559    V. CAROLINE,⁸ born Jan. 10, 1845; died March, 1865.

**418. SHELDON⁷ TOMLINSON,** son of Philo,⁶ (Dan,⁵ Noah,⁴ Isaac,³ Jonas,² Henry,¹) and Harriet (Atwell) Tomlinson, married Abby *Morrell,* of Stonington, Conn., Feb. 18, 1829. She was born Nov. 24, 1807. Their residence was in Stonington, six years; Utica, N. Y., four years; Springfield, Mass., fourteen years, when they removed to Alton, Ills. He died at Ann Arbor, Mich., Sept. 5, 1876, aged 70 years, and was buried at Springfield, Mass.

*Their children were:*

560    I. JANE ELIZABETH,⁸ born Nov. 17, 1829, in Stonington; married, Jan. 14, 1851, George **Wilcox**. He died in Springfield, Mass., June 26, 1857, aged 28 years. She married (2d) Winslow B. **Bent,** Mar. 10, 1859, and had :

## Line of Henry Tomlinson.

    I. Sheldon Tomlinson⁹ Bent, born July 25, 1860, in San Francisco, Cal.

    II. Alice⁹ Bent, born June 2, 1862, in San Francisco, Cal., and married Ezra Conway Felton, of Steelton, Pa., June 2, 1884.

    III. Jeanie⁹ Bent, born Aug. 28, 1866, in Ann Arbor, Mich., and died aged 2 months, 17 days.

    IV. Edith⁹ Bent, born Oct., 18. 1873, in Ann Arbor, Mich.

561    II. MARY BURROWS,⁸ born May 11, 1832; died Nov. 8, 1837.

562    III. ANN JOSEPHINE,⁸ born May 19, 1834, at Stonington, married Emerson W. Price, Mar. 23, 1881.

563    IV. CARLTON,⁸ born Sept. 8, 1836, at Norwich, N. Y.; died June 24, 1847.

564    V. JASON COYE,⁸ born Sept. 28, 1838, at Utica, N. Y.; died Aug. 4, 1839.

565    VI. ELIZA MORRELL,⁸ born Mar. 27, 1840, in Springfield; married Aug. 1, 1861, James R. Burgesser, and died April 3, 1878. Their children were:

    I. Josephine⁹ Burgesser, born Mar. 9, 1863.

    II. Abby Ella⁹ Burgesser, born Dec. 9, 1864.

    III. Jane Bent⁹ Burgesser, born April 2, 1867.

    IV. James Edward⁹ Burgesser, born Mar. 10, 1870; died Aug. 12, 1870.

566    VII. HENRY LEE,⁸ born Sept. 19, 1842, in Springfield; died Feb. 23, 1844.

567    VIII. CHARLES SHELDON,⁸ born Mar. 3, 1846, at Springfield; died Mar. 2, 1847.

*421. REV. GEORGE TOMLINSON,* son of
*Abijah,⁶ (Dan,⁵ Noah,¹ Isaac,³ Jonas,² Henry,¹)* and
Betsey (Tomlinson) Tomlinson, married Ann M.
Taylor, April 13, 1841, and resided at the old homestead of his father, at Marbledale.

*Their child was:*

568    I. GEORGE ABIJAH,⁹ born April 5, 1844; married Sarah Noble, Jan. 6, 1868.

*433. ROMULUS TOMLINSON,* son of
*Eliphalet,⁶ (Dan,⁵ Noah,¹ Isaac,³ Jonas,² Henry,¹)*
and Polly (Logan) Tomlinson, married Harriet S.
*Chittenden,* Oct. 16, 1849.

*Their child was:*

569    I. HARRIET EMILY,⁸ born Sept. 26, 1850; married Rev. Alfred Lee Royce, Sept. 21, 1872.

*436. CLARK TOMLINSON,* son of *William,⁶ (Henry, Jr.,⁵ Henry,¹ Samuel,³ Jonas,² Henry,¹)* and Amy (Curtiss) Tomlinson, married Sarah *Hawkins,* Nov. 2, 1822. She died Dec. 25, 1835, aged 31 years. He died July 20, 1878.

*Their children were:*

582    I. GEORGE,⁸ born Dec. 29, 1823; died unmarried, July 7, 1876.
583    II. WILLIAM A.,⁸ born Oct. 30, 1825.+
584    III. MARTHA M.,⁸ born Aug. 7, 1827; died Feb. 11, 1829.
585    IV. HENRIETTA,⁸ born Sept. 2, 1828; died June 14, 1829.

*437. WILLIAM H.⁶ TOMLINSON*, (called Harry) son of *William,⁵ (Henry, Jr.,⁵ Henry,⁴ Samuel,³ Jonas,² Henry,¹*) and Amy (Curtiss) Tomlinson, married Betsey Maria, daughter of Capt. Micah *Poole*, of Derby, Nov. 22, 1824. She was born Oct. 6, 1800, and died Feb. 8, 1845. They removed to Naugatuck, Ct., where they resided more than twenty years. He was an active member of the Episcopal Church, and held many offices of public trust; was interested in the building of the Naugatuck Railroad, and after its completion removed to Bridgeport, Ct. He married (2d) Mrs. Louisa Caroline *Bassell*, of New Haven. She was a lovely and devoted wife and mother, and died May 8, 1850. He married (3d) Elizabeth Ann *Baldwin*, of Bridgeport, who died Sept. 3, 1882. In 1856 he removed to Stratford, where he resided until the death of his wife Elizabeth and their daughter Louisa, who both died within the same week of dysentery, when he went to the house of his eldest daughter, Mrs. L. N. Middlebrook, in Bridgeport, where he resided, enjoying a green old age, active and useful, bearing his many trials and bereavements with cheerful fortitude, happy in the society of the children and friends who remained, and rich in the love and esteem of all who knew him. He died January 16, 1890, at the advanced age of 88 years and 10 months.

*Their children were:*

586   I. JULIETTE,⁵ born Mar. 22, 1827; married Louis N. Middlebrook, Dec. 9, 1857, and had three children:

      I. Louis Burton⁶ Middlebrook, born March 4, 1860; died Dec. 23, 1866.

      II. Jenny⁶ Middlebrook, born May 23, 1862; married Frank Brown Weeks, Oct. 11, 1883, and had Juliette, born Aug. 2, 1884; died May 13, 1885.

      III. Albert James⁶ Middlebrook, born July 24, 1864; married Isabel Maria Shelton, Sept. 2, 1890.

587.   II. JANE MARIA,⁵ born Nov. 10, 1833; married Albert F. Spencer, Aug. 3, 1858.

*By second wife:*

588   III. MARIA LOUISA,⁵ died in infancy.

589   IV. HENRY,⁵ died in infancy.

*By third wife:*

590   V. MARY LOUISA,⁵ born Oct. 25, 1853; died Aug. 27, 1882.

**438. STEPHEN⁷ TOMLINSON,** son of *William,*⁶ *(Henry, Jr.,*⁵ *Henry,*⁴ *Samuel,*³ *Jonas,*² *Henry,*¹*)* and Amy (Curtiss) Tomlinson, married Olivia, daughter of Capt. Ira *Peck* of Bridgeport. She died Aug. 31, 1833, at the early age of 22 years and 3 months, leaving one son. He married (2d) Mary Hall, daughter of William and Sophronia *Falconer,* June 18, 1846. She was born Sept. 6, 1817. He died Mar. 26, 1872.

Stephen Tomlinson was born in Woodbury, Ct., in 1803, came to Bridgeport at an early age, and for some years lived in the family of Mr. Eli Walker. He was early apprenticed with the firm of Currier & Potter, then engaged in manufacturing carriages in a small shop at the corner of Middle and Wall streets. At the expiration of his time with them the business was removed to the present site of the Standard Association building, where Mr. Tomlinson entered into partnership with Mr. Jerry Judson, under the firm name of Judson & Tomlinson. He being an expert mechanic and draftsman, the firm was highly successful, and five years later removed their factory to the corner of Broad and Cannon Streets.

After several years Mr. Judson retired when Mr. Augustus Wood entered the partnership under the firm name of Tomlinson & Wood.

Mr. Russell Tomlinson, a brother, and also Mr. Frederick Wood, brother to Augustus Wood, were afterwards admitted as partners in this firm.

Stephen Tomlinson was elected the first president of the Farmers' Bank, now the First National Bank of the city of Bridgeport, and held that position for several years. At the time of his decease he was president of the Bridgeport Patent Leather Company.

Mr. Tomlinson was emphatically the pioneer of the carriage manufacturing business in Bridgeport. He built the trade, which for years was the principal manufacturing enterprise in the city, and established the reputation for his firm second to none in the United States. He was truly a self-made man, the sole architect of his own fortune. Withal he was a true Christian, and gifted by nature with rare social qualities and refined tastes as evidenced by the elegant home on Golden Hill built by him, now owned by Mrs. E. F. Bishop, where his many friends were ever cordially welcomed and hospitably entertained, and in whose hearts his memory lingers with an exceeding fragrance. He died March 26, 1872.

*Children by first wife:*

591  I. OLIVER KIRTLAND,[a] born Aug. 12, 1833; married Mary F. Thatcher, Nov. 1, 1877.

*Children by second wife:*

592  II. WILLIAM FALCONER,[a] born March 24, 1848; died Feb. 6, 1857.

593  III. MARY LINSLY,[a] born April 4, 1850; married John F. Forsyth, June 8, 1881.

594  IV. ELIZABETH BALDWIN,[a] born Jan. 1, 1856; married Clarence H. Kelsey, Dec. 1, 1885, and had:

    I. Stephen Tomlinson **Kelsey**.

    II. Courtland **Kelsey**.

## Line of Henry Tomlinson.

**439. CYRUS B. TOMLINSON**, son of *William C.*,[6] (*Henry, Jr.*,[5] *Henry*,[4] *Samuel*,[3] *Jonas*,[2] *Henry*,[1]) and Amy (Curtiss) Tomlinson, married ———, and died Sept. 18, 1878, in Chatham, Columbia Co., N. Y.

- 595    I. CAROLINE A.,[8] married Henry L. Champlin, and resides in Chelsea, Massachusetts.
- 596    II. WILLIAM L.,[8] born Aug. 2, 1833; married and has one married daughter.
- 597    III. CHARLES H.,[8] died young.
- 598    IV. CHARLES H.,[8] "was killed in the late war at the battle of Irish Bend."
- 599    V. BENNETT F.,[8] is in the Soldier's Home at Noroton, Conn.

**440. RUSSELL TOMLINSON**, son of *William*[6] (*Henry, Jr.*,[5] *Henry*,[4] *Samuel*,[3] *Jonas*,[2] *Henry*,[1]) and Amy (Curtiss) Tomlinson, married, Feb. 10, 1831, Martha Maria, daughter of Capt. Lent Munson *Hitchcock* and his wife Martha *Newell*, of Bridgeport, Ct. Captain Hitchcock was a native of Southington, Ct., was a sea captain, sailing from Bridgeport many years.

Russell Tomlinson was born in 1807, and his father died in 1819. After working on the farm under different employers some years, he learned the blacksmith trade, and followed it in several places, uniting with it the manufacture of wagons

in a small way. He was a pioneer in the construction of steel carriage springs, and is said to have made with his own hands the first set put to successful use in Bridgeport. He became a partner in the firm of Tomlinson and Wood about the year 1837, and remained in that connection fifteen years. The firm increased its business largely and became noted for its fine and reliable work, second to none in the country, attaining great financial success. In 1852 he sold that interest and turned his attention to the manufacture of carriage springs and axles, founding the Tomlinson Spring and Axle Company, on Cannon street.

While bearing his full share in the conduct of extensive manufacturing and business interests, he did not lack in public spirit, and few men have been oftener called to public office and positions of trust, or given more and better service therein. He served in the Common Council in the years 1839 and 1840, and from that time to 1861, he served eight terms as councilman and five as alderman, and was most of the time on the important committtes of finance and the street department. He was selectman of the town at the period of the late war, and active in filling the quota of recruits required of the town. He was elected town auditor in 1857, and a member of the Board of Relief in 1858, in both of which he did much service, being a member of the Board of Relief at the time of his

death. He often served as moderator of town meetings. On the resignation of Hon. Dwight Morris in 1860, he was appointed, by the State, trustee of the fund for the benefit of the remnant of the Golden Hill Indians, which he retained to the time of his decease. He was representative to the Legislature, senator from the Fourteenth District, director and president in the Naugatuck Railroad Company, director in the Bridgeport Bank, also in the first National Bank and the Mountain Grove Cemetery Association. He was a large contributor to the building of Christ Church, on Courtland Street, and was the first junior warden of the parish, and at his death was vestryman in Trinity Church, and delegate to the Diocesan Convention.

He was a man of genial, kindly and sympathetic character, of excellent business judgment, and much respected by all his fellow-citizens.

Martha Maria, wife of Russell Tomlinson, was born June 2, 1812, and died June 25, 1881. He married (2d) Mahalah Warriner *Ball*, June 1, 1882. He died April 23, 1885.

Children of Russell and Martha M. Tomlinson were:

600    I. Julia Ann,[5] married Hon. William Darius Bishop, son of Alfred and his wife Mary Ferris Bishop, of Bridgeport, Ct., where they reside, Mr. Bishop being engaged in railroad enterprises.

Their children were:

1. Mary Ferris[9] Bishop.

II. Alfred[9] Bishop, died April 18, 1854.

III. Russell Tomlinson[9] Bishop, married Elizabeth Ford, No children. He married (2d) Minnie, daughter of George W. Lockwood, and had:

    I. Sophia Halsey[10] Bishop.

    II. Julian Tomlinson[10] Bishop.

IV. William Darius[9] Bishop, married Susan Adile Washburne, daughter of Hon. Elihu B. Washburne, and his wife Adile Gratiot, and had:

    I. Natalie Washburne[10] Bishop.

    II. William Darius[10] Bishop.

V. Henry Alfred[9] Bishop, married Jessie Alvord Trubee, daughter of William Edgar Trubee, and his wife, Susan Curtis Alvord. They had:

    I. William Alfred[10] Bishop, died Aug. 24, 1886.

    II. Margarite Alvord[10] Bishop.

VI. Nathaniel Wheeler[9] Bishop; married Annie Lucetta Warner, only daughter of J. De Ver Warner, M. D., and his wife, Lucetta Grumman.

601  II. Munson Hitchcock,[8] born Jan. 7, 1834.+

602  III. Caroline Augusta,[8] born Dec. 22, 1835; died Aug. 13, 1836.

603  IV. Maria Louisa,[8] born Aug. 8, 1837; died Feb. 7, 1838.

604  V. Stephen Russell,[8] born Jan. 11, 1846.+

*Line of Henry Tomlinson.* 171

**442. BENNETT TOMLINSON**, son of William,⁶(*Henry*,⁵ *Henry*,⁴ *Samuel*,³ *Jonas*,² *Henry*,¹) and Amy (Curtiss) Tomlinson, married Martha.

*Their child was:*

601½ I. SARAH;⁸ married.

**443. WILLIAM⁷ TOMLINSON**, son of William,⁶(*Henry*,⁵ *Henry*,⁴ *Samuel*,³ *Jonas*,² *Henry*,¹) and Amy (Curtiss) Tomlinson, married Elizabeth, daughter of David and Mary *Hawkins*, of Derby, Ct., Oct. 21, 1835. He died July 7, 1881.

*Their children were:*

604¼ I. JAMES FRANKLIN,⁸ born Nov. 21, 1836.

604½ II. RUSSELL HENRY,⁸ born Sept. 28, 1838, in Oxford, Ct.; died Nov. 13, 1838.

**444. WILLIAM A.⁷ TOMLINSON**, son of William A.⁶(*William A.*,⁵ *Doct. Agur*,⁴ *Zachariah*,³ *Agur*,² *Henry*,¹) and Susan (Walker) Tomlinson, married (1st) Amelia D., daughter of Sylvester D. *Russell*, of Morristown, N. J., in 1844. She died in 1852, and he married (2d) Maria R., daughter of Israel *Russell*, of Morristown, N. J., in 1854. She died in 1860, and he married (3d) Elizabeth T., daughter of Robert M. *Russell*, of Morristown, N. J., in 1863.

*Children of Wm. A. and Maria R. Tomlinson:*

603½  I. ELIZABETH RUSSELL,⁴ born in 1855; died in 1877.

604¼  II. AMELIA D.,⁵ born in 1858; died in 1875.

*Children of Wm. A. and Elizabeth T. Tomlinson:*

604½  III. WILLIAM AGUR,⁵ born in 1863.

604¾  IV. ELEANOR SMITH,⁵ born in 1867.

**461. JOSEPH⁷ TOMLINSON,** (4th), son of *Joseph,* (3d)⁶ (*Joseph,⁵ Joseph,⁴ Zechariah,³ Agur,² Henry,¹*) and Sally E. (Bennett) Tomlinson, married Dec. 2, 1857, Annie *Tappan*, daughter of Rev. Cyrus *Brewster.*

*Their children were:*

605  I. NELLIE.⁸

606  II. ROSALIE,⁸ married Rev. Charles W. Shelton, Mar. 17, 1881, and had: 1 Winona⁹ Shelton; 2 Willie⁹ Shelton.

607  III. JOSEPH.⁸

608  IV. ANNIE.⁸

609  V. CYRUS.⁸

**467. HENRY W.⁷ TOMLINSON,** son of *David,⁶* (*Henry,⁵ Capt. Beach,⁴ Zechariah,³ Agur,² Henry,¹*) and Betsey (Bostwick) Tomlinson, married Lucy *Perkins,* who died in Waterbury, Ct., in 1878.

*They had:*

610  ERNEST,⁸ born Sept. 14, 1864.

## Line of Henry Tomlinson.

**468. NATHAN W.⁷ TOMLINSON,** son of David,⁶ (Henry,⁵ Capt. Beach,⁴ Zechariah,³ Agur,² Henry,¹) and Betsey (Bostwick) Tomlinson, married Sarah *Nichols*. They reside in Waterbury, Ct.

*Their children were:*

611    I. CHARLES HENRY,⁸ born April 6, 1860.

612    II. MARY E.,⁸ born Sept. 10, 1861; died 1863.

613    III. WALTER H.,⁸ born May 3, 1863.

614    IV. IDA E.,⁸ born May 21, 1865.

615    V. ALBERT W.,⁸ born Nov. 26, 1868.

616    VI. CHARLES H.,⁸ born April 14, 1869.

617    VII. EDSON E.,⁸ born July 26, 1870; died 1870.

618    VIII. CARRIE E.,⁸ born Oct. 24, 1873; died 1874.

**475. CHARLES⁷ TOMLINSON,** son of Doct. John,⁶ (Agur,⁵ Capt. Beach,⁴ Zechariah,³ Agur,² Henry¹,) and —— (Perry) Tomlinson, married Anna *Pearce*, lived in Huntington, Ct., and died June 11, 1842.

619    I. NELSON.⁸

620    II. ANNA MARIA.⁸

621    III. WILLIAM.⁸

622    IV. CAROLINE.⁸

623    V. EMILY.⁸

*477. NELSON⁷ TOMLINSON*, son of *Charles,⁶ (Agur,⁵ Beach,⁴ Zechariah,³ Agur,² Henry,¹)* and Anna (Pearce), Tomlinson, married Nov. 10, 1842, Charity Maria, daughter of James *Drew*, of Monroe, Ct. She was born April 11, 1821. They settled in Upper White Hills, Huntington, Ct.

*Their children were:*

624    I. GEORGE N.,⁸ born Aug. 31, 1844; was a soldier in the late war, a private of Co. B., 20th Regiment, C. V., was killed by a sharp shooter at Atlanta, Ga., July 25, 1864.

625    II. JULIET M.,⁸ born Aug. 30, 1846; married Sturges B. **Clarke**, of Monroe, Ct., Jan 1, 1867. They have :

      I. Myra S.⁹ **Clarke**, born Jan. 14, 1870.

626    III. JOHN D.,⁸ born Nov. 5, 1848; married Sept. 16, 1885, Caroline E. **Canfield**, of South Britain, Ct., and have :

      I. Charles M.⁹ **Canfield**, born Sept. 11, 1887.

627    IV. Emma L.,⁸ born Feb. 15, 1851; married May 7, 1873, Walter **Hubbell**, of Huntington, Ct., and have :

      I. Susie M.⁹ **Hubbell**, born Feb. 9, 1874.

628    V. CHARLES ELBERT,⁸ born Dec. 5, 1853.

629    VI. MARY ELLEN,⁸ born Sept. 19, 1855.

630    VII. HARRIET M.,⁸ born Oct. 25, 1859; married Jan. 1, 1885, Homer B. **Curtis**, of Trumbull, Ct. They have:

      I. Maurice Tomlinson⁹ **Curtis**, born June 21, 1886.

631    VIII. GEORGIANA,⁸ born Aug. 23, 1864.

## Line of Henry Tomlinson.

**478. WILLIAM⁷ TOMLINSON**, son of Charles,⁶ (Agur,⁵ Beach,⁴ Zechariah,³ Agur,² Henry,¹) and Anna (Pearce) Tomlinson, married Ruth Eliza, daughter of Dea. Ferris *Drew*, of Huntington, Ct., June 7, 1846, in the church at Upper White Hills, in Huntington, Ct., where they resided a time, then removed to Woodbridge, Ct. She was born Feb. 15, 1829.

*Their children were:*

632  I. Son,⁸ born March 22, 1848; died same day.

633  II. Warren E.,⁸ born Feb. 25, 1850.+

634  III. Frank E.,⁸ born April 24, 1854.+

635  IV. Wilbur F.,⁸ born May 15, 1856.+

636  V. Royal D.,⁸ born Dec. 28, 1860.+

637  VI. Charles,⁸ born Oct. 11, 1863; died Sept. 24, 1866.

638  VII. Herbert H.,⁸ born April 25, 1869.

**491. GIDEON M. TOMLINSON,** son of Huntington,[6] (Jabez H.,[5] Capt. Gideon,[4] Zechariah,[3] Agur,[2] Henry,[1]) and Elizabeth T. (Mills) Tomlinson, married Abigail, daughter of Gideon and Lydia (Lewis) Welles, of Monroe, Ct., Sept. 2, 1840, and lived in Oronoke, in Stratford. Ct.

*Their children were:*

639   I. SARAH,[8] born Jan. 4, 1841; married William Ezra **Wheeler,** and had:

    I. William[9] **Wheeler.**

    II. Robert Tomlinson[9] **Wheeler.**

    III. Elizabeth[9] **Wheeler.**

640   II. REBECCA,[8] born July 6, 1843; married (1st) Charles **Burritt,** and had:

    I. Lillie[9] **Burritt,** married (2d) William **Wilkinson,** of Shelton, Ct.

641   III. GEORGE HUNTINGTON,[8] born Sept. 12, 1845.+

642   IV. ELIZA MILLS,[8] born Oct. 7, 1848; married Alfred Beach **Fairchild,** and had:

    I. Ralph Tomlinson[9] **Fairchild,** born June 24, 1880.

    II. Alfred Huntington[9] **Fairchild,** born May 26, 1886.

643   V. GIDEON,[8] born Feb. 3, 1852.+

644   VI. WILLIAM WRIGHT,[8] born March 14, 1856.+

645   VII. JABEZ HUNTINGTON,[8] born Oct. 27, 1862; died.

**496. HENRY T. TOMLINSON**, son of Caleb,⁷ (Abraham, M. D.,⁶ Abraham, M. D.,⁵ Jonah,⁴ Abraham,³ Jonas,² Henry,¹) and Susan (Meeker) Tomlinson, married Dec. 1, 1849, Elizabeth Brown, daughter of Dr. John *Temple* (who was for 20 years Dean of the Homeopathic Medical Faculty, of St. Louis) and his wife Elizabeth Staughton, whose father, the Rev. Wm. *Staughton*, was one of the founders of the Baptist School of Divinity, in Philadelphia.

The inscription on the monument reads: "Henry T. Tomlinson, died Feb. 10, 1877, aged 50 years, 1 month and 10 days."

*Their children are:*

646    I. JOHN TEMPLE.⁹ died.

647    II. HENRY THEODORE,⁹ died in infancy.

648    III. HENRY THEODORE,⁹ died in infancy.

649    IV. SAMUEL,⁹ died in infancy.

650    V. ELEANOR CHARLOTTE,⁹ married June 20, 1877, James Hillhouse, son of Dr. Henry S. Hewit, and grandson of the Rev. Nathaniel Hewit. Mr. James H. Hewit is descended, through his mother, from Agur Tomlinson, No. 181.

651    VI. HENRY LEWIS.⁹

652    VII. THOMAS HOYNE.⁹

653   VIII. CHARLES DOUGLAS.⁹

**502. CHARLES A. TOMLINSON**, son of Nathan Camp,[7] (David,[6] Doct. Abraham,[5] Jonah,[4] Abraham,[3] Jonas,[2] Henry,[1]) and Susan Catharine (Baldwin) Tomlinson, married Lucia E., daughter of Fowler *Sperry*, of Milford, Ct., Oct. 27, 1869. He resides on his father's homestead, in Milford village; is a coal merchant; has served four terms in the State Legislature.

654    I. EDWARD SPERRY,[9] born Sept. 20, 1870.

655    II. KATE LOUISE,[9] born Nov. 6, 1872.

656    III. ARTHUR SPERRY,[9] born June 19, 1876; died Aug. 6, 1876.

657    IV. ADA MAY,[9] born Sept. 5, 1877.

658    V. BERTHA HART,[9] born June 1, 1882.

**510. DAVID[8] TOMLINSON**, son of Hon. Theodore E.,[7] (David,[6] Joseph,[5] Agur,[4] Abraham,[3] Jonas,[2] Henry,[1]) and Abbie (Walden) Tomlinson, married Gertrude R. *Jenkins*, July 11, 1872.

659    I. THEODORE E.,[9] born April 15, 1873.

660    II. RADCLIFF,[9] born Nov. 26, 1876; died Oct. 19, 1884.

661    III. ELLA VANNESS,[9] born Jan. 4, 1878.

662    IV. GERTRUDE HYNCH,[9] born July 28, 1882.

**514. JOHN C.[7] TOMLINSON**, son of Theodore E.,[7] (David,[6] Joseph,[5] Agur,[4] Abraham,[3] Jonas,[2] Henry,[1]) and Abbey Esther (Walden) Tomlinson, was graduated at the New York University with the degree of A.B. in 1875, and from the University Law School with the degree LL.B. in 1877. In 1882 the honorary degree of A.M. was conferred on him by the same college.

He married Nov. 10, 1879, Frances French *Adams*, daughter of Charles W. Adams of Boston, and of his wife Frances Barker French, of Bangor, Maine. This wife, Frances F., died April 1, 1886, and he married (2d) Dora Morrell *Grant*, a daughter of Daniel J. Grant of Boston, and of his wife Elizabeth *Crane*, July 20, 1888.

*Children of John C. and Frances F. Tomlinson.*

663    I. John C.,[9] born Aug. 8, 1880.
664    II. Esther Walden,[9] born Dec. 4, 1884.

*Child of John C. and Dora M. Tomlinson.*

665    III. Daniel G.,[9] born May 1, 1889.

**535. EDWARD H.[7] TOMLINSON**, son of Abijah,[7] (Philo,[6] Daniel,[5] Noah,[4] Isaac,[3] Jonas,[2] Henry,[1]) and Marian (Wright) Tomlinson, married July, 1869, Fannie St. ———. He died April 3, 1882.

666    I. Edward S.,[9] born in 1871, and is living with his mother at St. Paul's, Minn.

**586. EVERETT S. TOMLINSON**, son of Abijah,⁷ (Philo,⁶ Daniel,⁵ Noah,⁴ Isaac,³ Jonas,² Henry,¹) and Marion (Wright) Tomlinson, married Dec. 12, 1876, at Champaign, Ills., Genevieve *Rush*. She was born Sept. 8, 1850.

667   I. LERAY, born Dec. 4, 1877.
668   II. ERNEST, born July 27, 1879.
669   III. GENEVIEVE, born Aug. 18, 1882.

**581. WILLIAM A. TOMLINSON**, son of Clark,⁷ (William,⁶ Henry, Jr.,⁵ Henry,⁴ Samuel,³ Jonas,² Henry,¹) and Sarah (Hawkins) Tomlinson, married Melissa *Wheeler*, of Trumbull, Ct., Oct. 11, 1854.

670   I. WALKER,⁸ born July 25, 1855; married Lillie C. *Downs*, Oct. 23, 1878.
671   II. WILLIAM A.,⁸ born Oct. 2, 1875.

**601. MUNSON H. TOMLINSON**, son of Russell,⁷ (William,⁶ Henry, Jr.,⁵ Henry,⁴ Samuel,³ Jonas,² Henry,¹) and Martha M. (Hitchcock) Tomlinson, married Sarah F., daughter of George *Wade*, April 11, 1855. He died June 19, 1874.

*Their children were:*

672   I. GEORGE WADE,⁸ born Jan. 14, 1856; died Oct. 31, 1862.
673   II. JULIAN MUNSON,⁸ born Dec. 24, 1859; married Fannie Eloise **Smith**, of New York, Jan. 2, 1889.
674   III. RUSSELL,⁸ born Feb. 12, 1866; married Lillian May Cynthia **Walters**, June 11, 1889. She died April 15, 1890. They had:
      I. Lillian Beatrice,¹⁰ born Mar. 29, 1890.
675   IV. MARGARET WADE,⁸ born Feb. 24, 1863.
676   V. FREDERICK,⁸ born Aug. 31, 1868.
677   VI. HENRY WADE,⁸ born June 23, 1870; died July 13, 1871.

*Line of Henry Tomlinson.* 181

**604. STEPHEN R.[8] TOMLINSON,** son of *Russell,[7] (William,[6] Henry, Jr.,[5] Henry,[4] Samuel,[3] Jonas,[2] Henry,[1])* and Martha M. (Hitchcock) Tomlinson, married Mary Katharine, daughter of Frederick Booth *Nichols*, and his wife Catharine Oaky *Sharpe*, Oct. 14, 1868. She was born Oct. 25, 1847, in New York City.

*Their children were:*

678    I. STEPHEN RUSSELL,[9] born Jan. 14, 1879.

679    II. WILLIAM HENRY,[9] born Oct. 20, 1876; died July 8, 1877.

680    III. ALICE LYMAN,[9] born June 24, 1879.

**633. WARREN E.[8] TOMLINSON,** son of *William[7] (Charles,[6] Agur,[5] Beach,[4] Zachariah,[3] Agur,[2] Henry,[1])* and Ruth Eliza (Drew) Tomlinson, married Aug. 2, 1876, Mary H. *Currie*, of Woodbridge, Ct. They reside in Shelton, Ct.

*Their children were:*

681    I. RUTH D.,[9] born May 29, 1883.

682    II. RALPH D.,[9] born May 23, 1886.

**634. FRANK E.⁸ TOMLINSON**, son of *William,⁷ (Charles,⁶ Agur,⁵ Beach,⁴ Zechariah,³ Agur,² Henry,¹)* and Ruth Eliza (Drew) Tomlinson, married Nov. 8, 1877, Sarah A. *Hotchkiss*, of New Haven, Ct. She died Oct. 27, 1878. He married (2d) April 6, 1881, Fannie L. *Ford*, of New Haven. They reside in South Dakota.

*Their children were:*

683    I. Eshel R.,⁹ born Sept. 28, 1883.

684    II. William Wallace,⁹ born May 13, 1886.

685    III. Harold Hotchkiss,⁹ born Mar. 20, 1888.

686    IV. Son,⁹ born Aug. 2, 1890.


**635. WILBUR F.⁸ TOMLINSON**, son of *William,⁷ (Charles,⁶ Agur,⁵ Beach,⁴ Zechariah,³ Agur,² Henry,¹)* and Ruth Eliza (Drew) Tomlinson, married Dec. 6, 1882, Antoinett B., daughter of Perkins *French*, of Easton, Ct. They reside in Danbury, Ct.

*Their child is:*

687    I. Carl Perkins,⁹ born June 6, 1886.

## Line of Henry Tomlinson.

**636. LOYAL D.[7] TOMLINSON,** son of *William,[7] (Charles,[6] Agur,[5] Beach,[4] Zechariah,[3] Agur,[2] Henry,[1]*) and Ruth Eliza (Drew) Tomlinson, married Jan. 16, 1884, Jennie *Sprague* of Danbury, Ct.

*Their child is:*

688    I. CHARLES BEACH,[9] born July 19, 1888; died Feb. 18, 1890.

**641. GEORGE H.[7] TOMLINSON,** son of *Gideon M.[7] (Huntington,[6] Jabez H.,[5] Capt. Gideon,[4] Zechariah,[3] Agur,[2] Henry,[1]*) and Abigail (Welles) Tomlinson, married Celestia *Booth*.

*Their children were:*

689    ELISHA MILLS.[9]

690    EDWARD BOOTH.[9]

691    ABIGAIL WELLES.[9]

692    ANNIE E.[9]

693    JABEZ HUNTINGTON.[9]

**643. GIDEON**[8] ***TOMLINSON***, son of *Gideon M.,*[7] (*Huntington,*[6] *Jabez H.,*[5] *Capt. Gideon,*[4] *Zachariah,*[3] *Agur,*[2] *Henry,*[1]) and Abigail (Welles) Tomlinson, married Idwilla I. *Nichols*, of Trumbull, Ct.

*Their children were:*

694    I. Josephine.[9]

695    II. Charles Henry.[9]

696    III. Jessie.[9]

697    IV. Lucius Nichols.[9]

**644.** ***WILLIAM W.***[8] ***TOMLINSON***, son of *Gideon M.,*[7] (*Huntington,*[6] *Jabez H.,*[5] *Capt. Gideon,*[4] *Zachariah,*[3] *Agur,*[2] *Henry,*[1]) married Alice *Russell*, of Huntington, Ct.

698    I. Ernest.[9]

699    II. George Welles.[9]

700    III. Florence.[9]

701    IV. Huntington,[9] born Oct. 27, 1863; died April 12, 1885, unmarried.

*Line of Henry Tomlinson.*

**348. JOHN L. TOMLINSON.**—(See p 152.) This family record not received at the time of going to press.

**354. LYMAN O. TOMLINSON.**—(See p 154.) This family record not received at the time of going to press, although promised weeks before.

**162.**—(See page 67.)

162 REBECCA TOMLINSON, married Thomas Rugles **Pyncheon**, Sept. 30, 1783, and had:

    I. William Henry **Ruggles**, born Feb. 16, 1786; died Dec. 11, 1831, in New Haven.

    II. Sophia Theresa **Ruggles**, born Nov. 1787; died Nov. 6, 1841, in New Haven.

    III. Marretta **Ruggles**, born Jan. 6, 1790.

    IV. Mertiminimia **Ruggles**, born Feb. 1, 1792; died Aug. 2, 1796.

**I. WILLIAM¹ TOMLINSON,** with a wife Abigail, was accepted in Derby, Ct., in December. 1677. There is a tradition that he was the nephew of Henry Tomlinson the first in Stratford, Ct., but no confirmation of this has been seen on any records.

He may have been the son of Robert Tomlinson of Milford, whose wife took a letter of dismission from Milford Church in 1648 to the church in Stratford, but of this relation no records have been found.

He was selectman in Derby in 1678 and filled that office several years.

March 20, 1711, he deeded his "lands, hereditaments, situate and being in the town of Derby," to his sons John and Isaac. There was a William junior, according to a document signed Nov. 2, 1707, by William Tomlinson, senior, and William Tomlinson, junior. Hence there were the following and perhaps other children.

*Children of William and Abigail Tomlinson.*

2  I. WILLIAM.²+

2½  II. JOHN.²

2½  III. ISAAC.²

**2. WILLIAM² TOMLINSON, JUN.**, son of *William*,¹ and Abigail Tomlinson, of Derby, Ct., resided in Derby, Ct., where he died in 1735 or 6, being about 66 years of age.

*The Will of William Tomlinson.*

Derby, March 10, 1734-5.

In the name of God Amen, I William Tomlinson of Derby being very Sick and Weak but through God's mercy I have my understanding perfectly. I do dispose of my outward estate firstly I commit my Body to y⁰ dust and my soul to God y' Gave it and as for my outward estate I do Give to my well beloved wife y⁰ use of my whole estate as long as she lives.

I do give to my Eldest son Benjamin all my Homestead after my wife's decease.

I do give to my two sons Ebenezer and Gideon two parcells of Land y⁰ one parcell lieing on a place Called East Hill and y⁰ other parcell Lying at Stonehill so called, to be equally divided between them Two sons forementioned and y⁰ Rest of my estate to be equally divided amongst my Daughters.

his<br>
WILLIAM X TOMLINSON.<br>
mark.

Signed, sealed and
delivered in presence of

JNO MUNSON

EPHRAIM SMITH

ROBERT SEALY    The Will was proved Oct. 11, 1736.

New Haven Probate Records, Vol. VI. p. 20.

The "rest of the estate of William Tomlinson to be equally divided amongst" his daughters was distributed as follows: To Elizabeth Pettitt, wife of Samuel Pettitt, £31; Ichabod Stockwell, heir of Robert Stockwell, son of Rebecca, one of the daughters of William Tomlinson, £32; Ruth Peck, wife of Isaac Peck, £31 18s.; Sarah Scott, wife of William Scott, £31 18s.; Abigail Scott (whose wife is not known), £31 18s.

*Children of William Tomlinson.*

3   I. BENJAMIN,[3] +

4   II. EBENEZER,[3] +

5   III. GIDEON,[3] +

6   IV. ELIZABETH,[3] married Samuel Pet it, Nov. 1, 1736, and they had:

    I. Eliad[4] Pettit, born July 19, 1737.

    II. Cyrus[4] Pettit, born Jan. 20, 1742.

    III. Catharine[4] Pettit, born June 23, 1744.

7   V. REBECCA,[3] married Ichabod Stockwell.

8   VI. RUTH,[3] married Isaac Peck.

9   VII. SARAH,[3] married William Scott.

10  VIII. ABIGAIL,[3] married —— Scott.

**3. BENJAMIN³ TOMLINSON**, son of William² (William¹) and —— Tomlinson, of Derby, married Jehoada, daughter of Jabez *Harger*, Jr., Nov. 16, 1742.

11    I. GIDEON,⁴ born Oct. 27, 1743.

12    II. JEREMIAH,⁴ born May 8, 1745.

13    III. ANNA,⁴ born July 1, 1747; died Jan. 8, 1749.

14    IV. COMFORT,⁴ born May 13, 1749.

15    V. BENJAMIN,⁴ born Aug. 30, 1752. +

16    VI. JABEZ,⁴ born Dec. 5, 1754.

17    VII. HANNAH,⁴ born April 26, 1757.

18    VIII. JOSEPH,⁴ born Nov. 7, 1758.

19    IX. DAVID,⁴ born Aug. 10, 1762.

*II. GIDEON TOMLINSON*, son of *Benjamin, Jr.³ (William,² William¹)*, resided in Derby, Ct., and had a war record as follows, reported in the Adjutant General's Record of *Connecticut Men* in the Revolution:

Gideon Tomlinson, of Derby, marched "for the Relief of Boston in the Lexington Alarm, in April, 1775," served two days.

"Gideon Tomlinson, a corporal, enlisted May 13, 1775; discharged Dec. 20, 1775; in the 3d Com-

pany, Gen. Wooster's Regiment." This company served at the siege of Boston, having in it five men by the name of Tomlinson, all of them, apparently, from Derby, Ct.

Gideon Tomlinson was in the First Company, or Capt. Nathaniel Johnson's, of Derby, in 1776, was at the battle of L. I., Aug. 27, stationed at Kips Bay 34th St. East River, and in the hurried retreat of the company from that place on September 15, he was missing.

15. *BENJAMIN*[1] *TOMLINSON, Jr.,* son of *Benjamin*[3] (*William,*[2] *William*[1]) and Jehoada (Harger) Tomlinson, married Mary *Harger,* Nov. 15, 1768. If this was the son of Benjamin, Senior, as above, he was only a little over sixteen years of age when he was married.

Benjamin Tomlinson enlisted May 15, 1775, and marched for the relief of Boston in the Lexington Alarm, and was discharged Dec. 20, 1775. This company served at the siege of Boston that year. He was in the list of pensioners of Connecticut in 1818.

The following extract from a letter of R. G. Tomlinson, who may have been grandson of the above Benjamin, is of interest, and the information offered should be secured:

"Battle Creek, Mich., Nov. 20, 1879.

Dr. Gilead Peet, . . . . . . . .

My father's name was Vincent Tomlinson; he settled in the town of Gaines, Orleans County, N. Y., in 1814, or thereabouts, with other Tomlinsons that were cousins. My father died in 1826, and all of the older stock of Tomlinsons that came from Connecticut are dead. There are four families scattered in the State of New York and other States that I can give you their whereabouts if you desire.

My grandfather's name was Benjamin Tomlinson; he resided on what was called Bunga or Great Hill in the town of Derby, Ct., died, I think, in 1836. He was a Revolutionary soldier, and was in the old Prison Ship in New York harbor, and took great pleasure in going to Derby on the Fourth of July, in his soldier's uniform, to show the people what Independence was and should be. . . . . . .

Yours respectfully,

R. G. TOMLINSON."

*Children of Benjamin and Mary Tomlinson:*

20  I. LUCINDA, born Aug. 11, 1769.

21  II. NABBY, born Aug. 12, 1771.

22  III. JEREMIAH, born April 15, 1774.

23  IV. GIDEON, born Mar. 18, 1777.

## MISCELLANEOUS.

The following were in the war of the Revolution, but it is not certain to what families they belong:

"WILLIAM TOMLINSON enlisted May 15, 1775, in the 3d Company of Genl. David Wooster's regiment, and was discharged Dec. 20, 1775. This company served in the siege of Boston."

"JOSHUA TOMLINSON was in the Continental Line of Connecticut, and received pay from Jan. 1, 1781, to Dec. 3, 1781."

"ELIPHALET TOMLINSON received pay from Jan. 1, 1781, to Dec. 3, 1781, in Capt. Richard's Company, Fifth Regiment, Connecticut Line."

"ELIPHALET TOMLINSON, of Derby, Ct., enlisted Dec. 22, 1780, for the war."

"ELIPHALET TOMLINSON was a pensioner of Connecticut in 1818, residing in Vermont."

"JABEZ TOMLINSON, of New Milford, enlisted in the Fourth Troop, October 23, 1780; had light complection, grey eyes, and dark hair."

"JABEZ TOMLINSON was a recruit in Sheldon's Draggoons, October, 1780, for the war, of New Milford, a clothier by trade, 5 feet 7 inches in

height, dark complection, light eyes, light hair." He was on the list of invalid pensioners in 1833-4, his residence not being given.

"LUCY TOMLINSON, of Derby, Ct., was a pensioner in Connecticut in the census of 1840, aged 69 years."

"PHEBE TOMLINSON was a pensioner in 1840, in Fairfield County, aged 75 years."

*CALEB TOMLINSON* married Abigail Fairchild, Nov. 5, 1795.

    I. LOCKY, born June 26, 1797, at Oxford, Ct.; married Sept. 15, 1818, Westover Hyde, of Hoosack, N. Y. They were residing at Cas'leton, Vermont, in 1856.

    II. SALLY, born Dec. 28, 1798; died April 7, 1799.

    III. SALLY, born in 1800.

    IV. SAMUEL, baptized May 22, 1803, in Oxford, Ct.; died Aug. 20, 1804.

*ELIZABETH TOMLINSON* of Derby, Ct., married David Tharp of Judea, Aug. 5, 1778.

*SEELEY TOMLINSON* of Oxford [Ct.], married Sarah Johnson, Nov. 28, 1822. (*Newtown Records.*)

**HORACE TOMLINSON** of Reading [Ct.], married Nancy *Hull*, Oct. 22, 1836. (*Newtown Records*.)

Interred at Quaker's Farm Burying-place, in the town of Oxford, Ct.:

ZALMON TOMLINSON, died July 1, 1805, aged 40.

PATIENCE, his wife [widow] died May 15, 1820, aged 53.

NANCY TOMLINSON, died Mar. 12, 1831, aged 35.

BALSORA TOMLINSON, died Feb. 26, 1822, aged 20 years.

Tomlinson graduates of Yale College:

| | | |
|---|---|---|
| AGUR, - - - in 1741. | ZACHARIAH, - - in 1805. |
| HEZEKIAH, - - " 1765. | JOHN LEWIS, - - " 1807. |
| JABEZ HUNTINGTON, - " 1780. | HENRY A., - - " 1828. |
| DANIEL, - - - " 1781. | GEORGE, - - " 1834. |
| ABRAHAM, - - - " 1785. | JOHN A., - - " 1856. |
| ZACHARIAH, - - " 1788. | CHARLES, - - " 1858. |
| GIDEON, - - - " 1802. | JOSEPH, - - " 1884. |
| AGUR, - - - " 1804. | WILLIAM T., - - " 1885. |

*Miscellaneous.*

*1. JOB TOMLINSON* was of Thurleston, Leicestershire, England, with the following brothers and sister:—

2. WILLIAM TOMLINSON, of Thurlston, Leicestershire, Eng.

3. GEORGE TOMLINSON, of Thurlston, Leicestershire, Eng.

4. JOSEPH TOMLINSON, of Thurlston, Leicestershire, Eng.

5. SARAH PERCIVAL was a Tomlinson of Derby, Derbyshire, Eng.

6. ANN PEASLY was a Tomlinson, of Leicester, Leicestershire, Eng.

Job Tomlinson was a resident of Thurleston, Leicestershire, England, and had the following children:

8   I. WILLIAM, born in Thurlston, Leicestershire, Eng.

9   II. ANN, born in Thurlston, Leicestershire, Eng.

10  III. JOSEPH B., born in Northampton, Northamptonshire, Eng.

11  IV. GEORGE, born in Northampton, Northamptonshire, Eng.

12  V. ELIZA, born in Northamptonshire, Eng.

13  VI. EDWIN, born in Chester, in Chestershire, Eng.

14  VII. OWEN, born in Melton, Mowbray, Leicestershire, Eng.

15  VIII. JOHN, born in Cold Harbor, Lincolnshire.

**10. JOSEPH B. TOMLINSON,** son of Job Tomlinson, of Leicestershire, England, married Elizabeth ——, who was born in Northamptonshire, England. They reside in Chicago, Illinois.

*Children of Joseph B. and Elizabeth Tomlinson:*

16    I. Sarah E., born at Salt Lake City, Utah, U. S. A., in 1854.
17    II. Marintha A., born at Calls Fort, Utah, U. S. A., in 1856.
18    III. Joseph B., Jr., born at Calls Fort, Utah, U. S. A., in 1858.+
19    IV. Lizzetta L., born at Fort Bridger, Wyoming, U. S. A., in 1859.

**18. JOSEPH B. TOMLINSON, Jr.,** son of Joseph B. and Elizabeth Tomlinson, married, and had:

20    I. Edward L., born at Boulder, Colo., in 1886, U. S. A.
21    II. Don J., born at Springfield, Colo., in 1887, U. S. A.

**I. JOHN TOMLINSON** of "Knight's Hulme, near Sandwich, Cheshire, England, where the family resided for a number of generations," and his wife was Anne *Whittingham* of Curtis Hulme, near Sandwich also. John Tomlinson's father's family is said to have consisted of thirteen children.

*John and Anne Tomlinson's children:*

2    I. William, never married.
3    II. Thomas,-|-
4    III. Anne, married William **Grapel**, a publisher in Liverpool, England. No children.
5    IV. Samuel.+

**3. THOMAS TOMLINSON**, son of *John* and Anne Tomlinson, married (1st) Charlotte *Wheeler*. He married (2d) Sept. 24, 1824, Emma Jones, daughter of Thomas *Jones*, builder of Liverpool, England. He was a corn merchant in Liverpool. He lived a time in Everton in Cheshire, near Liverpool, then removed to the latter place, where he died in 1844.

*Child by first wife:*

6    I. CHARLOTTE, married Frank Maxwell, of Drum Park, Dumfriesshire, Scotland, a corn merchant of Liverpool, and had two daughters and a son.

*Children by the second wife:*

7    II. WILLIAM.+

8    III. THOMAS.+

9    IV. PRISCILLA.

10    V. JULIA EMMA, married Frederick Martin, hide merchant in Liverpool, and had Norman Martin, Jessie Martin, and George Martin.

11    VI. FRANCES ANN, married Charles Martin, brother of Frederick, also a hide merchant.

**5. SAMUEL TOMLINSON**, son of *John* and Anne Tomlinson, married Ann, daughter of Thomas *Rhines*, of Liverpool, England.

12    I. GEORGE, died.

13    II. JOHN, died.

**7. WILLIAM TOMLINSON,** son of *Thomas,*[2] (*John,*[1]) and Emma (Jones) Tomlinson, married Anne Jane, daughter of Edwin *Rigy*, gentleman, of Liverpool.

14    I. PRISCILLA, married H. E. **Benson**, spice merchant, and died. No children.

**8. THOMAS TOMLINSON,**[3] son of *Thomas,*[2] (*John,*[1]) and Emma (Jones) Tomlinson, married May 1, 1855, Ellen, daughter of George *Gurden*, of Trueman Street Brewery, Liverpool. They were married at Walton Church, Liverpool, England. They now (1890), reside in Buffalo, New York State, in the U. S. A.

*Their children are:*

15    I. JOHN.[4]

16    II. MARION ADELAIDE, married William **Ray**, a tanner of Runcorn, Cheshire, Eng., and had William **Ray**.

*Miscellaneous.*

**1. THOMAS TOMLINSON** was born in Jarrow, South Shield, England. He was Superintendent of Police for 21 years.

2   I. THOMAS.
3   II. ROBERT; Captain of a boat on the Tyne river.
4   III. WILLIAM, born Sept. 27, 1824, in England.+
5   IV. JAMES.
6   V. HANNAH; married Mr. Cuthert, master of Tyne dock.
7   VI. ANN.

**4. WILLIAM TOMLINSON**, son of *Thomas* Tomlinson, was apprenticed to a shoemaker; ran away and enlisted in the English army; ran away and married Elizabeth *Vans* in 1846. Shortly after this they came to America, and settled in Philadelphia, Pa. He enlisted in the Union army in the 29th Regiment, Pennsylvania Volunteers, Co. F., and died of disease contracted in the army, Dec. 9, 1869. His widow, Elizabeth, died by the explosion of a lamp in 1873.

8   I. THOMAS W., born Sept. 25, 1847.+
9   II. ROBERT; died in his 23d year, in 1882.
10   II. ALFRED R., is married, and has five children.
11   III. ELIZABETH V., married H. Y. **Still**, has three children.
12   IV. CHRISTINA, married Nelson **Gavit**.
13   V. WILLIAM II., died in infancy.
14   VI. CHRISTINA V., died in infancy.
15   VII. JAMES II., is married and has one child.

**8. THOMAS W. TOMLINSON,** son of William (Thomas) and Elizabeth (Vans) Tomlinson, married Mary E. *Van Leenmen* in 1871. They reside in New York City, and have children, all born in New York except the first:

16    I. WILLIAM H., aged 19 years.

17    II. ALFRED R., aged 17 years.

18    III. MARY E., aged 13 years.

19    IV. CLARA P., died in infancy.

20    V. KITTIE P., aged 5 years.

21    VI. CLARA L., died in infancy

23    VII. FRANK W., aged 3 years.

**1. WILLIAM TOMLINSON** was born in England, removed to the North of Ireland when a child and settled there; married there and had a family of nine sons and four daughters. His son:

2     WILLIAM, resides in Chicago, Ills.

**BARNARD H. TOMLINSON**, son of James and Elizabeth Tomlinson, was born in England. His father, a bookseller of Newark,[1] county of Nottingham. Eng., died in 1767. Barnard H. Tomlinson was a midshipman in the British Navy, but came to America in early manhood; married Caroline Dudly *Knott*, an English lady, and made his home in Washington, D. C., in 1806, where his descendants reside.

---

[1] See Dickinson's Antiquities of Newark, England.

**1. WILLIAM TOMLINSON** was a methodist minister in England, and married Mary *Nixon*. They resided in Cheshire, England, and had several sons, all ministers.

*Their children were:*

2   I. JAMES.
3   II. JOHN.
4   III. THOMAS.+
5   IV. WILLIAM.
6   V. MARGARET.
7   VI. REBECCA.

**4. THOMAS TOMLINSON,** born in 1805, in Cheshire, England, where he married, in 1824, Mary *Donald*, and, in 1843, removed to America with his wife and six children. He was a Methodist minister and died in 1868. His widow, Mary, died in 1890, aged 86 years.

*Their children were:*

8   I. ESTHER; married —— **Molineaux**.
9   II. SARAH; married —— **Eull**.
10   III. HEPZIBAH; married —— **Babcock**.
11   IV. SOLOMON BYRON.+
12   V. JABEZ M.; an artist, lived at the South; was in the Confederate Army, and died, it was supposed, from injuries received in the army.
13   VI. JOSEPH W., is living in the West, engaged in railroad business.

**11. SOLOMON B. TOMLINSON,** son of Thomas and Mary (Donald) Tomlinson, married Delinda P., daughter of John G. and Margaret *Rice*, Sept. 7, 1853. Their home was in Elmira, N. Y., where he died June 8, 1887, and where she still resides.

*Their children were:*

14    I. CHARLES H., a lawyer in Albany, N. Y.

15    II. CLARA L; married Wilber G. **Griffes**, a merchant. They reside in Elmira, N. Y., and have children:

        I. Katie C. **Griffes.**

        II. Florence B. **Griffes.**

        III. Charles H. T. **Griffes.**

        IV. Alice Marguerite **Griffes.**

**1. JOHN TOMLINSON** resided in the Parish of Blythe, Nottinghamshire, England, where his father and ancestors resided before him. He had one brother, Joseph, and one sister, Mary; all born in the parish of Blythe.

*His children were:*

2  I. JOSEPH, resides in Lancashire, Eng.
3  II. WILLIAM, deceased.
4  III. THOMAS, deceased.
5  IV. ELIZA, deceased.
6  V. GEORGE, born February, 1828, in Nottinghamshire.+
7  VI. Daughter, residing now (1891) at Meaford, Ontario, Canada.

**6. GEORGE TOMLINSON**, son of John Tomlinson, of Nottinghamshire, is residing in Meafor, Ontario, Canada, with his family.

*His children are:*

8  I. JOHN, resides in Meaford, Ca.
9  II. WILLIAM, resides in Meaford, Ca.
10  III. GEORGE ALBERT, resides in Meaford, Ca.
11  IV. HENRY ALFRED, resides in Meaford, Ca.
12  V. "EDGIN," resides in Meaford, Ca.
13  VI. ELIZABETH, resides in Meaford, Ca.
14  VII. ANNA MARIA, resides in Philadelphia, Pa.
15  VIII. MARY JANE, married W. E. Smith, and is residing in Buffalo, N. Y.

*Miscellaneous.*

**1. HENRY TOMLINSON**, born in England according to tradition, came to America and resided in or near Philadelphia, Pa.

*His children are said to have been:*

2   I. Son, who went South.

3   II. Son, place of residence not known.

4   III. James, born in America.+

**4. LT. JAMES TOMLINSON**, son of *Henry* of Philadelphia, or thereabouts, married (1st) Barbara *Brown*, and she died March 26, 1808, in the 72d year of her age. He married (2d) Dorothy *Furness*. The inscription on his grave-stone in Shiloh, N. J., states that he was born in 1735 and died May 31, 1811, in the 76th year of his age.

He lived at one time on a farm in Pennsylvania, which is now within the limits of the city of Philadelphia, but afterwards he removed to Cumberland County, New Jersey, where he spent the remainder of his life as a farmer, except when he served his country as a soldier, for during the war of the Revolution he was first lieutenant in Captain Bennett's Company, in Colonel Enos Seeley's Battalion, N. J. State troops, and his son Samuel was with him.

*Children of James and Barbara Tomlinson:*

5    I. SAMUEL, born Feb. 16, 1762, in Frankfort, Pennsylvania.+

6    II. THOMAS, born Sept. 22, 1764.+

7    III. MARGARET, born Sept. 5, 1766; married Ebenezer Davis, Dec. 12 1787, and had children.

8    IV. JANE, died in 1772.

9    V. ELIZABETH, died in 1772.

10    VI. NATHAN, married; died Feb. 6, 1862, age 86 years.

**5. SAMUEL TOMLINSON,** son of Lt. *James* and Barbara Brown Tomlinson, married Ann *Garrison*. She was born Dec. 1, 1761, and died March 15, 1824. He was a farmer, but later in life became a merchant, and died in Bridgeton, N. J.

*Children of Samuel and Ann Tomlinson.*

11    I. JAMES, was a farmer and afterwards a blacksmith, and married Prudence ———, and died March 13, 1831, in his 48th year.

12    II. WILLIAM.

13    III. SARAH, married William Brookfield.

14    IV. LEWIS, married.

15    V. SAMUEL, born March 12, 1793, in Bridgeton, N. J.+

16    VI. MARGARET.

17    VII. DAVID.

18    VIII. JOHN.

**6. *THOMAS TOMLINSON*,** son of Lt. *James* and Barbara Tomlinson, married Rachel, daughter of Jonathan and Phebe *Ayres*, Feb. 16, 1789. She was born Sept. 21, 1769, and died March 20, 1839. He resided in Cumberland County, N. J., and was a farmer. He died April 5, 1812. All their children were residents of Cumberland County, N. J., except Jane.

*Children of Thomas and Rachel Tomlinson:*

19   I. Lemuel, born Jan. 4, 1790; married Abigail **Sheppard**, Mar. 22, 1814, had children, and died Dec. 9, 1833. He was a farmer.

20   II. Jane, born Feb. 3, 1792; married John F. **Randolph**, Dec. 16, 1813, had children, and died Feb. 19, 1836.

21   III. Phebe, born Oct. 11, 1794; married Jonathan **Davis**, May 13, 1817, had three children, and died Feb. 6, 1865.

22   IV. Joseph, born June 19, 1797; married Mary **Burt**. He was a merchant. She died Nov. 22, 1831.

23   V. Nathan, born Jan. 24, 1800; married Louisa **Bishop**, Mar. 11, 1824, had two children, and died Jan. 17, 1844. He was a tailor by trade.

24   VI. Seeley, born Nov. 18, 1802; married (1st) Rachel **Davis** Jan. 5, 1821, and (2d) Mary **Duffield** Oct. 2, 1834. He was a farmer, and died Dec. 1, 1874.

25   VII. Abel Sheppard, born Aug. 31, 1805.+

26   VIII. George, born Mar. 26, 1808.+

**15. SAMUEL TOMLINSON,** son of *Samuel,* (*James,*[2] *Henry,*[1]) and Ann (Garrison) Tomlinson, married Rebecca *Biddle,* April 8, 1818. She was born in New Jersey in 1794, and died in Cincinnati in 1834. They resided in New Jersey until 1834, when they removed to a locality ten miles north of Cincinnati, Ohio, where she died that same year. He died at the home of his son Samuel B., in Cincinnati, O., March 31, 1878, aged 85 years and 19 days.

*Children of Samuel and Ann Tomlinson:*

27    I. SARAH ANN, born Jan. 10, 1819, in New Jersey, and married John Gans, a farmer, Jan. 10, 1839, and died Feb. 20, 1890. They had:

       I. Emma Gans, married James Butler, a farmer of Rushville, Ind.

       II. Harriet J. Gans, married Rev. E. Spencer, of Moores Hill, Ind.

       III. Joseph Gans, a farmer at Canaan, Indiana.

       IV. Edward S. Gans, a farmer at Canaan, Indiana.

       V. Annie M. Gans, married Benjamin Stewart, a farmer of Indiana.

       VI. Kate G. Gans, married Rev. Braden, of Garden City, Kansas.

28    II. WILLIAM MILLER.

29  III. EMELINE B., born Mar. 19, 1822; married Rev. David M. Wilson, Oct. 16, 1847, and they went as missionaries to Syria, where they remained 14 years. Ill health of Mrs. Wilson caused their return to the U. S. They had :

    I. Daughter Wilson, born April 30, 1852, in Beirut, Syria; was graduated at Maryville College, Tenn., and married, Oct. 16, 1876, Hon. William A. McTeer, an attorney of Knoxville and Maryville, Tenn. Mr. McTeer was born Sept. 13, 1843.

    II. Samuel Tyndale Wilson (Rev.), born Feb. 17, 1858, at Hums, Syria, graduated at Maryville College, Tenn., and Lane Theological Seminary in Cincinnati, O.; went as a missionary to Mexico, but ill health caused his return. He is now Professor in Maryville College. He married Hattie M. Silsby, June 8, 1887.

30  IV. ISAAC HAMPTON (Rev.), born May 12, 1824, in New Jersey; was educated in Cincinnati, and entered the ministry quite young. He married, Jan. 1846, Martha Lemmon, and died in Cincinnati, Feb. 26, 1882. They had :

30½  I. SAMUEL L. (Tomlinson) (Rev.), who is living in Illinois.

31  V. REBECCA B., born Oct. 6, 1826, in New Jersey, was graduated at the Female College, at Oxford, Ohio, and married, Dec. 8, 1852, Rev. N. C. McDill, and died in Richland, Ind., Feb. 12, 1865. Mr. Dill is pastor of the church at Richland, to which he was called in 1852. They had :

    I. Samuel H. McDill (Rev.), pastor at Elizabeth, Ind.

32  VI. SAMUEL BIDDLE, born Jan. 11, 1829, in Philadelphia, Pa.+

33 VII. FANNIE HAMPTON, born April 6, 1831, was graduated at the Female College, Cincinnati; married, Jan. 7, 1858, Rev. Edward C. **Johnston**, who was educated at Wabash College, Indiana, and Lane Theological Seminary. He died in Petersburg, Ind., Aug. 14, 1878. Residence, Cincinnati. They had:

> I. J. Ambrose **Johnston**, educated at Wabash College, and graduated at Cincinnati College of Medicine and Surgery, where he lectures on his specialty—Gynecology.
>
> II. Emma R. **Johnston**, educated in Cincinnati, and is a teacher in that city.
>
> III. Mary L. **Johnston**, educated in Cincinnati, and is a teacher in that city.
>
> IV. Edward S. **Johnston**, educated in Cincinnati, and is a book merchant in that city.
>
> V. Herbert Lincoln **Johnston**, is a Student of Electrical Engineering at Ohio University, Columbus, O.
>
> VI. Edith G. **Johnston**, born Jan. 14, 1876; died May 19, 1883.

**25. ALBERT S. TOMLINSON,** son of *Thomas (James, Henry)* and Rachel (Ayres) Tomlinson, married Lois *Davis*, and resided all his life in Cumberland County, N. J., as a farmer. He was quiet and unassuming in his manner, but possessed more than ordinary intellectual strength. His son, when a student in college, went to him when perplexed with difficult mathematical problems, and always found aid, although he was untrained in the mathematics of the schools. He died January 12, 1880.

*Children of Abel S. and Lois Tomlinson.*

34   I. REUBEN, born Aug. 1, 1828; died Dec. 6, 1845.

35   II. LUCINDA M., born June 23, 1832; married Reuben T. **Barrett**, and died Jan. 9, 1859. They had Wilbert H. **Barrett.**

36   III. GEORGE EDWIN (Rev.), born June 27, 1837.+

37   IV. LOIS ANNA, born Sept. 17, 1841; married Dr. Volney R. **Stanton** of Philadelphia, Pa., who died Dec. 30, 1868. She has been a frequent contributor to the literary papers.

**26. GEORGE TOMLINSON,** M. D., son of *Thomas (James, Henry)* and Rachel (Ayres) Tomlinson, was born in Cumberland County, N. J.; attended medical lectures at the College of Physicians and Surgeons of the Western District of the State of New York, in Fairfield, Herkimer County, N. Y., where he graduated in the spring of 1831.

He married (1st) Sophronia A. *Davis* of Brookfield, N. Y., April 27, 1831, who died Nov. 8, 1832. He married (2d) Phebe Mulford, March 11, 1834, who died Feb. 2, 1864. He married (3d) Mrs. Rebecca Frazieur.

In June, 1831, he commenced the practice of medicine in Roadstown, N. J., where he continued until a few years ago, when he removed to the adjacent village of Shiloh, where he now (1891) resides.

*Children of George and Phebe Tomlinson.*

38   I. THOMAS H. (M. D.), born Sept. 26, 1836.-|-

39   II. SOPHIA A. (M. D.), born Dec. 17, 1838; was graduated at the Woman's Medical College in Philadelphia, and is practicing medicine in Providence, Rhode Island.

40   III. HORATIO M., born Dec. 2, 1840, and has done some very clever work as an artist.

41   IV. EDWARD M., born Oct. 22, 1842; was graduated at Bucknell University, Lewisburg, Pa., in 1867, and later pursued studies at the University of Berlin, Germany. He is now Professor of Greek in Alfred University, at Alfred Centre, N. Y. He married May E. Brown, March 12, 1884.

42   V. EMMA M., born Feb. 11, 1845; married the Rev. A. E. Main, and died Jan. 1, 1871.

43   VI. GEORGE, born Feb. 23, 1847.+

44   VII. MARY J., born June 8, 1849; was graduated at Elmira Female College, and died June 22, 1879.

45   VIII. JOSEPH, born Aug. 15, 1851.-|-

**32. SAMUEL B. TOMLINSON, M. D.,** son of *Samuel*, (*James*,² *Henry*,¹) and Rebecca (Biddle) Tomlinson, pursued a classical course of five years after he was fifteen, in Bellmont College, Ohio, then attended the Ohio Medical College at Cincinnati and received the degree of M. D. in 1855. Two years previous to graduating he was appointed by the Faculty as assistant anatomist and curator to the College Museum, which position he held four years, and then established himself in the practice of medicine, where he still retains his office, in Cincinnati, Ohio.

He married Athelia M., daughter of E. M. and Sarah E. (Edwards) *Spencer*, who was born Feb. 7, 1846, in Hillsboro, Ohio, educated in the public schools of Cincinnati, and is the author of an illustrated book of her poems, entitled "Summer Land and other Poems."

Her father, E. M. Spencer, was born in Dutchess County, N. Y., settled in Cincinnati, where for many years he was a member of the editorial staff of one of the daily papers.

Immediately upon their marriage they started on a tour through Europe, visiting various places in England, Belgium, Prussia, Switzerland, ascending the Alps, thence to Genoa, thence by steamer to France, and thence home to Cincinnati.

*Children of Samuel B. and Athelia M. Tomlinson.*

46   I. DAUGHTER, died aged 6 years.

47   II. DAUGHTER, died aged 6 years.

48   III. FANNIE MAY, born May 9, 1876.

49   IV. SAMUEL SPENCER, born Sept. 10, 1878.

*36. REV. GEORGE E. TOMLINSON,* son of *Abel S. (Thomas, James, Henry)* and Lois (Davis) Tomlinson, was educated at Union College, Schenectady, N. Y., where he made a brilliant record as a student. Afterwards he was for a time engaged in literary and educational work, and for one year was professor of Greek in Alfred University, N. Y., a position the trustees very much desired him to retain, but he preferred the work of the pastorate, in which he was highly successful. A biography, which will contain the history of his life, and selections from his sermons and writing is being prepared for publication.

He married Amanda P. *Titsworth*, and his early decease occurred at Westerly, R. I., May 11, 1876.

*Children of Rev. George E. and Amanda Tomlinson:*

50   I. EVERETT TITSWORTH (Rev.), born May 23, 1859.+

51   II. LAURA, born Jan. 17, 1862.

52   III. CORA, born Aug. 23, 1863.

54  IV. GEORGE EDWIN, Jr., born Aug. 4, 1868, and was educated at Rutgers College, New Brunswick, N. J., and is assistant superintendent of the Chicago and Aurora Smelting Company, at Chicago, Ill., where he resides.

55  V. HAROLD, born Nov. 30, 1871. He is engaged in business in New York City, and resides with his mother at Plainfield, N. J.

## 38. *THOMAS H. TOMLINSON, M. D.,*

son of Doct. *George (Thomas, James, Henry)* and Phebe (Mulford) Tomlinson, was graduated at the Medical Department of the University of Pennsylvania at Philadelphia, and afterwards studied at the Bucknell University of Lewisburg, Pa., and is now practicing medicine in Plainfield, N. J. He married (1st) Cornelia *Gillette,* and (2d) Mary E. *Davis.*

*Children of Doct. Thomas H. and Cornelia Tomlinson:*

56  I. MAY, born June 14, 1862.

*Children of Doct. Thomas H. and Mary E. Tomlinson:*

57  II. MINEOLIA, born Sept. 10, 1869.

58  III. EDWARD M., born June 11, 1873.

59  IV. ROLLAND D., born June 29, 1877.

**43. GEORGE TOMLINSON,** son of Doct. George (*Thomas, James, Henry*) and Phebe (Mulford) Tomlinson, married Emma M. *Bonham*, Dec. 24, 1868.

*Children of George and Emma M. Tomlinson:*

60   I. IRA M., born Mar. 2, 1870.

61   II. ARTHUR M., born April 4, 1873.

62   III. HENRY M., born Mar. 27, 1875.

63   IV. EUGENE J., born July 14, 1877.

64   V. JOSEPH W., born Feb. 10, 1879.

65   VI. MARY G., born April 5, 1882.

66   VII. EDWIN, born July 4, 1884.

67   VIII. ABEL, born Sept. 29, 1886.

**45. JOSEPH TOMLINSON, M. D.,** son of Doct. George (*Thomas, James, Henry*), and Phebe (Mulford) Tomlinson, was graduated at Williams College, and at the College of Physicians and Surgeons in New York City, and is practicing medicine in Roadstown, N. J.

He married Carrie *Lawrence*.

*Children of Doct. Joseph and Carrie Tomlinson.*

68   I. GEORGE.

69   II. DE VOE.

**50. REV. EVERETT T. TOMLINSON, M. D.**, son of Rev. *George E.* (*Abel S., Thomas, James, Henry*), and Amanda (Titsworth) Tomlinson, was educated at Williams College, and was for several years engaged in educational work.

In 1881-83, he was Head Master of the Auburn High School, at Auburn, N. Y., and from 1883 to 1888 was Head Master of the preparatory department of Rutger's College, New Brunswick, N. J. While there he prepared two Latin text books which have been extremely used.

In 1888 he accepted a call to the pastorate of a church at Elizabeth, N. J., where he was ordained in June, 1888, which position he still holds. He is a regular contributor to several leading religious papers. The degree of Doctor of Philosophy has been conferred upon him by Colgate University and Milton College.

He married Anna M., daughter of O. D. *Green* of Adams, N. Y.

*Children of Everett T. and Anna M. Tomlinson.*

70   I. Ruth.

71   II. Everett Titsworth, Jr.+

72   III. Paul Greene.

*1. ALEXANDER TOMLINSON*, and his wife Ellen, reside in the County of Derry, Ireland. He is the son of James Tomlinson, of England, who was in the English Army, and had four children, Alexander, John, James and Margaret.

*Children of Alexander and Ellen Tomlinson:*

2    I. Margaret.
3    II. James.+
4    III. John, deceased.
5    IV. John, deceased.
6    V. Jonathan Hughes, deceased.
7    VI. Esther.
8    VII. Alexander; resides in Yonkers, N. Y., U. S. A.; and one of his sisters.
9    VIII. Robert.
10    IX. Ellen.

*3. JAMES TOMLINSON,* son of *Alexander,* (*James*), and Ellen Tomlinson, came to America in 1880, married Mary ———, in 1885, and resides in Albany, N. Y., and one of his sisters.

*Children of James and Mary Tomlinson:*

11    I. Nellie; born Jan. 10, 1887; died Feb. 16, 1890.
12    II. Mildred; born in 1889; died Feb. 10, 1890.
13    III. James; born May 10, 1890.

# INDEX.

### GIVEN NAMES IN HENRY TOMLINSON'S LINE.

ABIGAIL, 30, 68, 119, 177, 266, 306
ABIGAIL WELLES, . . . 691
ABIJAH, . . . . . 233, 417
ABRAHAM, 2, 10, 11, 21, 54, 60, 73, 171
ADA MARY, . . . . . . 657
AGNES, . . . . . 374, 535
AGNES CHARLOTTE, . . . 427
AGNES CORTELYOU, . . . 379
AGUR, 8, 20, 48, 125, 127, 143, 181, 184
ALBERT W., . . . . . 615
ALEXANDER, . . . . . 160
ALICE, . . . . 15, 414, 546
ALICE LYMAN, . . . . . 680
ALONZO WALLER, . . . 483
ALVA DAVIS, . . . . . 400
AMARILLA, . . . . . . 100
AMELIA, . . . . . . 188
AMMON, . . . . . . 205
ANDREW KIDSTON, . . . 552
ANN, . . . . 34, 130, 284
ANNA, . 301, 311, 315, 500, 620
ANN ELIZA, . . . . . 508
ANNIE, . . . . . 455, 608
ANNE, . 66, 116, 120, 156, 169
ANNIE E., . . . . . . 692
ANN MARIA, . . 473, 479, 484
ANN JOSEPHINE . . . . 562
ANN REBECCA, . . . . 267
ANTOINETT, . . . . . 277
ARTHUR, . . . . . . 539
ARTHUR SPERRY, . . . . 656
AUGUSTUS, . . . . . 338
AVICE CAROLINE, . . . 480

BATHSHEBA, . . . . 9, 26
BEACH, . . 51, 257, 276
BEERS, . . . . . . 104
BENJAMIN, . . . . . 82
BENNETT, . . . . . 443
BENNETT BENEDICT, . . 224
BURNETT F., . . . . . 509
BERTHA HART, . . . . 658
BETSEY, 186, 200, 210, 271, 341, 366, 474
BETSEY JENNETTE, . . . 390
BETTY, . . . 76, 117, 187

CALEB, . 46, 65, 174, 295, 297
CARL PERKINS, . . . . 687
CARLTON, . . . . . 563
CAROLINE, 250, 333, 420, 559, 622
CAROLINE A., . . . . 595
CAROLINE AUGUSTA, . . 602
CORNELIA L., . . . . 323
CARRIE, . . . . 453, 536
CARRIE E., . . . . . 618
CATHARINE, . 244, 317, 375
CELIA, . . . . . . 312
CELIA HAWLEY, . . . . 503
CHARITY, . . . 148, 260
CHARLES, 167, 218, 241, 272, 290½, 340, 369, 419, 426, 441, 474, 637
CHARLES ABRAHAM, . . 502
CHARLES AUGUSTUS, . . 404
CHARLES BEACH, . . . 688
CHARLES C., . . . . 251
CHARLES DOUGLAS, . . 653
CHARLES ELBERT, . . . 628
CHARLES H., . . 597, 598, 616

Charles Henry, 255, 611, 695
Charles Lambert, . . . 309
Charles Sheldon, . . . 567
Charilla, . . . . . 398
Clarissa, . . . . . 531
Clark, . . . . . . 436
Cornelia, . . . . . 332
Cyrus, . . . . . . 609
Cyrus Burton, . . . 489
Curtiss, . . . . 135, 435
Curtiss William, . . 448

Damaris, . . . . . 81
Dan, . . . . . 101, 231
Daniel, . . 86, 186, 425, 665
David, 72, 79, 97, 165, 172, 179,
183, 219, 221, 261,
334, 337, 494, 510
David Austin, . . . 405
David Gibson, . . 304, 504
David Joseph N., . . 154
David Welles, . . . 409
Deborah, . . . . . 190

Edson E., . . . . . 617
Edward Booth, . . . 690
Edward Delavan, . . 382
Edward G., . . . . 542
Edward H., . . . . 556
Edward Kidston, . . 553
Edward Rutledge, . . 497
Edward S., . . . . 666
Edward Sperry, . . . 654
Edwin, . . . . . . 465
Eleanor Charlotte, . . 650
Eliphalet, . . . . . 236
Elisha Mills, . . . . 689
Elisha Patterson, . . 391
Eliza, . . . 314, 335, 424
Eliza Catharine, . . . 228
Eliza Mills, . . . . 642
Eliza Morrell, . . . 565

Elizabeth, 16, 28, 42, 138, 150,
152, 168, 256, 447
Elizabeth Maria, . . . 470
Elizabeth Baldwin, . . 594
Ella Vanness, . . . . 661
Ellen A., . . . . . 393
Ellen Adams, . . . 326
Ellen Candee, . . . . 411
Emeline C., . . . . 548
Elmer, . . . . . . 489
Emily, . . . . 357, 623
Emily Rebecca, . . . 486
Emma, . . . . . . 529
Emma L., . . . . . 627
Eloisa, . . . . . . 262
Ernest, . . 610, 668, 698
Estiel R., . . . . . 683
Esther Candee, . . . 551
Esther Walden, . 513, 664
Eunice, . 43, 112, 144, 274
Everett S., . . . . 557

Fannie E., . . . . 549
Florence, . . . . . 700
Francelia, . . . . . 458
Frank, . . . . . . 415
Frank E., . . . . . 634
Fred, . . . . . . 545
Frederick, . . . . . 676
Frederick David, . . 482

George, 370, 395, 401, 421, 582
George Abijah, . . . 568
George Albert, . . 227, 408
Geo. Huntington, . . 641
Georgina, . . . . . 631
George N., . . . . 624
George Wade, . . . 672
George Wallace, . . 554
George Welles, . . . 699
Genevieve, . . . . 669
Gertrude Hynch, . . 662

INDEX.    221

GIDEON,       53, 151, 153, 282,
                        491, 643
GILES HAWKINS, . . . .   423
GOULD, . . . . . . .     280
GRACE C., . . . . . . .  368
HANNAH, 44, 75, 111, 124, 139,
                   147, 283, 316
HAROLD HOTCHKISS, . .    685
HARRIET, . . . . . .     530
HARRIET EMILY, . . .     569
HARRIET M., . . . . .    630
HARRISON, . . . . . .    358
HENRIETTA, . . . . . .   460
HENRIETTA LOUISA, . . .  229
HENRY, 1, 41, 55, 57, 115, 128,
              142, 254, 264, 290, 589
HENRY ABRAHAM, . .       164
HENRY HARRISON, . . .    532
HENRY LEE, . . . . .     566
HENRY LEWIS, . . .       651
HENRY S., . . . . .      544
HENRY T., . . . . . .    496
HENRY TALMAGE, .  321, 511
HENRY THEODORE,  647, 648
HENRY WADE, . . .        677
HENRY WARREN, . . .      467
HERBERT H., . . . .      638
HEZEKIAH, . . . . .  29, 123
HOMER S., . . . . . .    392
HORACE, . . . . . . .    386
HORACE ELISHA, . . .     406
HULDAH, . . . . . .      163
HUNTINGTON, . .     286, 701

ICHABOD, . . . . . .      22
IDA E., . . . . . . .    614
ISAAC, 13, 33, 38, 93, 203, 207,
              216, 259, 343, 462
ISAAC CORNELL, . .       383
ISABELL ANDREW, . .      505
JABEZ HUNTINGTON,    158, 490,
                        645, 693

JAMES, . . .   209, 363, 451
JAMES C., . . . . . . .  212
JAMES HENRY, . . . .     403
JAMES T., . . . . . .    543
JAMES WILLARD, . . .     381
JANE, . . . . . . .  331, 339
JANE CAROLINE, . . .     223
JANE ELIZABETH, . . .    560
JANE MARIA, . . . . .    587
JASON COVE, . . . . .    561
JEANNETTE, . . .    293, 300
JENNETT, . . . . . .     402
JENNETTE ADELAIDE, . .   226
JESSIE, . . . . . . .    696
JESSIE ALZENA, . .       506
JEMIMA, . . . . . . .    157
JERUSHA, . . . . . .     159
JONAH, . . . . . . .      19
JONAS, . . . . . . .       3
JOHN, .   12, 31, 247, 270, 452
JOHN BRAINARD, . . . .   472
JOHN C., . . . . . . .   663
JOHN CANFIELD, . . .     514
JOHN D., . . . . .  394, 626
JOHN G., . . . . . .     361
JOHN GIBSON, . .    173, 175
JOHN L., . . . . .   85, 538
JOHN LEWIS, . . . . .    194
JOHN RUSSELL, . . .      377
JOHN TEMPLE, . . .       646
JOHN VICTORY, . . . .    485½
JOHNSON LOGAN (REV.), .  431
JOSEPHINE, . . . . .     694
JOSEPH,  27, 50, 70, 77, 136, 215,
              252, 329, 461, 555, 607
JOSEPH BOWERS, . . . .   178
JOSIAH, . . . . . . .    141
JULIA, . .  307, 328, 388, 533
JULIA CAROLINE, . . .    325
JULIA ANN, . . . . . .   600
JULIETTE, . . . . . .    586
JULIETTE M., . . . . .   625

# INDEX.

| | | |
|---|---|---|
| Julian Munson, | | 673 |
| | | |
| Katee, | | 122 |
| Katy, | | 140 |
| Kate Louise, | | 655 |
| | | |
| Laura, | | 350, 540 |
| Laura Cornelia, | | 384 |
| Lemuel Etheridge, | | 488 |
| Leray, | | 667 |
| Levi, | 83, 191, | 197 |
| Lewis, | 196, | 242 |
| Louisa, | | 305 |
| Lovena, | 222, | 413 |
| Lucinda, | | 397 |
| Lucius, | 253, | 263 |
| Lucius Nichols, | | 697 |
| Lucretia W., | | 558 |
| Lucy, | 107, 108, 249, | 534 |
| Luthenia, | 81, | 199 |
| Lydia Augusta, | | 211 |
| Lydia J., | | 456 |
| | | |
| Margaret, | | 4 |
| Margaret Wade, | | 675 |
| Maria, | 278, 291, 298, | 446 |
| Maria A., | | 324 |
| Maria Antoinette, | | 410 |
| Maria Louisa, | 588, | 603 |
| Maria Theresa, | | 220 |
| Marietta, | | 372 |
| Mark, | | 240 |
| Martha, 23, 62, 292, 299, 308, | | 430 |
| Martha Bates, | | 525 |
| Matilda, | | 399 |
| Mary, 37, 58, 61, 126, 129, 146, 160, 176, 204, 248, 255, 265, 330, 336, 356, 429, 457, 493, 528, | | 524 |
| Mary Alice, | | 132 |
| Mary Ann, 98, 225, 289, 364, 380, | | 387 |
| Mary Burrows, | | 561 |

| | | |
|---|---|---|
| Mary Burwell, | | 376 |
| Mary E., | | 612 |
| Mary Elizabeth, | | 281 |
| Mary Ellen, | | 629 |
| Mary Gibson, | | 499 |
| Mary Jane, | | 287 |
| Mary Linsly, | | 593 |
| Mary Louisa, | | 590 |
| Mehetable, | | 303 |
| Melinda, | | 327 |
| Millard Gould, | | 485 |
| Minerva, | 360, | 416 |
| Munson Hitchcock, | | 601 |
| | | |
| Nabby, | 64, | 102 |
| Nancy, | 185, 269, | 279 |
| Nancy Maria Bates, | | 527 |
| Nancy Sophia, | | 428 |
| Nathan, | 106, | 346 |
| Nathan Camp, | | 310 |
| Nathaniel, | 69, | 217 |
| Nathan Welles, | | 468 |
| Nellie, | | 605 |
| Nelson, | 385, 619, | 477 |
| Noah, | 38, 103, | 165 |
| | | |
| Oliver Kirtland, | | 591 |
| Oliver Mead, | | 313 |
| Oscar Watson, | | 469 |
| | | |
| Patience, | 35, | 114 |
| Permelia, | | 238 |
| Peter, | | 207½ |
| Peter Cortelyou, | | 365 |
| Phebe, | 7, 82, 25, 134, | 192 |
| Philo, | | 232 |
| Philo Bostwick, | | 466 |
| Polly, | 80, | 302 |
| | | |
| Rachel, | | 36 |
| Radcliff, | | 660 |
| Ralph D., | | 682 |

INDEX.                                   223

Ransom, . . . . . . 355
Ransom Perry Bates, . 526
Rebecca, . . . 121, 162, 650
Remus, . . . . . . 432
Robert S., . . . . . 557
Romulus, . . . . . 433
Rosalie, . . . . . 606
Royal D., . . . . . 636
Russell, 94, 211, 240, 243, 675
Russell Henry, . . . 604½
Ruth, . . . . . . 189
Ruth Ann, . . . . 422
Ruth D., . . . . . 681

Sally, . . 137, 318, 431, 450
Sally J., . . . . . 362
Samuel, 14, 45, 63, 110, 118, 195,
                     214, 619
Samuel C., . . . . . 517
Sammy, . . . . . 67, 96
Samuel Perry, . . . . 471
Sarah, 18, 47, 49, 74, 99, 113,
       155, 161, 198, 206, 268,
       342, 373, 463, 464,
                     492, 639
Sarah Ann, . . . . . 407
Sarah Elizabeth, . . 378, 396
Sarah Jane, . . . . 389
Sarah Lewis, . . . . 285
Sarah Louisa, . . . . 481
Sheldon, . . . . 239, 418
Sibyl, . . . . . 92, 109
Silas, . . . . . . 202
Simon, . . . . . 208, 344
Sophia, . . . 273, 459, 476
Statira, . . . . . 509
Stephen, . . . 133, 246, 438
Stephen Martin, . . . 449
Stephen R., . . . . 678

Stephen Russell, . . . 604
Susan, . 231, 235, 319, 412, 445
Susan Catharine, . . . 498
Tabitha, . . . . . 6
Theodore E., . . . . 659
Theodore Edwin, . 322, 512
Thomas Hayne, . . . 652
Thomas Jefferson, . . 250¼
Timothy, . . . . 95, 213
Truman, . . . . . 204

Urania, . . . . . 193

Victory, . . . . . 145
Victory Leander, . . . 507

Walker, . . . . . 670
Walter H., . . . . 613
Warren E., . . . . . 633
Webb, . . . . . 71, 78
Wilbur F., . . . . 635
Willard, . . . . . 550
Willard L., . . . . 541
William, 170, 294, 296, 337, 443,
         454, 478, 495, 621
William A., . . 245, 583, 671
William Agur, . . 131, 444
William Augustus, . . 230
Wilber Beach, . . . . 487
Wm. Falconer, . . . 592
Wm. Henry, . . 437, 670
William L., . . . . 596
Wm. Russell, . . . 371
Wm. Sherman, . . . 367
Wm. Wallace, . . . 681
Wm. Walter, . . . 501
Wm. Wright, . . . 644

Zachariah, 17, 40, 52, 149, 205¼,
                 259¼, 275

# INDEX.

SURNAMES OTHER THAN TOMLINSON. THE FIGURES REFER TO PAGES AND NOT TO NUMBERS, AS IN THE PREVIOUS INDEX.

| | PAGE | | PAGE |
|---|---|---|---|
| ADAMS, | 108, 149 | BENNET | 138, 139, 125, 172 |
| ACKLEY, | 89 | BENT | 160, 161 |
| ALCOTT | 14, 15 | BENTON | 109, 125 |
| ALDERMAN, | 140 | BIRDSEYE | 13, 29, 52, 53, 65 |
| ALLEN, | 53, 54 | BISHOP | 3, 166, 169, 170 |
| ALLEY | 132 | BLACKLEACH | 13 |
| ALLIS | 156 | BLACKLIDG | 10, 11 |
| ALLYN | 80 | BLACKNEY | 48 |
| ALVORD | 170 | BLAKEMAN, | 15, 106, 137, 141, 142 |
| AMBLER | 43 | BLOW | 109 |
| AMES | 57 | BLISS | 117 |
| ANDRE | 100, 101 | BRADLEY | 132, 145 |
| ANDREWS | 121 | BRADY | 150 |
| ARMSTRONG | 107 | BRECK | 120 |
| ATWOOD | 83, 138, 131, 160 | BREWSTER | 48, 172 |
| | | BRISCO | 103, 156 |
| BACKUS | 79 | BRONSON | 30 |
| BACON | 74, 75 | BROOKS | 97 |
| BALDWIN, | 101, 104, 115, 133, 148, 163, 178 | BROWN | 18 |
| | | BROWNELL | 140, 147 |
| BAILEY | 121 | BRUSH | 76 |
| BALL | 170 | BRYAN | 6, 7, 43 |
| BARBER | 32 | BOLLEO | 132 |
| BARNET | 91 | BOOTH | 58, 64, 75, 127, 184 |
| BARRY | 40 | BOSTWICK, | 48, 56, 57, 135, 140, 172, 173 |
| BARTHOLOMEW | 87 | BOTSFORD | 155 |
| BASSET, | 22, 31, 34, 38, 39, 72, 73, 80, 81, 84, 122, 124, 125, 163 | BOWERS | 32, 69 |
| BATES | 154 | BUCKINGHAM | 140 |
| BAYLIS | 116 | BUNNELL | 129 |
| BEACH | 22, 44, 50, 55, 62, 83 | BURGESSER | 161 |
| BEARD | 53, 122 | BURNO | 105 |
| BEARDSLEY | 42, 56, 84, 96, 144 | BURLOCK | 54 |
| BEERS, | 37, 41, 70, 80, 81, 100, 101, 120 | BURR | 144 |
| BENJAMIN | 67 | BURRITT | 84, 12, 176 |
| BELKNAP | 137 | BURWELL | 120 |

# INDEX. 225

| | PAGE | | PAGE |
|---|---|---|---|
| CAMP | 104, 116, 148 | EAST | 7 |
| CANDEE | 77, 78, 129, 130, 156, 159 | EDWARDS | 37 |
| CASE | 113 | ELLIS | 106, 132 |
| CHAMBERLAIN | 43 | ELY | 56 |
| CANFIELD | 19, 22, 108, 116, 125, 174 | EMMERSON | 132 |
| CHAMPLIN | 157 | ENGLISH | 116 |
| CHAPMAN | 95, 138, 139, 140 | ENSIGN | 133 |
| CHAPPELL | 106 | FAIRCHILD | 112, 176 |
| CHAUNCEY | 13 | FALCONER | 104 |
| CHATFIELD | 13, 21, 22, 123, 155, 159 | FARMER | 33, 37 |
| CHITWOOD | 83 | FARRINGTON | 81 |
| CLARK | 12, 65, 96, 105, 159, 174 | FENN | 147 |
| CLAY | 159 | FELTON | 161 |
| COBB | 119 | FESSENDEN | 109 |
| COGSWELL | 115, 116 | FILLEY | 139 |
| COLE | 159 | FITCH | 61 |
| COLES | 90 | FOLSOM | 65 |
| COLT | 125 | FORD | 134, 170, 183 |
| COOK | 87 | FORSYTH | 166 |
| CORTELYOU | 74, 126, 115 | FOWLER | 37, 128 |
| CRANE | 170 | FRANCIS | 108 |
| CRAWFORD | 106 | FREEMAN | 34, 35 |
| CREIGHTON | 60 | FRENCH | 55, 170, 183 |
| CROFUT | 156 | FROUDE | 4 |
| CROSSMAN | 126 | GARRIGUS | 94 |
| CUNNINGHAM | 125 | GIBSON | 19, 67, 86, 104 |
| CURRIE | 182 | GLOVER | 69, 107, 130 |
| CURTISS | 16, 29, 47, 49, 51, 53, 56, 64, 65, 90, 83, 84, 134, 138, 140, 158, 162, 163, 164, 167, 171, 174 | GOFFE | 71 |
| | | GOLD | 20, 44, 65, 82, 103 |
| | | GOODSELL | 131 |
| | | GOODYEAR | 8, 77, 85 |
| DAY | 106 | GORHAM | 30 |
| DARCEY | 78 | GRANT | 170 |
| DARROW | 56, 57 | GRATIST | 170 |
| DAVIS | 20, 37, 81, 128, 132, 155, 159 | GRAHAM | 150 |
| DAYTON | 100 | GREELEY | 150 |
| DECK | 70 | GREENLEAF | 142 |
| DUDLEY | 72 | GRIFFIN | 27 |
| DE FOREST | 53, 54, 77, 79, 114 | GRUMMAN | 170 |
| DIBBLE | 95, 96 | GUNN | 92, 142 |
| DOWNS | 130, 138, 139, 160 | HALL | 71 |
| DREW | 87, 174, 175, 182, 183, 184 | HARD | 85 |
| DUNBAR | 92 | HARGER | 10, 14, 15, 189, 190 |
| DUNHAM | 113 | HARRAL | 60 |
| DURAND | 21, 22, 34, 43, 44, 144 | HAWLEY | 7, 10, 11, 12, 18, 24, 51, 54, 56, 70, 97 |
| DWIGHT | 44 | | |

# INDEX.

| | PAGE | | PAGE |
|---|---|---|---|
| HAWKINS, | 21, 22, 33, 34, 37, 43, 70, 78, 133, 117, 136, 153, 153, 162, 171, 180 | KIP | 139 |
| | | LABORIE | 88 |
| | | LACEY | 62 |
| HAYES | 110 | LANE | 116 |
| HAZELTON | 134 | LAMBERT | 104 |
| HEDDEN | 103 | LEAVENWORTH, | 42, 44, 57, 97, 127, 134, 150 |
| HENRYS | 42 | | |
| HEWIT | 177 | LEWIS, | 46, 55, 76, 82, 88, 96, 97, 142, 145, 146 |
| HIBBARD | 127 | | |
| HILL | 11, 103 | LIVINGSTON | 107, 110 |
| HILLHOUSE | 177 | LOCKWOOD | 58, 112, 170 |
| HINE | 48 | LOGAN | 134, 162 |
| HINSDELL | 59 | LONGWORTH | 57 |
| HITCHCOCK | 107, 181, 182 | LUM | 23, 33, 76, 137 |
| HOAG | 115 | | |
| HOLBROOK | 74, 123, 124, 143 | MALLETT | 106 |
| HOLMAN | 110 | MALTMAN | 149 |
| HOLMS | 24 | MANSFIELD | 33, 43 |
| HOMANS | 53 | MARSH | 48, 49 |
| HOPKINS | 37 | MARTIN | 33 |
| HOTCHKISS | 77, 78, 79, 80, 85, 163 | MAUWEHU | 32 |
| HOVEY | 49 | McLANE | 140 |
| HUBBARD | 44 | McMAHON | 49 |
| HUBBELL | 57, 90, 91, 174 | McMANUS | 95 |
| HULL | 37, 116, 143 | McEWIN | 46, 67 |
| HUMPHREY | 22, 84 | MEAD | 60, 106, 149 |
| HUMPHREYS | 30 | MEIGS | 41, 70 |
| HUNT | 135 | MENARD | 57 |
| HUNTINGTON | 26, 62, 63, 64, 97 | MERWIN | 68 |
| HURD | 113, 114, 125, 136 | MEEKER | 113, 147, 177 |
| | | MIDDLEBROOK | 164 |
| INGRAHAM | 23 | MILES | 125 |
| INCH | 96 | MILLER | 103, 146 |
| INDIAN NAMES | 8 | MILLS, | 48, 51, 67, 86, 88, 93, 97, 146, 176 |
| IVES | 103 | | |
| JOHNSON | 71, 102, 103, 125, 190 | MITCHELL | 103 |
| JUDD | 133 | MONTAGUE | 130 |
| JUDSON, | 16, 18, 30, 51, 128, 129, 135, 144 | MORRELL | 160 |
| | | MORRIS | 54, 170 |
| KEELER | 114 | MOORE | 47, 86, 146 |
| KELLOGG | 27, 30, 31, 97 | MORSE | 24, 55, 91 |
| KELSEY | 166 | MOSS | 31, 66 |
| KENEDY | 151 | MOTT | 108 |
| KNIES | 71 | MUNSON | 187 |
| KNOX | 58 | MYGATT | 48 |
| KIMBALL | 109, 110 | NEWELL | 167 |

## INDEX. 227

| | PAGE |
|---|---|
| NEWMAN | 103 |
| NORTHROP | 48, 114 |
| NICHOLS | 23, 64, 56, 96, 102, 130, 124, 173, 182, 185 |
| NOBLE | 162 |
| NOYES | 150 |
| OLCOTT | 27, 29 |
| OSBORN | 117, 110 |
| PAGE | 124 |
| PALMER | 136, 137 |
| PARROTT | 97 |
| PARTREE | 127, 128 |
| PATTERSON | 157, 158 |
| PAULDING | 132 |
| PEARCE | 173, 174, 175, 143 |
| PEASE | 91 |
| PECK | 67, 89, 127, 164, 188 |
| PERRY | 42, 43, 112, 123, 121, 137, 141, 155, 173 |
| PEET | 56, 57, 58, 59, 60 |
| PERKINS | 172, 178 |
| PETTIT | 183 |
| PIERCE | 132 |
| PIERPONT | 94, 95, 96 |
| PIERSON | 10, 15 |
| PIPER | 78 |
| PIXLEE | 55 |
| PLANT | 83, 148 |
| PRESCOTT | 125 |
| PRICE | 161 |
| POOLE | 81, 163 |
| POTTER | 102, 107 |
| PUTNAM | 132 |
| PYNCHEON | 67, 221 |
| QUEEN | 100 |
| QUENBY | 7 |
| QUOSH | 32, 33, 34, 35, 36, 39 |
| RAY | 106 |
| READING | 157 |
| RECE | 142 |
| REESE | 92 |
| REXFORD | 82 |
| RICHARDS | 94 |
| RIDER | 81, 136 |

| | PAGE |
|---|---|
| RINDGE | 53 |
| RIGGS | 18, 76, 126 |
| ROE | 58 |
| ROUNDSLEVE | 97 |
| ROYCE | 102 |
| RUDD | 54 |
| RUSH | 180 |
| RUSSELL | 5, 40, 74, 75, 110, 171, 185 |
| SAMPSON | 109 |
| SANFORD | 72, 85, 86 |
| SAYRE | 53 |
| SCHELL | 149 |
| SCHWANGLER | 60 |
| SCHUBERT | 144 |
| SCOTT | 189 |
| SEALY | 187 |
| SHELEY | 143 |
| SHELDON | 130 |
| SHELTON | 42, 40, 50, 54, 85, 86, 90, 92, 95, 96, 125, 139, 164, 172 |
| SHEPARD | 31 |
| SHERMAN | 12, 143 |
| SKEELS | 125 |
| SMITH | 6, 21, 22, 34, 43, 49, 58, 72, 101, 105, 135, 135, 148, 157, 181, 187 |
| SOMERS | 58 |
| SPENCER | 104 |
| SPERRY | 133, 178 |
| SPRAGUE | 164 |
| STAFFORD | 70 |
| STAPLES | 127, 149 |
| STARK | 132 |
| STARR | 48 |
| STAUGHTON | 177 |
| STERLING | 103 |
| STEVENS | 134 |
| STILES | 10, 16 |
| STILLMAN | 91 |
| STOCKWELL | 188 |
| STONE | 92, 143 |
| STRINGHAM | 100 |
| STRONG | 42 |
| SUMMER | 20 |
| TALBOT | 44 |
| TEMPLE | 177 |

## INDEX.

| | PAGE | | PAGE |
|---|---|---|---|
| THATCHER | 166 | WATSON | 49 |
| TAYLOR | 20, 127, 102 | WATTS | 37 |
| THOMPSON | 29, 30, 62, 107, 137 | WEBB | 26 |
| THORP | 114 | WELCH | 79 |
| THRALL | 57 | WEED | 108, 109 |
| TIBBALS | 103 | WEEKS | 104 |
| TOBY | 52 | WELLES | 16, 18, 48, 49, 51, 62, 64, 86, 176, 184, 185 |
| TOWNSEND | 86 | | |
| TRACEY | 44 | WELTON | 94, 95 |
| TREAT | 103 | WETMORE | 28, 46, 62, 64 |
| TRUBEE | 170 | WHEATON | 115, 131 |
| TRYON | 38, 64 | WHEELER | 10, 18, 19, 51, 97, 107, 117, 144, 176, 180 |
| TUCKER | 81 | | |
| TUTHILL | 80 | WHITTELSEY | 110 |
| TUTTLE | 76 | WIGGINS | 78 |
| TWITCHELL | 20, 15 | WILCOX | 157, 160 |
| WADE | 181 | WILCOCKSON | 12, 18, 125 |
| WADSWORTH | 71 | WILKINSON | 170 |
| WAGNER | 125 | WILMOT | 57 |
| WAKELEE | 26, 70 | WILLYS | 61 |
| WAKELEY | 136 | WILLES | 60 |
| WALDEN | 151, 170, 175 | WOOD | 167 |
| WALKER | 99, 136, 171 | WOODRUFF | 31, 104 |
| WALTERS | 181 | WOOSTER | 10, 15, 16, 19, 38, 40, 62, 63, 68, 69, 156 |
| WARNER | 92, 94, 170 | | |
| WARREN | 110 | WORDIN | 122 |
| WASHBURN | 16, 17, 170 | WRIGHT | 53, 58, 160, 179, 180 |
| WASHINGTON | 68, 69, 145 | | |
| WATERS | 24 | YALE | 34, 35, 43 |

www.ingramcontent.com/pod-product-compliance
Lightning Source LLC
Chambersburg PA
CBHW021421300426
44114CB00010B/588